THE
CHELSEA
YEAR
1988/9

THE CHELSEA YEAR
1988/9

The Yearbook of
The Royal Horticultural
Society

General Editor
David Joyce

Chatto & Windus
LONDON

Half-title: Begonia 'Sugar Candy'

Frontispiece: A Countrywoman's Garden, for which a Gold
Medal was awarded to the National Federation of Women's
Institutes, Chelsea 1988

First published in 1988
by Chatto & Windus Ltd
30 Bedford Square
London WC1B 3SG

A CIP catalogue record for this book
is available from the British Library.

ISBN 0 7011 3387 2

Designed by Heather Garioch & Ruth Prentice

Colour origination, typesetting and printing by
Butler & Tanner Ltd, Frome and London

*Opinions expressed by authors are not specifically endorsed
by the Royal Horticultural Society.*

CONTENTS

Contributors 6

Foreword 7
R. A. E. Herbert, VMH
President of the Royal Horticultural Society

CHELSEA FLOWER SHOW 9

Anniversary Year *13*
Priscilla Boniface & David Joyce

Cottager's Plot and Tycoon's Whim *19*
David Joyce

Plant Cinderellas Discovered *31*
Stephen Lacey

The Flower-arranger's Garden *39*
Christopher Lloyd

Old and New in Vegetables and Herbs *49*
Joy Larkcom

Fruit Trees to Measure *61*
Brian Self

Conservation-minded Gardening *69*
Francesca Greenoak

Greenhouse Improvements *77*
George Sheard

Pleasing the Public *85*
Deborah Kellaway

WESTMINSTER & REGIONAL SHOWS 93

Friendly Competition *97*
Marigold Assinder

Bulbs for Four Seasons *103*
Jack Elliott

Evergreen Choice *113*
Kenneth A. Beckett

Starting with Orchids *123*
Phillip Cribb & Joyce Stewart

A Storm to Remember: October 1987 *129*
Arthur Hellyer

Roses in the Autumn *137*
Michael Gibson

PERSPECTIVE 1987–1988 *147*

Beth Chatto
An Unusual Talent with Plants *151*
David Joyce

Recipients of Cups, Trophies,
Medals and Prizes *152*

PREVIEW 1988–1989 *155*

Calendar of Shows *156*

EXHIBITORS

at Chelsea and Westminster Shows
June 1987 to May 1988 *158*

Index *175*

Acknowledgements *176*

CONTRIBUTORS

MARIGOLD ASSINDER was born and brought up at Chyverton, near Truro in Cornwall, where her twin brother, Nigel Holman, continues the garden started by her father. She has gardened at her Putney home since 1957 and in recent years she has shown regularly at the Society's shows.

KENNETH A. BECKETT, who gardens in Norfolk, is a horticulturist and writer with a wide knowledge of ornamental plants grown in Britain. In the past ten years he has been a member of five RHS Committees. In 1987 he was awarded the Veitch Memorial Medal in gold.

PRISCILLA BONIFACE has written a number of books and articles reflecting her interest in the conservation of historic buildings and gardens. *In Search of English Gardens*, published recently, is a critical edition of the writings of Loudon in *The Gardener's Magazine*.

DR PHILLIP CRIBB is Curator of the Orchid Herbarium at the Royal Botanic Gardens, Kew. He is joint author of, among other works, *The Manual of Cultivated Orchid Species*, *The Genus Pleione* and *The Genus Paphiopedilum*.

DR JACK ELLIOTT, a retired general practitioner who gardens in Kent, has had a life-long interest in bulbs. He is a member of the RHS Council, Chairman of the Rock Garden Committee, President of the Alpine Garden Society and past Chairman of the Hardy Plant Society.

MICHAEL GIBSON, DHM, is a gardening writer who has specialized in roses and their history. In 1985 and 1986 he was President of the Royal National Rose Society. His most recent book is *The Rose Gardens of England*.

FRANCESCA GREENOAK is a gardener and naturalist who has written several books on wildlife and its relationship with human beings, including *All the Birds of the Air* and *God's Acre*. She is currently Gardening Correspondent of *The Times*.

ARTHUR HELLYER, MBE, VMH, FLS, is a practical gardener and prolific writer on horticultural subjects. Until his retirement, in 1966, he was Editor of *Amateur Gardening* and he is Gardening Correspondent of the *Financial Times*.

DEBORAH KELLAWAY, who was born in Melbourne, Australia, has taught and gardened in London and Norfolk. Her first book on gardening, *The Making of an English Country Garden*, was published in 1988.

STEPHEN LACEY is the author of *The Startling Jungle: Colour and Scent in the Romantic Garden*. He has a one-acre cottage garden in North Wales and a small garden in Oxford.

JOY LARKCOM, who with her husband runs an organic market garden in Suffolk, has written several books and numerous articles on vegetable growing. She has travelled widely in Europe and the Far East in search of interesting vegetables and has experience of new and traditional techniques of cultivation.

CHRISTOPHER LLOYD, VMH, horticultural journalist and author of classics such as *The Well-tempered Garden*, writes a weekly column in *Country Life* and contributes regularly to the *Guardian* and the *Observer Magazine*. His house and garden at Great Dixter, East Sussex, are open to the public.

BRIAN SELF, BSC, MI HORT., is Liaison Officer at the AFRC Institute of Horticultural Research, East Malling (formerly East Malling Research Station). He is currently one of the two Vice-Chairmen of the RHS Fruit and Vegetable Committee and Chairman of its Fruit Group.

JOYCE STEWART, MSC, FLS, MI HORT., currently the Sainsbury Orchid Fellow at the Royal Botanic Gardens, Kew, is a member of the RHS Council and of the Orchid Committee. She has written and lectured about orchids and frequently judges them. Her particular interest is wild orchids.

FOREWORD

R. A. E. Herbert, VMH
President of the Royal Horticultural Society

Chelsea Flower Show is the highlight of the gardening year for members of the Royal Horticultural Society. It is the finest flower show in the world and brings together on one compact site an amazing range of gardens and plants, all demonstrating in their own way the current peaks achieved by the art of horticulture. As leisure and wealth increase, this annual showcase becomes even more important for the way in which it demonstrates the ever-widening range of choice open to gardeners.

The aim of this book is to capture the essence of the 1988 Show within months of it taking place. This year's Show was a milestone for the Society because it marked the seventy-fifth anniversary of the first Show held at Chelsea in 1913 and, due to the new admission arrangements, visitors were able to see the wonderful range of exhibits in exceptional comfort.

The articles in this book draw the reader's attention to outstanding exhibits and features of the Show and as such will be appreciated as a reminder to those who were visitors as well as an indication of what they missed to those unable to attend.

Chelsea is not, however, the Society's only flower show, as the many visitors who come to our Westminster Halls each month well know. These regular shows, where plants may be purchased, offer all gardeners the opportunity to keep abreast of the current season. The Society will also be extending its presence to other shows outside London, starting with Glasgow in August.

The importance of this book lies in its ability to synthesize many of the current horticultural trends of Chelsea and our other shows. The skill with which so many distinguished horticultural writers have picked out and emphasized significant features will undoubtedly be of great value to all those who wish to apply the expertise and experience of the Society's shows to their own gardens.

CHELSEA FLOWER SHOW

Anniversaries are not always the better for being celebrated. They may provide copy material for desperate journalists and give an excuse for strident commercial attention-seeking, but their genuine interest is often very limited. There was good reason for approaching Chelsea 1988 with some misgivings.

It was a relief to discover that the anniversary dimension to the Great Spring Show was not a monstrous imposition on an event that is a perennial source of interest and pleasure. True, it may have provided the nostalgic inspiration for a number of exhibits. One had the feeling, though, that the cottage theme, for example, so insistent in the anniversary year, reflected a general swing in interest to traditional ways of gardening in a limited space. The anniversary celebration was at its most valuable when it encouraged the staging of exhibits with an historical and unsentimental slant that helped to put the current state of British horticulture in a broader context.

To be fair, there was much to celebrate in this anniversary year, for the Great Spring Show has had a phenomenal and sustained popular success without the collapse of the standards that justify it horticulturally. The anniversary year took on particular significance because this occasion was the test of measures introduced by the Society's Council to deal with the problem of overcrowding that has risked making the Show unmanageable on the Chelsea site. Some way had to be found to limit the number of visitors. In retrospect, the old arrangement whereby a relay of friends,

The staging of exhibits at the Great Spring Show must be completed during the Monday afternoon of Chelsea week, in time for judging to take place.

aunts, uncles and distant country cousins could use to exhaustion a transferrable membership ticket permitting free entry throughout Chelsea week seems extraordinary.

Judged purely on the ease with which visitors could get about and use facilities, there can be no doubt that the Great Spring Show was much more pleasant and successful than it has been for a number of years. Satisfying exhibitors is, of course, just as important as pleasing visitors. Exhibitors need not just the glory of awards but also full order books to justify the enormous investment in time and money that is put in to staging a Chelsea exhibit. Reports from nurserymen and other exhibitors this year suggest that results have been somewhat uneven, some down on previous years while others have done exceptionally well.

The Society's Council recognizes that there is room for refining the arrangements, in particular so as to lift the number of visitors attending at off-peak hours. The opportunity is taken elsewhere to encourage Chelsea visitors who are in a position to be flexible about the time they attend to plan their visits for early morning or late afternoon. They will enjoy the benefit of seeing Chelsea at its uncluttered best and they will be helping the Society to make the most of all the hours that the Show is open.

A fully comprehensive survey of the last Chelsea would require a mammoth volume at least on the scale of the *Horticultural Record*, which commemorated the Royal International Horticultural Exhibition, the 1912 precursor of the first Great Spring Show at the Chelsea site. The articles that follow should be read as a first instalment of a progressive review of Chelsea shows, for in subsequent issues there will be opportunities of taking up quite different subjects to those dealt with here.

It is, nonetheless, cause for regret that some truly outstanding exhibits of 1988 are not covered more fully. Exhibitors from abroad, such as the Kirstenbosch Botanical Gardens and the Barbados Horticultural Society brought fascinating plants that are not so familiar to British gardeners. The co-operative exhibit staged by three orchid nurseries – Burnham Nurseries Ltd, McBeans Orchids Ltd and Wyld Court Orchids – in association with the tropical plant specialists Anmore Exotics was one of the most successful treatments there has been in recent years of the notoriously difficult Monument site. Perhaps on the strength of this success there will be a trend towards more co-operative exhibits at subsequent Chelsea Shows.

There is no shortage of other exhibits that could be listed among the outstanding, from well researched scientific displays to glorious assemblies of ornamental plants. For many, however, the essential memory of Chelsea is not so much the broad view but a series of delightful details, a well-planted hanging basket, a pot of herbs, a striking contrast of foliage and hard surface and familiar and cherished flowers that vie with the quirkish and unknown for a hold on the imagination. Chelsea in 1988 was as rich in these details as it always is.

One does, however, come away from the Great Spring Show every year staggered not only by visions of a multi-seasoned temperate and tropical horticultural paradise but also by the awfulness of plants one would never want in the garden or house, by garden designs of numbing aridity, in fact by a thousand and one things, from florists' sundries to luxury conservatories, that do not conform to one's own prejudices. A criticism levelled at the organizers of Chelsea that they let 'bad taste' go unchecked should not, though, be taken too seriously. In between having your own prejudices confirmed, there is just the chance that you will discover how silly and trivial they have been and that another person's way of looking at gardens and plants may after all be valid.

Detail of the exhibit staged by the Torbay Parks and Recreation Department.

Anniversary Year

Priscilla Boniface and David Joyce

The Great Spring Show has always been a blockbuster. Even before 1913, when it was moved to the Chelsea site from the gardens of the Inner Temple on the Embankment, it justified superlatives. The first of the Temple shows, held a century ago this year, was enthusiastically reported in the *Gardener's Chronicle*: 'We are aware that we have not been so sparing of adjectives as it is our duty to be on ordinary occasions, but this new departure ... is so remarkable, and the circumstances are so peculiar, that a few superlatives are more than admissible.' The Society was just recovering from a period of financial crisis and horticultural decline. The revival of the Society's fortunes and the success of the Temple shows was largely due to a return to the original policy of 1804, 'horticulture pure and simple', which had been lost sight of in an extravagant development, Kensington Garden.

The immediate forerunner to the 1913 show had been the Royal International Horticultural Exhibition, which had been staged in the grounds of the Royal Hospital, Chelsea, the previous year. Although the Society was not responsible for organizing this 'landmark of horticultural progress', it was closely associated with it and many prominent Fellows took a leading role in its management. The 1912 spectacular set the standard and style that the Society was to follow in 1913.

The first Chelsea was a great triumph. The site proved an admirable venue: Sir Christopher Wren's dignified Royal Hospital buildings provided a fitting backcloth while the leafy gardens were an ideal setting for displays of gardens and plants. The sense of being in a mature garden set apart from the bustle of the capital was, as it still is, part of the charm of Chelsea. There had been some concern that the show had gone too

For seventy-five years the uniformed pensioners of
the Royal Hospital, Chelsea, have added a slightly
formal but cheerful note to the Great Spring Show.

far west, but the success of the International Show had proved crowds would not be deterred. Carriages could 'set down' at the south entrance, while pedestrians, most of whom travelled by public transport, were admitted through the north entrance.

Apart from the suitability of the location there were three factors principally responsible for the success of Chelsea in 1913. Firstly, despite a few hitches, the organization worked smoothly. Not everyone could be satisfied. Only half the space applied for could be allotted, such was the demand. The *Gardener's Magazine* found the tent too small – it was erected, as the marquee still is, by the firm of Piggott Bros. But in a layout that in essence was very similar to that of today, exhibitors worked to a tight schedule to create gardens and mount displays that delighted an enthusiastic public. Exhibitors arrived with horses and carts so that at times the show ground must have more resembled a shire horse show than a prestigious gardening exhibition. The keenly admired rock gardens were major feats of instant landscaping, for lifting and moving equipment was, by modern standards, primitive. The authority of head gardeners and leading nurserymen ensured that plants of every description were shown in their prime.

A second explanation for the success of the first Chelsea, and for many Chelseas to come, was that it proved a great social event. At the end of May Chelsea was *the* place to be. A love of plants and gardens is, happily, a great leveller; at the time of the International Exhibition Sir Trevor Lawrence, President of the Society, alluded somewhat pompously to 'the way in which the love of Horticulture pervades every class'. But what counted in 1913 was the support of Society, and royal patronage helped to ensure that the Show was an event in the social calendar that could not be ignored. As subsequent royal interest has shown, Chelsea was not simply an obligatory ritual. King George V may sometimes have been difficult to humour but Queen Mary and later Edward VIII, George VI and Queen Elizabeth the Queen Mother are among royals who have shown a deep interest in plants and gardens.

Outweighing by far the organizational and social explanations for the success of the first Chelsea and its successors was its horticultural excellence. The rivalry – in general, friendly – between the owners of great gardens, in 1913 still being created and developed in considerable numbers, gave a competitive edge to their own showing and also to that of the displays of nurserymen eager to promote their special lines of ornamental and useful plants.

Despite the great flow of introductions that had reached Europe in the eighteenth and nineteenth centuries, gardeners were still avid for new plants and to that end were willing to sponsor collecting. In the first half of this century the most outstanding introductions to British gardens were from China, Burma and the Himalayas. At the turn of the century the first E. H. Wilson expedition to China – he was sent by the firm of Veitch – brought back the

handkerchief tree, *Davidia involucrata*. Other introductions from this and subsequent Wilson expeditions included *Acer griseum*, *Clematis armandii*, *Lilium regale* and *Rhododendron fargesii*. Between 1904 and 1932 George Forrest made several expeditions to western China, his introductions including over 300 new species of rhododendrons, 150 species of primula (of which the most significant was probably *Primula malacoides*), *Gentiana sino-ornata* (the introduction he prized above all others), *Camellia saluensis* (a parent of *C.* × *williamsii*) and *Magnolia campbellii* var. *mollicomata* (which comes into flowering as a much younger tree than *M. campbellii*). Introductions from the Sino-Himalayan region were continued by Captain Frank Kingdon Ward during the period 1911 to 1958. He was initially sponsored by A. K. Bulley, the owner of the Liverpool-based nursery firm of Bees Ltd, and his introductions included the blue poppy, *Meconopsis betonicifolia*, primulas, including *Primula bulleyana* and *P. florindae*, and numerous rhododendrons. Another influential figure, Reginald Farrer, stimulated an interest in the growing of alpines and rock garden plants through his writings, notably *My Rock Garden* (1907) and *The English Rock Garden* (1919).

ABOVE The gardens of the Inner Temple on the Embankment, the site of the Great Spring Show before its move to the grounds of the Royal Hospital in Chelsea, offered little scope for rock garden exhibits. At the early shows on the new site the many examples exhibited testified to their popularity.

RIGHT Notcutts is one of several firms that have been showing regularly at Chelsea since 1913. In 1988 part of their stand was a recreation of their exhibit at the first Chelsea Show.

Anticipation of new introductions from China and elsewhere was not the only cause of excitement in the horticultural world at the time of the early Chelsea Shows. A fascination with the results of increasingly sophisticated plant breeding went hand in hand with an appetite for new introductions. Orchids were a case in point. For many years at Chelsea these were displayed more lavishly than almost any other category of plant. In 1913 the exhibits mounted by Sir Jeremiah Colman of Gatton Park and Sir George Holford of Westonbirt showed orchid breeding at its most advanced.

Among other aristocratic passions were conservatory plants and rhododendrons. But hardy and half-hardy annuals and perennials were not neglected. The sensation of 1900 had been the first waved and frilled sweet pea, 'Countess Spencer'; the subsequent regular introduction of new colours kept this plant in the public eye. In 1904 the firm of Blackmore and Langdon, founded in 1901 and still showing at Chelsea in 1988, began the serious breeding of delphiniums; they also raised tuberous begonias, cyclamen, phlox and polyanthus. At Amos Perry's nursery a wide range of herbaceous perennials was bred selectively, including oriental poppies. The first white-flowered selection, 'Silver Queen', was shown at the International Exhibition; two years later came 'Perry's White'. Perry, W.R. Dykes and others were responsible for breeding new types of bearded irises; the first with velvet-textured falls was raised in 1910 by A.J. Bliss. In the same year Montagu Allwood began a programme of crossing perpetual-flowering carnations with *Dianthus plumarius*, which led eventually to the Allwoodii pinks that are still shown by Allwoods at Chelsea. A year later George Russell, an allotment gardener, began experiments with lupins that led to the sensation of the 1937 Chelsea, the Russell lupins shown by Messrs Baker Ltd.

Roses, tulips, daffodils, Michaelmas daisies and many other ornamentals were the subject of intensive breeding programmes and so, too, were fruit and vegetables. The early catalogues of seed firms such as Messrs Sutton & Sons Ltd show the intense competition for the market of such seeds as peas, beans and cucumbers. In the long term, even more significant than the fruit and vegetable breeding programmes of individual nurseries was the research initiated by a cluster of scientific institutions founded close to 1913. The John Innes Horticultural Institute dates from 1909, the founder, John Innes, leaving his fortune 'for the study of the growth of trees and for the improvement of horticulture by experiment and research'. Much later the name of the Institute became familiar to gardeners through the standardized potting and seed composts that it formulated, but its first field of study was plant genetics. Almost contemporary with the first Chelsea were the East Malling and Long Ashton Research Stations, which were to have such an important impact on fruit growing in the temperate areas of the world. The Cheshunt Experimental and Research Station, later the Glass-house Crops Research Unit, was also founded in 1913, and did major research on the growing of crops under glass.

It is clear that the transfer of the Great Spring Show to Chelsea occurred at a time of major developments in horticulture. The climate was favourable for success. What is remarkable is that the standard of excellence established at the first Shows has been maintained so consistently since. Although it is hard to believe it in the apparent chaos in the grounds during the week immediately before Chelsea, the arrangements for staging the show are so fine-tuned that, if there are hitches, these are not apparent to the visitor. The greatest threat to Chelsea has been posed by its own success. Gardeners on the grand scale will still find more than enough to interest them but there is no mistaking the shift in favour of those gardening in a limited space. The democratization and media coverage of Chelsea – it was first televised in 1958 – have resulted in many more visitors wanting to come and see for themselves the most important annual horticultural event in Britain. Changes to the entrance arrangements in 1988 made visiting much more pleasurable than it has been for several years. Because of the crowds it draws there is always the possibility that the Great Spring Show could be moved to another venue but the likelihood is that the Chelsea site will be retained and not simply out of sentimentality.

What really counts for the success of Chelsea in the future, as it has in the past, is adherence to the Society's prime horticultural objective. There will be changes of emphasis, as there have been already. For example, the rate of new introductions has slowed but to compensate there has been, in the last decade especially, a renewed interest in good garden plants that have unaccountably fallen into neglect. To improve upon a superlative is difficult but that is what organizers and exhibitors aim to do at each succeeding Chelsea.

The Chelsea Show remains a shop window for new introductions and successes in breeding, as these bearded irises, *c.* 1920.

Cottager's Plot
and
Tycoon's Whim

David Joyce

The art of passive gardening is easily perfected. You swan about the pleasure grounds of stately homes critically attentive to lapses in maintenance; you view with satisfaction from your front window the flawless velvet of your neighbour's lawn; you peer unabashed into the idyllic country gardens of complete strangers. And at Chelsea you comment loudly on the failure of designers to realize your own vision of paradise as though, were it there, you would buy it off the peg. At Chelsea, however, you will find a lot of jostling competition to view garden exhibits and much of it from practical gardeners keen to take home ideas extracted from designs differing widely in scale and style.

In an anniversary year passive and practical gardeners alike should not have been surprised to find a number of designers looking to the past for their inspiration. What could be more evocatively traditional than the cottage garden?

Distinguishing the myth from the reality of this simplest of traditional gardens is in fact no easy business. Victorian and Edwardian artists, gentry playing at the simple life and, more recently, weekenders creating havens of rustic charm have all done their bit to idealize a style of gardening born out of the harsh realities of rural life. Vegetables and fruit for food, herbs for physic and flavouring, poultry for eggs and meat, a beehive for honey, perhaps even a pig, all these were as much part of the cottager's plot as homely flowers. It might be said that the old spirit of cottage gardening is now more truly expressed in urban and suburban allotments than in country gardens. What is certain is that before the cataclysm of the First World War the simple cottage garden, with its lovingly tended and exuberant mixture of plants, was a much more

A Countrywoman's Garden, designed by Jacqui Moon and John Ravenscroft, had a nostalgic and practical appeal for Chelsea visitors.

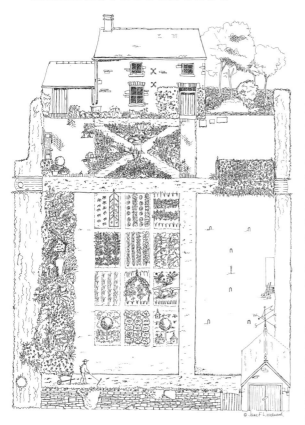

common feature of rural Britain than it is now. Many have forecast that these traditional gardens would fade away completely, leaving no more than a legacy of cheerful flowers, but exhibits at Chelsea 1988 showed that the cottage style still offers an appealing mix of nostalgia and practicality.

A 'designed' cottage garden is very nearly a contradiction in terms. Much of the appeal of one of the most popular exhibits of the show, the Women's Institute and Bridgemere 'Countrywoman's Garden', lay in the simplicity of its conception. Straight brick and cinder paths divided up a front garden measuring approximately 8·5 by 9 m (28 by 30 ft) into a vegetable patch and beds with flowers, herbs and fruit. Items to catch the eye included a beehive, forcing pots for rhubarb, a weathered picket fence and, outside it, an edging of wild flowers in grass. The real pleasure of the garden did not depend, however, on obvious details of window dressing but rather on the sweet order of a plot in which culinary delights rubbed shoulders with 'good-tempered and pleasing' flowers of the kind advocated by Margery Fish.

Despite taking its inspiration from the past, this was unmistakably a gardener's garden. Jacqui Moon, who devised it – and who in 1987 won the Design Award Cup of the National Federation of Women's Institutes for the scheme that was later taken to Chelsea – drew on her experience of garden making at Puddington in Cheshire. The result made points that could be applied to many small gardens, including those less deliberately nostalgic: the advantages of close planting in well-cultivated ground; the happy effect of mixing ornamentals with useful plants; and the merits of a simple and unpretentious layout that is easily managed and lets plants speak for themselves.

Ryl Nowell's 'A Cottage in the Country, 1913' presented a traditional garden on a larger scale, vegetables, herbs and flowers arranged either side of a serpentine path and stream sloping away from an old cottage. This exhibit included many lovely plants, assembled from many sources, angelica among others proving itself a highly ornamental herb. Although firmly based on a country tradition, the element of conscious design made this a cottage garden of the 1980s rather than one of seventy-five years ago.

If these exhibits had whetted your appetite for sound herbaceous perennials suitable for the cottage style, Carlile's Hardy Plants in the marquee had just the sort of things to please. Here were flowers of subtle and harmonious colouring, in many cases selected forms of kinds treasured by the humble cottager but free from the strident brashness that is sometimes the result of 'improvement'. Achilleas, aquilegias, campanulas, delphiniums, geraniums and lupins were all prominently featured but perhaps the most striking plants were the verbascums, including the lovely apricot-pink 'Cotswold Beauty'. Cottage enthusiasts must not be allowed a monopoly, though; like so many plants on this stand, this is too good to be reserved for one style of gardening only.

The cottage theme as a celebration of seventy-five years at Chelsea was also taken up by Highfield Nurseries in an exhibit designed by Julian Dowle. Their '1913 Garden Restored' used a Cotswold garden setting to demonstrate how

OPPOSITE Thomas Woodward, the garden design business of Roger Thomas and Jane Woodward, exhibited a scheme drawing directly on the cottage tradition.

ABOVE A mixture of flowers, herbs and vegetables struck an authentic note in Ryl Nowell's version of a 1913 country garden.

LEFT The designer Julian Dowle updated a Cotswold cottage garden for Highfield Nurseries, incorporating fruit trees on modern rootstocks.

The British Trust for
Conservation Volunteers
used recycled materials in a
scheme reconciling the
needs of wildlife with those
of a suburban household

fruit can be grown in a small space using modern varieties, rootstocks and training methods. It was worth getting beyond the country presentation of this exhibit, for town and suburban gardeners could apply modern techniques of fruit growing to make their gardens productive and – as the fruit tunnel, fans, espaliers and short standards of this garden showed – pleasing to the eye. A much more ambitious scheme featuring fruit was shown in a plan for a kitchen garden in Co. Wexford, by the Dublin-based designer Patrick Bowe. This scheme, the drawing and colouring beautifully executed by Kieran O'Neill, harked back to a scale of gardening commonplace in 1913 but now rare.

The cottager's range of plants was limited, partly a question of money and availability, but restricted also, perhaps, by a distrust of the foreign and unknown. Wildlife gardeners sometimes share this point of view, seeing all intro-

ductions as displacing native species as well as failing to provide a habitat in which native insects, birds and animals will thrive. The British Trust for Conservation Volunteers were not so scrupulously patriotic, allowing a few foreigners to mingle with a predominantly native collection of plants in their 'Wildlife Water Garden'. This was a garden that would need to be left for months and years rather than days and weeks to prove its success. At Chelsea it made a pleasant cool green pause, despite its hard surfaces and sleeper-edged beds. A remarkable feature of this exhibit was that, unlike almost all others at Chelsea, it was put together by volunteers, who worked under the direction of landscape designer Andrew Halksworth.

The Gale's 'Honeybee Garden', designed by Appleton Deeley Partnership, contained a pretty planting of natives from the wildflower seed specialist John Chambers. Ragged robin, red campion, foxglove, wild columbine,

A Plant Lover's Garden, designed by Bressingham
Landscapes, brought together an outstanding
collection of foliage and flowering plants.

poppies and oxeye daisies were among species that stood up well in a garden that also included cultivated plants loved by bees. A nice touch was a verge of wild flowers outside the garden, nestling under a wall of golden stone.

Unlike the cottager in the past or, for that matter, the conservationist constrained by convictions, the modern gardener can choose from a vast range of plants that will give the garden interest and variety through twelve months of the year. Many exhibitors exploited this wealth of material in inventive planting schemes, none with a stronger sense of the intrinsic worth of plants than Bressingham Landscapes. Much of the interest shown in their exhibit focused on the new golden-leaved birch, *Betula pendula* 'Golden Cloud', one of many plants with golden or variegated foliage included in their choice selection. The attention lavished on this new star was disproportionate, given that Bressingham Landscapes, a comparatively new department of Blooms of Bressingham Ltd,

had been able to draw on the great resources of the parent nursery to show so many plants of sterling qualities. Beneath a core planting of shrubs and conifers, giving height and substance, the underplanting was grouped according to growing conditions and interesting associations of texture, form and colour. This truly was 'A Plant Lover's Garden', warranting long and close scrutiny for the use of plants of discreet beauty, such as the lovely hosta 'Frances Williams' (glaucous leaves with a pale cream variegation), as well as eyecatchers, such as the bicoloured bronze-red and yellow broom *Cytisus* 'Lena'.

The Bressingham garden was outstanding in the way it catered for the plant enthusiast. There were, however, other gardens of suburban scale which, though stressing ease of

Tim Newberry, the designer of a Plantsman's Garden for Cramphorn PLC, used dense planting in a low-maintenance scheme.

maintenance, showed imaginative planting schemes. Foliage played an important role in the garden design by Tim Newberry for Cramphorns. A thick planting of interesting shrubs and perennials formed an easily managed backing to a scheme incorporating pool, area of decking and summerhouse linked by winding paths on a sloping site. The *Daily Mirror*'s promise of 'gardening without tears' was underwritten by a planting scheme, devised by John Plummer. He set out to show that by choosing the right plant almost any area of the garden, shaded and dry, sunny and moist, and every variation, can be made attractive. The silver birch is in danger of becoming the token tree of suburbia but the multi-stemmed specimens used to give height and a light canopy in limited areas of the garden created the impression of a glade. They were more successful in giving the garden a structure than the miniaturized sinuous line of path and beds derived from the broad sweeps of the eighteenth-century landscapists.

The town and suburban gardens of the reasonably affluent increasingly become extensions of the indoor living area. Plant beds and lawns give way to paved areas for sitting out and entertaining, sun rooms, pergolas, barbecues, and pools that are more architecture than water garden. This tendency is, if anything, exaggerated at Chelsea, where the costs of mounting an exhibit are reduced by getting sponsorship in one form or another from manufacturers. There is the risk of design being subordinated to the requirements of the shop window but at least the Chelsea visitor has an opportunity to compare results and prices. And every garden holds its lessons: solutions for difficult corners, effective and cheaper options to York stone; the use of slight changes of level; ways of creating shelter and privacy.

In most cases the shop window is quite simply a view over the fence, few small gardens being able to cope with the customary Chelsea crowds. Roddy Llewellyn's design for *Homes and Garden* made a welcome exception. This

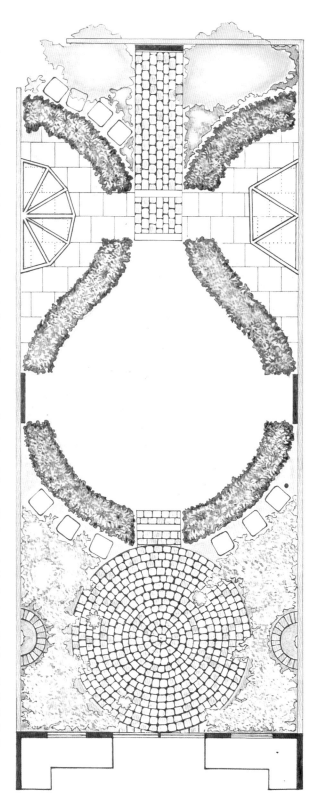

Mirrors helped to give a feeling of spaciousness in the town garden of linked compartments designed by Roddy Llewellyn for *Homes and Garden*.

The formal design of the Secret Garden by the Landscape Students of Merrist Wood Agricultural College was underlined by skilful planting.

formal town garden could only be seen by walking through it. Entrance was through a kitchen (apparently still the most voguish room of the house) into a paved area with symmetrically arranged wall fountains and beds planted predominantly with deciduous azaleas – rather bitty, despite their pastel colours. A sequence of three compartments followed, created by curving hedges 1·8 m (6 feet) high of *Thuja plicata*, the points of transition from one to the other marked by arches. A pair of mirrors in the lawn compartment and a single mirror at the end facing the kitchen helped to make the garden seem larger than its real size (the problem of keeping them clean left many visitors uneasy). In a second paved compartment a specially designed greenhouse faced a greenshed, and the last compartment was planted to suggest a woodland glade. Although details might prove irritating to many garden-

ers, the formal division of a space to create a succession of contrasting areas is something that could be adapted to many unpromising town gardens.

Despite the current renewed interest in formal gardens, there was only one other design based on a symmetrical layout, that exhibited by Merrist Wood College. The title, 'The Secret Garden', was puzzling, but this was still a beautifully presented design suitable for many small sites or as a delightful element within a larger scheme. It was a refreshing reminder that a calm formality can be achieved without relying on obvious historical allusions in the form of topiary or an army of 'Renaissance' figures. A simple rectangular garden with a gazebo at one end and a gravelled path running across the width at the other was divided into two pairs of planting compartments by length-wise and crosswise axes with, at their point of

For Help the Aged
Robin Williams
designed a small
sheltered housing
communal garden
which had as its focal
point a pool and
fountain.

meeting, a pool round which ran a brick-edged path of setts. The pool and its surround of sunken garden, lavender hedge and circular path were the dominant features of the garden while the symmetry was reinforced by a pair of pools flanking the path to the gazebo, urns at either end of the cross axis and a pair of sculptures in the foreground. Thoughtful understated symmetry in the planting sustained the formal scheme, for example, variegated *Cornus* *alba* 'Elegantissima' either side of the gazebo and paired planting of *Spiraea japonica* 'Gold Flame' in the front beds.

Town gardens at Chelsea tend to rely on ingenious utilization of space to appeal, with hard surfaces softened by an extravagant use of short-term planting. In the *Daily Telegraph* 'Patio Garden' paving, decking, pergola and water were important elements but the range of interesting plants supplied by Starborough

ing tender bamboos in pots, made subtle arching variations of leaf and stem. It is difficult to dissociate the use of bamboos from the rigorous aesthetic of Japanese gardens, which so often in its European interpretations seems crude pastiche. It remains to be seen whether, in the current revival of interest in these plants, they can be divorced from their oriental associations.

The active gardener who happily submits to the gentle tyranny of the vegetable world easily forgets the quieter pleasure of simply being among plants enjoyed by those who cannot garden. The designs presented by Help the Aged and the London Association for the Blind (LAB) were a reminder of what can be done to make a garden a pleasant place for the old and those who are blind or partially sighted. The small sheltered-housing communal garden designed by Robin Williams for Help the Aged provided ample seating in a richly planted scheme that focused on a raised pool with fountain and a Victorian-style summer house. Colour, scent, sound and movement, all these ingredients contributed to a setting where one would be happy to sit even when still capable of wielding a garden fork. Peter Rogers' design for LAB used changes of texture in the paving to alert the partially sighted or blind to the proximity of obstructions. Aromatic herbs, scented and brightly coloured flowers and plants with distinctive tactile qualities gave a dimension to the garden that could be appreciated equally by the blind and sighted.

Chelsea would not be Chelsea without an element of fantasy. One gardener's fantasy, however, is another's reality. Large rock gardens on the scale of Douglas G. Knight's gold-winning exhibit can be no more than a dream for many suburban gardeners, and yet, with the right financial resources and a site of adequate size, this might be just the thing. The swimming pool, increasingly *de rigueur* in Australia and America, is yet to be accepted as a standard feature of gardens in Britain. Climate, rather than the expense of installation, may be the explanation. Nonetheless, the swimming pool still suggests high living, even when the lining is a sombre black (as in the case of the *Sunday Times* 'Swimming Pool Garden') rather

Nursery showed that there is scope for planting the unusual even with just a few containers and small beds. Among the finds to be made here were some uncommon forms of the Japanese maple, *Acer palmatum*, including a tub-grown specimen of the variegated 'Butterfly', light and airy as its name suggests. A low shrub with leaves as finely dissected as many maples proved to be a birch, *Betula* 'Trost's Dwarf'. The climbers included the fine variegated form of *Trachelospermum jasminoides*, a plant for a sheltered and sunny position.

Even less conventionally planted was the little courtyard of bamboos exhibited by the European Bamboo Society, formerly the Bamboo Network, and designed by Michael Hirsh. In a tiny area measuring only 3·4 by 4·3 m (11 by 14 feet), several graceful species, includ-

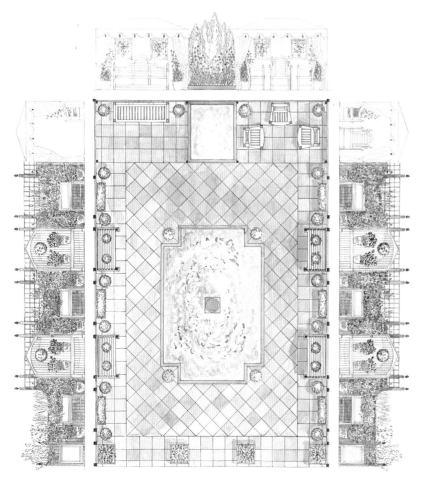

OPPOSITE At early Chelsea Shows there were numerous rock garden exhibits, and interest in this kind of gardening was stimulated by the books and articles of Reginald Farrer. Douglas G. Knight's gold-winning exhibit was one of two rock gardens in 1988.

LEFT Leonie Highton and John Bridges, who designed the Blue and White Garden for *House and Garden Magazine*, created a lavish theatrical set for entertaining.

than the conventional Californian blue. A compact garden largely taken up by a swimming pool is certainly a more feasible proposition than a romantic lakeside extravaganza like the nostalgic garden created by B & Q to celebrate 'The Glorious Twenties'. Although a garden well beyond the ambitions of the average Chelsea visitor, there were nice details (for instance, the bridge over the feeder stream) that perhaps could be adapted to something on a modest scale.

For pure theatre nothing could match the blue-and-white scheme presented by *House and Garden*. This was not a garden for every day. The colour scheme, which, we were told, was inspired by seventeenth-century Delft tiles, might pall after less than a year and the planting, dominated by delphiniums, marguerites,

petunias and lobelia, might quickly pass its zenith. But these strictures are misdirected. This was party time. How impressed one might be, as a tycoon's guest, sipping champagne and circulating with the *beau monde* in a stage set prodigally designed for a brief sensation.

On the strength of gardens shown in 1988 it is difficult to discern future trends. This year, in particular, many designers have honoured seventy-five years at Chelsea by looking back rather than forward. The Pershore College garden, 'Encompassing Britain into the 1990s', is unlikely to be the last word, the bold architectural features overwhelming interesting plants. Is it perverse to want to see more designers grappling with schemes that rely very little on structural elements – and some that make allowances for a child or two?

Plant Cinderellas Discovered

Stephen Lacey

It is to the credit of British nurserymen that so many tickets to the annual Chelsea ball are given to the Cinderellas of the plant world. While their ugly sisters elbow their way into customers' trolleys, these retiring individuals spend most of the year sitting in their nursery rows, neglected and forgotten. It is only for a brief few days in May that they enter the public arena, escorted into the limelight of the Great Marquee, and their names, emblazoned on black labels, come to the lips of amateur gardeners. Even here they are inclined to be upstaged by acrobatic bromeliads and performing cauliflowers and it is all too easy for us to forget everything about them by the time we get home.

Of course, there are good reasons why many plants remain obscure: they may have a weak constitution, an untidy manner of growth, or territorial ambitions; they may have been superseded by more modern cultivars or they may be just plain difficult to cultivate. But other plants are obscure simply because they always have been or because fashions have changed and left them behind; they may be lovely and easy garden plants. These are the Cinderellas I want to describe here.

The rose acacia, *Robinia hispida*, shown by Notcutts, received the Royal Horticultural Society's Award of Merit in 1934 yet still takes people by surprise. It is like a bright pink Chinese wisteria (for which it is an interesting companion on a warm wall) with elegant cut foliage and dangling racemes of pea-flowers. Though perfectly hardy, its brittle branches are easily snapped in the wind and need wall protection. It is by nature a suckering shrub but when grafted onto the common false acacia, it turns into a tree – an alternative to the ubiquitous golden 'Frisia', perhaps?

An old deciduous azalea hybrid, 'Narcissiflorum',
makes a compact bush and its semi-double flowers,
with a darker tone in the centre, are sweetly scented.

The rose acacia (*Robinia hispida*), best given a sheltered position because of its brittle branches, flowers in late spring and early summer.

With all eyes focused on the new golden birch shown by Blooms, I wonder how many people spotted the golden oak, *Quercus robur* 'Concordia', tucked into the Fortescue Garden Trust's stand. This has been around since 1843 and received a First Class Certificate, the RHS's highest award, in 1868. But how often do you see it today? It keeps its colour well, the young leaves beginning bright yellow and maturing to old gold, and it slowly forms a neat rounded tree, little more than 4·5 m (15 ft) high; an unusual subject for the modern small garden, in other words. Like most golden-leafed plants it objects to strong sunlight, so a position in part-shade is required.

There are a number of horse chestnuts in cultivation which you would have thought would have been seized upon by today's gardeners. Hillier Nurseries were showing *Aesculus* × *mutabilis* 'Induta' (Award of Merit 1959). This has cones of apricot flowers, marked with yellow – apricot is always a rare and desirable colour in gardens – and they appear in late May when the red and white displays provided by the giant horse chestnuts

are over. The foliage is typically broad and umbrella-like. Growth stops at around 4·5 m (15 ft).

Also on Hillier's stand was a selection of shrubs which normally find their way only into plantsmen's gardens. *Jasminum humile* 'Revolutum' is a topnotch subject which I first met in the herbaceous border of Arley Hall in Cheshire some years ago. It makes a free-standing mound of fine ferny leaves which are studded during the summer with comparatively large, bright yellow trumpets; they are only slightly fragrant, alas. Hardy except in the coldest areas, it enjoys a sunny position; grown against a wall it will attain 1·5 m (5 ft) or more in height. It was introduced in 1814 but got its Award of Merit as recently as 1976.

Denis Woodland drew my attention to *Pittosporum tenuifolium* 'Garnettii', which, he said, ought to be far more widely grown. He thought people were frightened away from these New Zealand evergreens because of their reputation for tenderness, but this form was reliably hardy in a sheltered spot. It is certainly a stunning foliage plant with leaves of pale green edged in

A close relative of the common horse chestnut, *Aesculus* × *mutabilis* 'Induta' makes a large shrub or small tree and its flowers are apricot in colour.

The yellow-flowered *Jasminum humile* 'Revolutum', an introduction from China in 1814, does well in full sun either free standing or against a wall.

white; in winter they are tinged with pink. It can grow to 3 m (10 ft) or more and mature plants bear tiny purplish-brown flowers, scented of honey, in late spring.

Another variegated evergreen on Hillier's stand was *Rhamnus alaterna* 'Argenteovariegata'. My plant always seemed to be dicing with death during its first few years in my garden but has subsequently proved a good inhabitant, coming through even quite hard winters with only the odd branch blackened. It is a dense vigorous shrub, growing to 4·5 m (15 ft) in a favourable corner, and its marbled grey-green leaves have white margins. It received an Award of Merit in 1976.

Halimium lasianthum (Award of Merit 1951) really is on the borderlines of hardiness, but what a sensation it is when buried in yellow, maroon-blotched saucers during July. If I lived in a very chilly area I would be prepared to grow it in a pot and put it into a cold frame for the winter. It makes a low sprawling mound and is ideal for the rock garden or the hot dry Mediterranean border, where it can lounge with cistuses, helianthemums and rosemaries.

Both Notcutts and Hillier Nurseries had the deciduous azalea 'Narcissiflorum' on their stands. This cultivar has been around for over a hundred years but it is still worth a place in the woodland garden; it received an Award of Garden Merit in 1969. Unlike many of its young cousins, it doesn't knock you for six with footballs of blazing cerise but provides a measured display of semi-double pale yellow funnels. The scent is sweet and delicious. For gardeners who cannot grow the tender scented rhododendrons 'Fragrantissimum' and 'Lady Alice Fitzwilliam', here is a substitute of grace and refinement.

Hopleys were showing *Ribes speciosum* (Award of Garden Merit 1925). Having spent much of my childhood in gardens reeking of fetid flowering-currant foliage, it was a happy surprise when I discovered that the family contained this gem. Its leaves are lobed, glossy and more or less evergreen, and in spring its spiny branches drip with a mass of miniature scarlet, fuchsia-like flowers. It is not as hardy as its vulgar relatives but is perfectly trustworthy against a sunny wall; if this is whitewashed the effect will be stunning. Plants can reach 3 m (10 ft) in height. I rate this shrub highly and it is a mystery to me why it is not more widely grown.

Ramparts Nursery always has some less obvious grey-leaved plants on display and this year Jack Gingell drew my attention to *Ptilotrichum spinosum roseum* (a plant also being shown by Potterton and Martin). This makes a neat, spiny, dome-shaped shrublet, 30 cm (12 in) high, and produces loose light heads of flower, rather like an alyssum or aethionema. On the species itself they are white; on this form clear rose-pink. It comes from the Mediterranean and wants good drainage and plenty of sunlight. It was given an Award of Merit in 1968 when shown by Valerie Finnis.

Mark Mattock told me that rose buyers seem to have lost interest in the modern hybrid shrubs which do not fit clearly into the currently perceived categories of perpetual-flowering bushes (hybrid teas and floribundas), ground-cover plants or old-fashioned shrubs. But many modern shrub roses also flower

Like many plants with grey leaves, *Ptilotrichum spinosum roseum* needs a well-drained sunny position. It forms a shrublet about 30 cm (12 in) high.

continuously and are trouble-free. Mattocks had 'Westerland' on their stand. This rose, introduced in 1969, bears clusters of large semi-double, bright orange blooms. Their catalogue lists many others including the single 'Golden Wings' and the semi-double magenta Yesterday'.

I wish I could remember which stand was exhibiting the rugosa rose 'Agnes'; my notes have let me down. This outstanding shrub, introduced in 1922, is always overshadowed by the famous white, pink and purple forms. Admittedly, it is not as luxuriant in growth or as free with its flowers as these, but how many of the older shrub roses bear double blooms of buff yellow? And their fragrance is unique, an astonishingly penetrating lemon cocktail; they are ideal for buttonholes.

Herbaceous perennials are enjoying a revival and there were plenty of interesting subjects in the marquee which might be taken up by gardeners. Blooms of Bressingham were showing *Hemerocallis dumortieri*, a neglected member of a currently very popular genus. It

was introduced in 1832 and received an Award of Merit in 1931. Like *H. flava* it has poise and quiet charm and is free from the coarseness of leaf and grossness of flower which characterizes so many of the recent cultivars. The small yellow, scented trumpets emerge from brown buds and blow above sprays of grassy foliage.

Smilacina racemosa (Award of Merit 1947) was also being shown. This is one of those useful perennials that can bring spring excitement to the summer herbaceous border without occupying too much ground space. In appearance it is similar to Solomon's seal but instead of producing white bells its tips erupt in cream blossom. It makes a stand 90 cm (3 ft) high and prefers a little shade; it dislikes limy soil.

Everyone grows lime-green *Alchemilla mollis* but, for some inexplicable reason, not *A. conjuncta*. The small alchemillas have never really caught on and nurseries are invariably muddled over their names. *Alchemilla conjuncta* is often sold as *A. alpina*, which is in fact just like a miniature *A. mollis*. Even Blooms had misnamed it on their stand! *Alchemilla conjuncta* is quite distinct from these soft hairy-leaved forms. Its leaves are dark, shiny and fingered, and have silver edges and silky silver undersides. Instead of forming clumps and seeding itself about, it spreads sideways, making a dense carpet, impenetrable to weeds. It is not invasive and makes a splendid edging to a border in sun or shade.

Hardy geraniums are all the rage as groundcover plants at present. They were in evidence all over the Show but the National Council for the Conservation of Plants and Gardens (NCCPG) made a special feature of them. One species that tends to be overlooked by gardeners is *Geranium maculatum*. It is not rare or endangered; it just lacks publicity. One of the earlier performers, it is also among the most attractive. The foliage is deeply lobed and the flowers an alluring shade of lilac-rose. It received an Award of Merit in 1967.

Also on the NCCPG stand was *Corydalis ochroleuca*. This is hard to find in nurseries and when you do see its name it has often been wrongly applied to its ferny-leaved cousin *C. ophiocarpa*. It is a cream counterpart to the

Geranium maculatum, a North American species, has been rather overlooked, despite the popularity of the genus. It comes into flower in late spring.

common yellow *C. lutea*, with exactly the same airy foliage, dainty flowerheads and seeding proclivities. It flowers non-stop and grows anywhere that isn't too hot and dry, so it is the friend of every ham-fisted gardener. Extraordinarily, Wisley grow plants of it in their new alpine house and perhaps this frightens people into thinking it is tricky.

A plant I have only recently acquired is *Carex riparia* 'Variegata' (Award of Merit 1974). I first saw it in the woodland garden of Knightshayes Court in Devon – and indeed it was sold to me elsewhere as the Knightshayes grass. It is an extremely pretty thing with very narrow leaves of almost pure white (it is certainly the whitest grass I have ever seen) and they make a beautiful show when flecked with their black flowerheads. It is really a sedge and likes moist conditions. It grows 90 cm (12 in) high and is best in part-shade. The Fortescue Garden Trust had it on their stand.

They also had *Tiarella wherryi* (Award of Merit 1948). Even the ordinary foam flower, *T. cordifolia*, is not used by gardeners as much as it might be. It is the ideal underplanting for woodland shrubs, carpeting quickly and thickly and providing a haze of cream for violently coloured azaleas. *Tiarella wherryi* has more deeply cut, ivy-shaped leaves with prominent brown veins, and it starts flowering later, in early summer, and continues for many weeks. Otherwise it has the same uses and creates the same effect.

Sorcery is practised at Chelsea by all the bulb firms, who turn Nature's calendar inside out and conjure up flowers on early spring bulbs for the last days of May. Snowdrops, crocuses and dwarf irises, only a memory the weekend before, are suddenly alive again; it is thrilling to see them back, but a touch sinister too.

The brightest colours catch the eye first and these usually belong to the tall hybrid tulips. By the time you have jotted down the names of all that take your fancy, you are ready for relief in the form of cool blue scillas and pale narcissi and your eyes tend to race over the dwarf species tulips nestling at their cousins' feet. It is true that many of these are unsatisfactory perennials for British gardens because our

summers are too damp and sunless for them, but several are trustworthy. Broadleigh and Avon Bulbs were showing red *Tulipa hageri*, rusty orange *T. whittallii* and scarlet *T. linifolia*, all of which received Awards of Merit in 1970. The latter is an especial favourite of mine and although grown in the tangle of a mixed border, pops up every spring to make a pool of flame between clumps of bronze fennel.

The best of all the species tulips is without doubt *T. sprengeri*, which was on the stands of Rupert Bowlby and the Fortescue Garden Trust. I have never understood why it is so expensive because it comes readily from seed and is an easy garden perennial in sun or shade. The last tulip to open, its flowers are guardsman's red within and buff green without and are supported on 90 cm (12 in) high stems. There is nothing like it for bringing drama to the early June border; I know a garden where it has seeded itself thickly between lime-green euphorbias and scarlet oriental poppies and the result is electrifying. It received an Award of Merit in 1948 but it had been recommended for another one at Chelsea this year!

Rupert Bowlby had a number of alliums on his stand, including the new 'Purple Sensation' which received an Award of Merit at Chelsea last year. As with tulips, it is the taller forms that tend to steal the show while the dwarf varieties twiddle their thumbs. Sky blue *Allium caeruleum* and pale pink *A. unifolium*, which ought to be in every garden, remain uncommon even though both have been around for ages. *Allium unifolium* received its Award of Merit as long ago as 1949. Both are easily cultivated on well-drained fertile soil and grow to about 45 cm (18 in) in height. They flower in June.

Ornithogalum nutans was on several stands. This Cinderella is a British wild plant and has probably been trodden on more times than it has been bought. Only in recent years have gardeners begun to recognize its worth. Of course, it is ideal for today's sophisticated palette – its silvery white stars are striped in olive-grey – and it is fitting that it was Sissinghurst Castle that submitted it for its Award of Merit in 1983. It naturalizes readily.

It is easy, as one becomes more knowledgeable about plants, to become snobbish too, to fill one's garden only with the rare and obscure and to scorn the familiar and the humble. I am not advocating here that gardeners should throw out their forsythia, purple buddleia and montbretia in favour of golden oak, rose acacia and smilacina; just that when the next vacancy occurs in a border, it is worth taking a panoramic view of British garden flora to find the right ingredient. Common old cerastium may strike the right silvery note but, well, ptilotrichum may be even better!

As an underplanting for shrubs, *Tiarella wherryi* has similar merits to its better known relative, the foam flower (*T. cordifolia*). Both spread quickly to form a thick carpet but they are not dangerously rampant. *Tiarella wherryi* has creamy flowers over a long season that starts in early summer.

The Flower-arranger's Garden

Christopher Lloyd

'There can't possibly be anything for you to look at there,' I exclaimed to a couple of members of the RHS Council who appeared to be transfixed in conversation before a stand consisting entirely of sweet peas. I had just arrived at the show on the Monday morning, the day when finishing touches are put to it and all the judging by innumerable committees and sub-committees is done.

Probably they weren't talking about the sweet peas in front of them at all. Walking round Chelsea with a friend is rather like walking round a garden. What you actually see before you acts as a trigger for discussion of the whole world of flowers and gardens, your own, your friend's and hordes of others that come to mind in a rapid-fire interchange of experience, opinion and fresh ideas.

In fact, when I had moved them on by my somewhat brash remark (I presently noticed that the owner of the stand was within hearing), I examined those sweet peas for quite a time, so fresh, each bowl a different variety and that incomparable fragrance (of what other flower can you say, 'It smells of sweet peas'?) floating off them in a continuous act of wooing.

Of all the thousands of gardeners who grow this much loved flower, quite a proportion have the show bench at their local horticultural society's exhibition in mind. Prize blooms are their ambition. But this was not an exhibit of prize blooms. It was clearly aimed at the majority of us who love the flower for itself, who want to be able to pick it in bunches from our own gardens and who arc willing slaves to this recurring task, as it becomes, picking all that have opened every three days, perhaps for three months on end, so that our plants continue to

Oriental poppies, shown here in Christopher Lloyd's garden at Great Dixter, are among the most sumptuous summer flowers for cutting.

grow and produce yet more flowers, rather than simply run to seed.

Shown in May, the sight and smell of sweet peas at Chelsea is a delightful reminder of pleasures to come at home. Or perhaps they bring a nostalgic pang, as we recall the days when we or our parents used to grow them, but our urban circumstances now preclude the possibility.

But we can still buy them in the market. As a nation, the British have never been great buyers of flowers as people are, for instance, on the Continent, where it is normal to present your hostess with a bunch whenever you have been invited out. But the great flower-arranging movement that gained momentum soon after the last war has had a tremendous impact on the trade.

Those who love 'doing the flowers', to put this little artistic act at its simplest, or who have

Regular cutting will ensure a long season from sweet peas, flowers of incomparable scent and available in a magnificent range of colours.

greater pretensions in the realm of floral art, can take in what they see at Chelsea in two different ways. They can either note flowers and foliage that are suited to the purpose and which they can easily grow in their own gardens, or they can note the use of flowers which they wouldn't dream of trying to grow, but which are, nonetheless, available to them in florists' shops. Something like the bird of paradise flower, *Strelitzia reginae*, will be expensive but exciting. For an occasion, why not splash out? Excuses are not hard to find.

There were lilies, *Lilium auratum*, in the friend's house where I dined after the last show. Were they expensive? I enquired. Quite, at £1.50 a stem. Actually, I didn't think that was really expensive at all. There were half a dozen enormous, exotic buds and blooms on each stem and they would be exhaling their rich scent for ten days at least.

One stand at Chelsea was devoted entirely to lilies. Since the techniques have been developed for producing them as cut flowers the year round, they have joined roses, chrysanthemums and carnations as the most popular of florists' flowers. However, their forced blooms are often misshapen, thin petalled and uncharacteristic, when flowered out of their normal season. They still look bright and they still pass as lilies. I wouldn't touch them myself, but many do.

Chelsea, of course, sees a great meeting of the seasons. Thanks to holding them back (crocuses, hyacinths, narcissi) or bringing them on (delphiniums, dahlias, michaelmas daisies), flowers of every season can be admired, but they may be quite uncharacteristic of the way they would look at their natural time. This doesn't really matter too much, so long as what we see is worth seeing.

Year-round flowers have advantages and disadvantages. Those perfectly-shaped tightly-furled rose buds shown, for instance, by Interflora, can be ordered and despatched to friends to mark a celebration at any time of the year and such dependability is a great convenience. But because they are always with us, they arouse no emotions. They become more of a ritual than an event. Whereas a few short-stemmed blooms of the old Bourbon rose 'Mme Isaac Pereire', flat-faced, crammed with petals, vivid magenta and with as rich a scent as any rose I know, are certainly something to get excited about, even if they only last in water for a couple of days. The florists wouldn't touch it, but we can grow it ourselves, and it was there, at the show, with little forcing necessary. Mme Isaac starts flowering in May, anyway, and many of the shrub roses are not far behind. So these are the roses to look at and to note, on Peter Beales', David Austin's and, to an extent, on Mattock's stands. I simply glaze when confronted by hybrid teas and floribundas, which I know will look nothing like they do here, when grown in my own garden. Later flower shows, when they have been gathered from the fields, is the time to assess them.

Carnations are worth looking at, and pinks. The distinction becomes ever more tenuous.

Year-round carnations are nothing new. So long as there is adequate light, it is natural for the perpetual-flowering carnation to make buds continuously and these are flowers which anyone can grow in a small greenhouse. Little heat is needed but plenty of ventilation. Air is not an expensive commodity. More than half a carnation's appeal is in its scent, or so I feel about it, but I must be in the minority. In the interests of other considerations, most florists' carnations have lost their scent entirely. But what's the use of a buttonhole if it isn't worth diving your nose into when a cigarette is lighted nearby? Many of the more unusually and interestingly coloured and marked carnations do still have a good scent, as I particularly noted in Steven Bailey's display. You may not find them at the florist's but you could grow some yourself.

Even though not lasting more than a few days in water, many old roses are lovely seen close to as cut flowers. 'Mme Isaac Pereire' is richly scented.

Alstroemerias have seen great developments of late and we'll be hearing more about them in the next few years. The new hybrids, tall, large-flowered and striped like schizanthus, were cornered by the Dutch cut-flower trade, and have only recently been released to the general public, Peter Smith being the first to retail them here as plants. He shows them and them alone at Chelsea, calling them Princess Lilies (they have no royal connections, however, and are not lilies). Now Steven Bailey has them and the range of varieties and availability is becoming wider. Although grown under glass by the florists, they appear to be pretty hardy, but can also be grown in large pots. After their first flowering and a cut back, they'll usually carry a smaller, secondary crop. In the garden, they have the advantage of being clump formers and clumps can be divided when necessary. The alstroemerias we are familiar with are runners.

These new hybrids grow 1·2 m (4 ft) tall or more and need support. They do not yet supersede the Ligtu hybrids, which have their own colour range and dainty charm, but greatly extend the seasonal range and are altogether more imposing.

Although our gardens owe much to South African flowers, exhibits from that country seem to come from another planet. In part, an other-worldly image is deliberately fostered but the flowers themselves are often strange. I have already mentioned strelitzias. Most of us feel that, by adoption, white arum lilies, *Zantedeschia aethiopica*, share a place in our inheritance. The personal identification could be closer still if more people realized that they can be treated as hardy plants. I can enthusiastically recommend the broad-spathed variety purveyed by Fibrex Nurseries which they have named 'White Sail'.

These arums enjoy a heavy, well-nourished, water-retentive soil. In the open their flowering is mainly in June–July and each bloom remains in condition for three weeks, unless scorched by hot sunshine. Therefore dappled shade suits them well. They can also be grown under water, to a depth of 23 cm (9 in) or so above their crowns, and this protects them in winter from any but the severest frosts. But there are many colourful hybrids on the market now, less hardy perhaps, but easily grown under frost-free glass. Protected in this way they flower a month or two earlier.

Gerberas have made stunning progress in recent years. These huge, glittering daisies, single or (even more compulsive) double, look almost too artificial to be real, and yet they patently are. For sheer glamour there are few flowers to beat them. The plant, with its coarse dandelion leaves, is hideous, but if you're simply interested in what it will produce for cutting, this may not matter. It is deep rooted and gives much the best results if grown in the ground. Under frost-free glass it will then give the minimum of trouble.

Protea is the South African national flower and it arouses great pride. For dried-flower arrangements, the English owner will keep a bloom for many years. Proteas certainly have their fascination but I find them slightly repulsive. Having seen my fill of them at Chelsea I feel I've earned a year's rest. Seeing that they grow on large shrubs, they hardly belong to the flower-arranger's garden unless you live in the maritime south-west. Tresco, in the Scilly Isles, is famed for them.

Gloriosa superba (or it may be *G. rothschildiana*) generally finds a place in some display at Chelsea, most likely with NAFAS (the National Association of Flower Arranging Societies). This is a lily-like, tuberous-rooted plant with orange and yellow Turk's-cap flowers on a climbing plant. The leaves have tendrils which enable the plant to scramble over shrubs in its native habitat. I remember it wild in Kenya and the thrill of being able to pick it in such quantities that I was able to make it the basis of a huge flower arrangement in a friend's house. That was in 1946, but I daresay it's still there.

Gloriosas can be grown like begonias, resting the tubers in a frost-free place in winter, then starting them off in moist peat under warm glass in spring. Subsequently they can be potted up with other summer flowerers like blue plumbago and purple *Polygala myrtifolia*, and stood against a warm wall in your courtyard or patio, allowing the lilies some trellis to climb over. Or you can plant them in the ground, against a wall, for the summer, as long as slugs are kept at bay. Whether you would then feel inclined to cut such precious material is doubtful.

Peonies at Chelsea are most strongly represented by the shrubby kinds, which we call tree peonies. They are at the height of their natural flowering season in May but are of doubtful value or availability as cut flowers. The herbaceous types then flowering are the *Paeonia officinalis* cultivars, of which the old double red 'Rubra Plena' is by far the most widespread. It is a splendid cut flower to give weight at the heart of a big arrangement. I find its rank smell a trifle off-putting but this is not generally too serious.

An old favourite among the herbaceous peonies is
Paeonia officinalis 'Rubra Plena', flowering in time
for Chelsea and good for cutting.

The best cut-flower peonies are the June-flowering *P. lactiflora* hybrids and they are still, as for many, many years, shown in force by the famous peony firm of Kelways. Well-grown peonies at the height of their season look splendid in any garden, but nowadays I exclude them from my borders. For one thing, they are not as easy to grow as they used to be. That may not be your experience, but in many gardens they suffer from peony botrytis, a disease which eats into and kills their flower buds, leaves and stems. You can spray against it but need to be more persistent than I am prepared to be.

Another disadvantage of peonies is their short and early flowering season. To have such large-growing passengers in a border from late June onwards is not on, as far as I'm concerned. But they are the ideal cut flower, to be gathered just as the buds are opening and before they have become drenched by rain. So I have my peonies in spare corners where they can sulk if they want to but surprise me with wonderful material when the mood is on them.

Most of the best flower-arranger's garden plants at Chelsea are in this hardy perennial range, and none are more important to us than

Part of the pleasure of Iceland poppies comes from watching the crinkled petals unfold from hairy buds.

'Mme Emile Debatène', one of the *Paeonia lactiflora* hybrids that flower in June.

the hostas, though we often grow them for their foliage alone. This is at its freshest and most beguiling in May. 'Wide Brim', in Blooms of Bressingham's excellent display, was new to me in 1988 and took my fancy, with its broad, lime-green margin to an otherwise darker and heart-shaped leaf. But exciting though variegated hostas undoubtedly are, they do not have it all their own way. The plain-leaved kinds can be lively, too, and yet act, arranged in generous clumps, as antidote and foil to brightly coloured flowers. The proudly upstanding 'Krossa Regal', with blue-grey foliage, carries itself like a torch bearer, while 'Royal Standard', a *Hosta plantaginea* hybrid, retains the fresh colouring of its lime-green foliage right into autumn. That is a valuable attribute both in the garden and for cutting. Its white, lily-like flowers open from August onwards and are deliciously

As foliage plants for the garden or for cutting, hostas, such as 'Krossa's Regal', are invaluable.

scented from night to morn.

Solomon's seal, *Polygonatum × hybridum*, has the same kind of presence and likes the same moist conditions, whether shaded or not. It is flowering at Chelsea time, its greenish bells hanging in a frieze below the two-ranked leaves. You see it used over and over again and I am not surprised. Common it may be, but it is inimitable. We can't be without it, nor without lilies-of-the-valley to grow in the same spot and to pick from for the house. You see some of the more unusual lilies-of-the-valley at Chelsea: *Convallaria majalis* 'Variegata' with yellow-striped leaves is good, though it reverts; the pink kind is distinctly grubby and the extra size in 'Fortin's Giant' has no extra appeal for me. The commonest is the best.

If you don't think of poppies as cut flowers, you should. Home Meadows shows the Iceland kind, *Papaver nudicaule*, in a strain that is neither too gross and unpractical nor too subtle. The colours are mainly straightforward in orange, yellow and white, with a few soft pink. Flower buds are included in their arrangements and these help. Each flower lasts for three or four days (pick them on the morning they open), which is as long as sweet peas give you.

Oriental poppies last as long, though you should always singe or boil the stem base before arranging them and it helps to give them a few hours' drink in a deep bucket before making your arrangement. Blooms showed an attractive variety with the unfortunate name of 'Beauty Queen'. It is a warm shade of apricot set off by dark stamens and held on slender stems.

Best of all for big arrangements is *Papaver bracteata* 'Goliath', with huge, blood-red blooms on long, sturdy stems. It seems almost too good to be true. An excellent associate is cardoon foliage (*Cynara cardunculus*) up to 1·5 m (5 ft) long, heavily toothed and of blue-grey colouring. Blooms show this and so does Beth Chatto, when she comes. Or you could bring the closely related globe artichoke (*C. scolymus*) into your plan, using the young globes as well as the foliage. That we saw on the RHS display of unusual vegetables from Wisley. Good to be able to eat your arrangement after admiring it; rather like a cat with a mouse.

When cutting rhododendrons, such as the old variety 'Sappho', removal of most of the leaves will help to keep the flowers from drooping prematurely.

Asphodeline luteus has spikes of starry yellow flowers that make an unusual addition to arrangements, and the seed heads are also decorative when dried.

No matter how often you go to Chelsea over the years, you always see things that are new to you. *Allium unifolium* was one such for me in 1988, shown by Rupert Bowlby. It makes a broad umbel of pink stars above a rod-straight stem 45 cm (18 in) tall. Many alliums, ornamental members of the onion tribe, are excellent for our purposes. *Allium caeruleum* has blue globes of quite tiny flowers while in 'Purple Globe' the sturdy flower head is 10 cm (4 in) across and of a rich purple colouring. This is a variety of *A. aflatunense* and grows 90 cm (3 ft) tall, so it associates well behind a group of glaucous-leaved hostas, which will cover its own foliage. As with many alliums, the foliage is dying by the time the flowers are reaching their peak. In none is this trait more evident than *A. giganteum*, which carries important-looking lilac globes on stems that are 1·5 m (5 ft) tall. I recommend growing it in a spare patch and using it entirely as a cut flower.

Not too distantly related are the asphodels, of which Blooms were showing *Asphodeline luteus*. It carries spikes of yellow stars that are 90 cm (3 ft) tall above grassy foliage in May and is a tough, clump-forming perennial of which I've planted a row to stand like sentinels along the top of a retaining wall. The seed heads are decorative, too, and can be gathered for drying.

Whether the trees and shrubs you see at Chelsea are suitable for flower arranging depends largely on whether the cut material will take up water. Even when given the full treatment by bashing and boiling their woody stems, followed by a long, deep drink, many will let you down. Such, I find, is the case with *Weigela florida* 'Variegata'; the ornamental crabs too are dicy. *Viburnum plicatum* in lacecap and snowball varieties is generally a great letdown, as could be seen even on the day of judging it with *V. plicatum* 'Shasta' in the awards marquee. *Euphorbia characias wulfenii* was perfectly happy, on the other hand, and won the highest First Class Certificate award.

I love to use rhododendrons in my arrangements when I have the chance. Notcutts were showing an old favourite, 'Sappho', which is almost white but with a large, deep purple blotch. Its stemmy, rangy habit suits it ideally

for cutting; so much easier to deal with than bushes of dense, congested growth. Obviously the flowers have a better chance of remaining turgid if most of the foliage is removed, but you would almost certainly want to do that anyway.

I find the variegated version of the Norway maple, *Acer platanoides* 'Drummondii', with a broad cream margin to its palmate leaves, ideal for cutting. The best material is usually near the top of a plant, so I keep mine as a tall bush, upper branches of which can be reached from a step ladder. There is another advantage to limiting its growth in this way. It readily reverts to branches of plain green foliage and these, being more vigorous than the variegated, soon take over if not removed. On a bush-tree, this is easily done.

The euphorbias include many fine garden plants and some, such as *Euphorbia characias wulfenii*, provide good material for bold arrangements.

Acer p. 'Drummondii' looks well when arranged with lilac. I now know, in my own garden, which lilac varieties are more likely to take up water and which will collapse (the late double white 'Mme Lemoine' is one of the worst offenders, alas). Notcutts are especially strong on lilacs. Their 'Firmament' is one I fancied, its pale 'blue' making it a most appropriate team mate for the acer, but what its behaviour is when cut, I do not know. I suppose I should visit the show on the last day, Friday, to find out. That would be an excellent test for a great deal of the cut material at Chelsea.

Old and New in Vegetables and Herbs

Joy Larkcom

One feature of the 1980s vegetable world is a tug of war between old and new varieties. Pulling strongly on the 'new' side are commercial pressures (there is money in developing and marketing new varieties) and the EEC seed legislation. Intentionally or not, the weighty hand of EEC bureaucracy is tending to squelch old varieties into oblivion. Pulling as strongly in the other direction are traditional amateur gardeners. Many men cling loyally to the old varieties they have always grown and know suit their conditions. OK, there are women vegetable growers as well, but I bet 99 per cent of the diehards are male!

Both teams were in evidence at Chelsea this year. They were face to face on the National Institute of Agricultural Botany (NIAB) stand, where, with true civil-service impartiality, the merits of old and new were clearly set forth. 'Oldies' which came in for praise included the leek 'Winterreuzen', with its long shaft, good yield and winter hardiness; that delicious calabrese 'Romanesco', with its unusual lime-green conical head and good culinary qualities (though its drawback of variability was mentioned); and the tomato 'Gardener's Delight', known for its sweet flavour and good skin finish even in poor conditions. 'Southport Globe' and 'White Lisbon' onion, 'Little Gem', 'Salad Bowl', 'Lobjoit's Green' cos and 'Red Lollo' lettuce all had honourable mentions, though I feel 'Red Lollo' had been pulled onto the wrong side. Surely this beautiful decorative Salad Bowl type of lettuce was selected relatively recently by an Italian seed company and is really 'new'.

Marshalls Seeds, a company rooted in the fertile Fen soil of Wisbech, were the only seedsmen to make a feature of vegetables. New and old were stacked high, shoulder to shoulder, on their traditional Fenland

The Highfield Nurseries cottage garden showed
a combination of traditional and modern ways of
growing old and new varieties of fruit and vegetables.

farm cart, the old represented by the rosy 'Purple Top' turnip, dating back to the last century, and their own, aptly named, 'Giant Fen Globe' onion, selected carefully over the last thirty years.

New varieties exhibited included the glasshouse lettuce 'Novita', the sweet pepper 'Clio', the fast-growing all-male asparagus 'Franklim', and potatoes 'Concorde' and 'Dunluce'. All of these were outstanding in their different ways and available to amateur gardeners through their catalogue.

It was up to the NIAB to spell out the advantages of modern varieties, the majority of which are now F_1 hybrids. Vigour, uniformity and high yield (partly because there are fewer unproductive plants), are their most notable characteristics, coupled frequently with resistance to disease and pests. With some vegetables the F_1 hybrids are now so good that virtually all the commercial crops are from F_1 seed. This is true of Brussels sprouts, Chinese cabbage, sweet corn, calabrese, cucumber and sweet pepper, and these F_1 varieties figure ever more prominently in amateur seed catalogues. They are undeniably good but the price is high – an inevitable consequence of the complex breeding

'Lobjoit's Green' is a reliable old variety of cos that is winter hardy and therefore suitable for autumn sowing to be used the following spring.

procedure which lies behind them.

The NIAB highlighted a few new varieties of outstanding value to amateurs, such as the Chinese cabbage 'Tip Top', which has large heads and, unlike the old varieties, won't run to seed at the drop of a hat. Another is the sweet corn 'Candle', one of the new 'supersweet' types. It must, however, be grown apart from the traditional varieties or crossing will occur and the sweetness be lost.

Old and new was the theme on the *Gardening from Which?* stand, which embraced the 100-year span between 1938 and 2038, looking backwards to the days when each cos lettuce was carefully tied to blanch it, and to a future when, it is hoped broad beans will have built-in resistance to blackfly. Their choice of varieties reflected the requirements of modern gardeners – notably the need for productivity and compactness to compensate for the small size of the average 1980s vegetable plot.

An example was the odd-looking, semi-leafless pea 'Bikini', in which many of the leaves have been reduced to claw-like tendrils. This characteristic was a naturally occurring break, which proved of great benefit in combine-harvesting commercial peas – less leaf to tangle with! But it is also useful for amateurs. The peas tend to be self-supporting, they are better 'ventilated' and therefore healthier, and the tendrils themselves make a tasty vegetable if steamed.

'Mini' cauliflowers are another new concept in vegetable growing illustrated here – again a spin-off from research into commercial vegetable growing. Certain summer varieties of cauliflower can be grown as close as 15 cm (6 in) apart to produce small curds about 7·5 cm (3 in) in diameter, which are ideal for deep freezing. As it is ready in about three months, the mini cauliflower gives far higher returns than a traditional cauliflower, which occupies a large patch of ground for many months, producing one solitary cauliflower at the end of it ... if you're lucky!

Dwarf varieties of vegetables are another development welcomed by space-pressed gardeners. Two good examples on the *Which?* stand were the high-yielding but compact broad bean 'The Sutton', and the new, pretty-leaved tomato 'Totem', ideally suited to pots on patios or to flowerbeds – an exceptionally sturdy, neat little plant.

When it comes to diversity in vegetables the twentieth century has been a dull stretch. Our ancestors used to cultivate a far wider range of vegetables than we do. Some of these were low yielding, which may explain their fall from favour, but many did nothing to deserve the fate of negligence. At last there are signs of a yearning for more 'interesting' vegetables, for colourful forms of those commonly grown and even for new kinds, and this was reflected in the choice of plants featured in the RHS exhibit of 'lesser grown' vegetables.

The range of vegetables grown commercially is limited but, as the RHS exhibit of lesser-grown vegetables showed, the amateur has a wide choice.

Those chosen ranged from the glamorous to the humble. In the glamour category was sea kale (enticing blanched samples peering through the top of a sea-kale pot), a lovely vegetable with a sadly short season. The same could be said of globe artichokes and even sweet fennel, all handsome, delectable vegetables with a stately-home aura about them. A striking old-timer was a clump of purple-podded peas. (The peas inside are an ordinary green – a minor disappointment!) Equally striking are the brilliant scarlet stems of rhubarb chard, displayed to full effect in a large terracotta pot. In practice its slightly less stunning cousin, white-stemmed Swiss chard, is better value as it is slower to bolt. In fact it is one of the most underrated of easily grown but 'lesser grown' vegetables, high yielding over a long period, with both stems and leaves being edible.

The old method of blanching wild sea kale, found in coastal areas, was to stack stones around the plant. The blanched shoots make a choice spring vegetable.

Two other old-fashioned vegetables were asparagus peas, with reddy brown flowers, clover-like leaves and quaint angled pods, and red orach, edible when young and a joy for flower arrangers when flowering and setting seed. It was surrounded by a patch of curly endive. This is an old vegetable which is now attracting the interest of plant breeders so new, naturally blanched and vastly improved varieties are becoming available.

Several belonged to the humble end of the scale: Good King Henry, the poor man's asparagus; nasturtiums, at last recognized again for the culinary qualities of both leaves and flowers; and the decorative American 'Gilfeather' turnip, in which leaves and root can be eaten. Salad plants were prominent, some still only one step removed from the wild: for example, dandelion, salad rocket, the continental 'Treviso' chicory and miner's lettuce (*Claytonia perfoliata*), an American native which became naturalized here in the nineteenth century. As I've been 'pushing' claytonia ever since I learnt about it in Europe nearly twelve years ago, seeing it in the RHS Chelsea exhibit was to me a notable milestone.

Coloured lettuces are enjoying a resurgence in popularity in shops, restaurants and gardens. I've never before seen so many featured at Chelsea, some even used as bedding plants. Most eye-catching in the RHS exhibit were the deep red tints of the old favourite 'Continuity', and a box of the beautiful, coyly frilled 'Red Lollo', mentioned previously. (Everyone seems to be ignoring its stablemate 'Green Lollo', an equally pretty, and slightly bulkier plant!)

There's a new look to tomatoes too. Several golden varieties were being grown in the RHS greenhouse – an old look really, as the first tomatoes to reach Europe in the sixteenth century were yellow. Strings of tiny yellow currant tomatoes were ready picked in baskets, alongside the thick-walled American 'Striped Cavern', sliced open to display the truly cavernous inside 'designed' for stuffing! A victim of EEC legislation, 'Striped Cavern' seed cannot yet be sold in this country, though seedsmen Thompson & Morgan are marketing the plantlets – which is allowed. On the Jersey States mouth-watering stand nearby was a new cherry tomato, 'Cherito', an improvement over the ever-popular 'Gardener's Delight'. It had been grown hydroponically, like so many commercial tomatoes, far removed from the contaminating influence of common garden soil that all gardeners used to rely on!

Perhaps this is the place to mention that other notable produce stand and perennial feature at Chelsea – the National Farmers' Union exhibit. As always it was a marvellous spectacle of home-grown fruit, vegetables, mushrooms and flowers, with superb blemish-free pyramids of red cabbage, creamy cauliflowers and Chinese cabbage towering elegantly into space.

Chinese cabbage gives an excuse for one last trip to the RHS stand, for oriental vegetables figured prominently in their 'lesser grown' collection. Some, like the tripartite-leaved herb

ABOVE A number of selections of dandelion, a traditional salad green, have been made by French growers. Blanching greatly improves the flavour.

LEFT High yield and uniform size are important considerations for commercial growers of tomatoes. A well-flavoured and dependable variety for the amateur is 'Gardener's Delight'.

'Mitsuba' are still virtually unknown to the gardening public; others, the Japanese mustard 'Mizuna' among them, are gaining a toehold in the affections of adventurous gardening cooks and are becoming more widely grown. Pak choi, flowering Chinese cabbage, and the 'Green Lance' flowering kale gave us a glimpse of an exciting world of oriental brassicas waiting to be taken up. I just wish there had been a few cut-and-come-again patches of oriental greens, as this is one of the easiest ways to grow them, producing lovely, tender juicy pickings for salad or cooking, and ideally suited to autumn and early spring, when our range of vegetables is at its most limited.

The RHS exhibit included more exotic oriental curiosities: the long roots of Japanese burdock; 'celtuce', or stem lettuce, the oriental lettuce grown for its fat swollen stem which has, perhaps not surprisingly, a refreshing lettuce flavour; the tiny, knobbly, nut-flavoured tubers of the Chinese artichoke; and giant radishes. Who knows, in ten years' time all these may have become as familiar as coloured lettuces are today.

A final thought on diversity. Could we find future gardeners cultivating mushrooms? In the scientific corner of the marquee the Institute of Horticultural Research were telling the tale of their research into the cultivation of novel mushrooms related to our common field mushroom. In other parts of the world gardeners can and do cultivate quite a range of mushrooms. Perhaps results of the Institute's work will eventually filter through to our vegetable plots and allotments.

Chelsea gives the gardening public clues on not only what is being grown, but *how* it is being grown. And here again new practices and old are jostling for attention, sometimes in competition, sometimes harnessed together. Vegetable growers have always utilized domestic materials in their gardening (how about the waxed calico on early garden frames?) and today the trendy gardener makes extensive use of plastics, unaesthetic though they may be. *Gardening from Which?* neatly married old with new in a patch of the continental salad mixture 'Saladini', which furnishes the kitchen with a won-

derful range of salad plants over many months, growing under the warm veil of a 'floating cloche' made from ultra-light, woven plastic film. This acts as a windbreak, protecting crops against the elements and bringing them on earlier. There are numerous modern materials welcomed and utilized by modern vegetable growers: plastic mulching films; perforated plastic films also used as floating cloches; 'growing bags'; and lightweight sterile potting composts. These are used along with artificial fertilizers, chemical insecticides, fungicides and weedkillers.

But there's a reverse side to the coin, with many gardeners reacting against chemicals and turning to 'organic' growing. In a recent survey carried out by *Gardening from Which?* among its 170,000 members, nearly a third said they used mainly organic methods. This growing band were well catered for at Chelsea. Wye College had a demonstration of compost making on an industrial scale; the Henry Doubleday Research Association – who have now established a national demonstration organic garden in Warwickshire – showed different mulching techniques, and many commercial stands offered organic manures.

Less reliance on chemical aids leads to more emphasis on building up the soil fertility and growing plants really well. As a means to this end there's a noticeable increase in gardeners adopting the 'bed system'. In this very old system a garden is laid out in (usually permanent) beds a yard or so wide, where instead of being planted in rows, plants are grown at equidistant intervals. This saves space, saves on manure and, above all, avoids the need to tread on the soil and so damage the soil structure. Moreover, when the plants are full-grown, their leaves form a shading canopy over the surface, preventing weed seed from germinating.

Energetic gardeners go one stage further, creating 'deep' beds raised above ground level by the incorporation of generous quantities of manure and compost. Again it was *Gardening from Which?* who chose to demonstrate this, by growing some of their modern varieties in a deep bed. Highfield Nurseries, in their 'updating' of a 1913 garden, demonstrated the

When choosing varieties the growers
represented on the National Farmers' Union
stand face commercial pressures the amateur can ignore.

The National Farmers' Union exhibit of commercially
grown produce is in the tradition of the exhibits
formerly staged by the major seed companies.

row-less, equidistant spacing concept, with a bed of sweet corn, dwarf broad beans, beetroot and coloured 'Salad Bowl' lettuce lying neatly behind their low 'step-over' hedge of apples.

In some ways the twentieth-century would-be organic gardener has an easier task than his predecessors, who, before the advent of artificial fertilizers and modern garden chemicals, were all, perforce, 'organic'. We have the men from the ministry to thank for enforcing high standards in vegetable seeds, all now complying with statutory minimum levels of germination and purity.

Less obvious is the work done by bodies like the Plant Health Inspectorate, who had a stand in the scientific section at Chelsea. Thanks to their eternal vigilance, we are still free from the Colorado beetle, which plagues European and American gardeners. A new threat to the beetroot family is *rhizomania*, a disease caused by a virus carried inside a microscopic fungus. It has already reached us from France and Holland and could become serious. However, control measures on the sale of beet seed, such as ensuring that beet seed is rubbed to remove the fungus, should prevent this happening.

Amateur gardeners, along with farmers and commercial growers, benefit from the Inspectorate's potato certification scheme, introduced in the late 1970s. All potato seed crops must now be grown on soil that has been tested to prove it is free of potato cyst nematodes, and seed crops are subject to testing once or twice during their growing season. Thus we are guaranteed disease-free potato seed, and are spared some of the horrendous scourges which can afflict the potato crop.

But to cheerier matters than potato eelworm. One of the happy repercussions of the small size of the average twentieth-century garden is a return to earlier approaches to vegetable growing, with the realization that flowers and vegetables don't *have* to be segregated, and that many vegetables are ornamental and can become a decorative feature in their own right. Mixing plants belongs to the centuries-old cottage-garden tradition, stemming from the days when almost all vegetables, flowers and herbs were grown for utilitarian purposes – whether culinary, medicinal or domestic. So they took pot luck together, cheek by jowl, creating the colourful hotchpot which epitomizes the cottage garden.

Using vegetables ornamentally probably began in the sixteenth century with the introduction of exotic, mainly American vegetables to the gardens of the European gentry. Like the flowers of the day, they were planted in elaborately patterned formal beds or parterres, boxed in with neat little hedges, so they would not offend any sensibilities if viewed from the drawing room. The classic modern example is the reconstructed Renaissance garden at Château Villandry in the Loire: closer to home there is Rosemary Verey's exquisite 'potager' at Barnsley House. Inspired by these models, vegetable plots with a consciously 'pretty' element are being created all over the country.

Certainly there were several examples at last year's Chelsea of little formal gardens making full use of decorative vegetables – from red lettuce, beetroot and purple-podded peas to climbing runner beans and ornamental kales. This year it was the turn of the cottage garden, personified in the Women's Institute garden designed by Jacqui Moon, which won the award for the best garden in the show. Here beetroot, cabbages, peas and rhubarb were barely separated by a brick path from the traditional cottage-garden herbs and aquilegias, pinks and lupins. This idea was also seen at work in Ryl Nowell's attractive 1913 cottage garden, where, under the cheery eye of a scarecrow, which received almost as much media attention as certain gnomes in a previous year, vegetables and cottage plants mingled happily together.

Herbs, too, have leapt back into fashion, and one couldn't help noticing how frequently at Chelsea they were being used decoratively. There was the lovely patch of purple sage, bronze fennel and purple-flowered chives in the Women's Institute garden, contrasting here with grey artemisia and the bold green of sorrel. In the Highfield Nurseries' garden nearby a lovely stone urn was planted with a fine bay, edged with the delicate variegated 'Silver Posie' thyme. Similar examples of herbs providing a decorative touch could be found all over

Chelsea. Occasionally they were in window boxes, to which many are well suited, being better adapted to the dry conditions which beset window boxes than some traditional window-box plants. There is now a huge demand for herbs, and Marshalls Seeds had a collection of mainly variegated herbs which they are supplying by mail order: 'Doone Valley' thyme, tricolour and purple sage, variegated apple mint, golden oregano and French tarragon (the good one!).

But herbs are essentially grown for their practical qualities. In the John Chambers'/Gale's 'Honey Bee Garden' borage, chives and various flowering thymes vied for the attention of the twelve or so *real* honey bees in the garden. Wells

A traditional approach to mixing herbs, vegetables and flowers, as in Ryl Nowell's exhibit, is fully consistent with an adventurous choice.

and Winter, regular exhibitors at Chelsea, featured a wide range of useful herbs, from tree onions, calamint and angelica to the golden-leaved elder, *Sambucus plumosa aurea*: the bark, leaves, flowers and berries of elder are all used in traditional herbal medicine.

The use of herbs – surely among the oldest plants cultivated by man – in modern medicine and allied fields, is another interesting case of old versus new. The British Herb Association stand highlighted the serious research into the properties of herbs now being undertaken at the West of Scotland College. It is quite possible that volatile oils from herbs may eventually replace some of the chemical sprays, medicines, artificial preservates and food flavourings which are causing public anxiety. Volatile herb oils can inhibit disease bacteria and the agents which bring about food poisoning and decay. In the case of salmonella, for example, oils from verbena, thyme and bay, in that order of effectiveness, can all inhibit quite dramatically the development of this food-poisoning bacterium.

Research is also being undertaken into the cultivation of herbs. It has been shown that the biochemical quality of herbs grown in Scotland is comparable to those from the Mediterranean and other European countries far more commonly associated with herb production. Indeed oil from Scottish-grown summer savory is superior to French and a close second to Hungarian, generally considered the best. The West of Scotland College are also looking into the possibility of juniper becoming a commercial crop in Scotland, and to the large-scale cultivation of warmth-loving herbs in greenhouses.

Perhaps the last word on herbs at Chelsea this year should go to Rosemary Titterington's Iden Croft Herb Farm stand, devoted to plants with fragrance and texture chosen for the enjoyment they can give to the visually handicapped. Rosemary Titterington is one of the largest producers of herbs in the country – more than 450 different varieties can be bought at the Iden Croft Herb Farm – and she is an acknowledged expert on many aspects of herb cultivation and use. When her mother started to lose her sight, Rosemary Titterington began to appreciate not just the fragrance of herbs, but their tactile qualities. This led to research into the whole subject, and eventually to the establishment of a new garden for disabled and blind people on the herb farm. The attractive Chelsea exhibit was crammed with many herbs with these qualities: from the familiar marjorams, sages, thymes and mints to many pelargoniums, with their variously scented leaves, the sedums and houseleeks, with their fleshy 'feelable' leaves, *Choisya ternata*, edelweiss, artemisias – all interesting to touch. For those who have sight there were colourful pinks, lavenders and much more besides. It was a fascinating collection, developing a new role for some of the best loved of old garden plants.

For those with little space herbs have much to offer,
as was shown in the courtyard garden exhibited by
the Lavers and District Horticultural Society.

Fruit Trees
to Measure

Brian Self

For hundreds of years gardeners have practised the technique of budding or grafting fruit trees on rooted shoots, known a rootstocks. According to one authority, the technique was 'used by the Chinese before 2000 BC, and even earlier by the first known citizens of Mesopotamia' (R. J. Garner, *The Grafter's Handbook,* 1947, new edition in preparation). Fruit trees do not generally come true from seed so this technique was essential for maintaining selected varieties.

It was recognized long ago that the rootstock influenced the way the grafted shoot or scion developed. In *A Treatise of Fruit Trees* of 1757, Thomas Hitt warned fruit growers, 'if they buy their trees of nurserymen, they should diligently inquire upon what stocks they are propagated. For stocks are in some measure a sort of soil to the kinds of tree raised on them.' However, until the selection of rootstocks was put on a scientific basis, fruit trees in an orchard were usually large and showed considerable variation in vigour and performance. Even seventy-five years ago it would have been virtually impossible to acquire trees on dwarf or semi-dwarf rootstocks; none would have been considered suitable for the intensive orchard or the small garden. In contrast to the early Chelsea shows, where there were no exhibits of dwarf fruit trees, displays at Chelsea in 1988 showed compact and manageable trees on a range of stocks.

Research carried out this century into the influence of the rootstock on the scion has given the professional and amateur fruit grower made-to-measure trees, whose size can be forecast in advance. Wherever temperate fruits are grown in the world the name of East Malling is associated with rootstock science and practice that has led to these developments.

Apple trees at Wisley. Amateur as well as commercial growers have benefited from the study of rootstocks carried out by the Research Station at East Malling.

As a result of the recent closer integration of horticultural research in England, the Research Station has changed its name to AFRC Institute of Horticultural Research, East Malling. But the name change does not alter the fact that in 1988, like the Royal Horticultural Society's Chelsea Show, the Research Station celebrates its seventy-fifth anniversary. Exhibits at this year's show demonstrated the way the amateur has benefited from the Station's long programme of research.

Before this century apples were the fruit trees for which rootstock selection was the most advanced. In the early 1900s two broad groups of rootstocks were recognized: Seedling, Crab or Free stocks and Paradise stocks. The former were usually raised from seed, derived from a variety of sources, including wild crab and cider pomace, the residue after pressing apples, which contained pips. The term Paradise was applied to the vegetatively multiplied stocks, which at that time were mistakenly thought to be dwarfing. It was not until the Paradise stocks were evaluated that different types were shown to have different vigour. The name Paradise was used as early as the seventeenth century. John Parkinson, in his *Paradisi in Sole*, published in 1629, described it as 'being a dwarfe Tree, whatsoever fruit shall be grafted on it, will keep the graft low, like unto itself and yet beare fruit reasonably well' (quoted by F. A. Roach in *Cultivated Fruits in Britain*, 1985).

The early work on the collection of Paradise rootstocks was initiated at East Malling by the first Director, R. Wellington, and continued by his successor, Dr R. G. Hatton, later Sir Ronald Hatton. Some 71 collections of apple stocks were obtained from nurseries in England, France, Germany and Holland. Many of these stocks were mixed or found not to be true to name. The stocks were firstly classified on their botanical characters and grouped into sixteen different types. Hatton's important first report summarizing work in progress at East Malling on Paradise apple stocks was published in the *Journal of the Royal Horticultural Society* in 1917. Hatton wrote at the time: 'Yet growers today are largely planting trees on stocks that are not guaranteed as true to name, and which

are, moreover, not infrequently mixed with several other varieties of "Paradise".'

Hatton saw the need to bring order from this confusion; he dropped the various trade names such as Broad-leaved, English Paradise, Doucin, French Paradise, etc. and awarded them East Malling type numbers, e.g. Malling Type I, II, III, etc. The 'Type IX', which had potential as a dwarfing stock, was originally received in four collections under the names Jaune de Metz from France and Paradise Mitzer and Paradise Gelber from Germany. It was not then grown by English nurserymen. In 1917, after three years' experience with 'Type IX', Hatton remained guarded: 'it seems quite possible that it might afford a useful dwarfing type, if suitable to this country. Further obser-

An ornamental and practical way of growing fruit was shown by Highfield Nurseries with cordon arches of apple cultivars on 'MM. 106' rootstock.

vation is required to establish this point.' In 1921 he was still cautious about recommending 'M.IX', though he favoured 'Type I', Broad-leaved, for permanent bush trees; 'Type II', Doucin, for bush fillers (short-term bushes to start cropping early) and general dwarf trees; and 'Type V', Doucin Ameloire, for cordons and garden trees.

Gradually the name and the word 'Type' ceased to be used and the stocks were distributed and known by their 'M' numbers all over the world. It was not, though, until 1971 that Roman numerals for rootstocks 'M.I' to 'M.XXV' were replaced by arabic equivalents.

During the 1930s Hatton was able to predict the influence of his selected stocks on the growth and cropping of varieties worked on

Highfield Nurseries showed the apple cultivars 'Bountiful' and 'Jupiter' on 'MM. 106' rootstock, and 'Greensleeves' as a step-over edging on 'M. 27'.

them. He came down in favour of 'M.IX' as the dwarfing type though he cautioned users on its anchorage: it has an extensive root system but the roots are brittle and the tree requires a permanent support. 'M.VII' was described as semi-dwarfing and 'M.IV' moderately vigorous. The latter stock was little used in Britain: its poor anchorage and nursery performance precluded Hatton from recommending it although it was planted on the Continent. Both the vigorous 'M.I' and M.II' were extensively used, the latter especially with 'Cox's Orange Pippin'. The very vigorous 'M.XII' and 'M.XVI' were both planted and the more precocious 'M.XVI' was favoured. However, the demand for strong rootstocks decreased as the advantages of less vigorous ones were demonstrated.

As a result of a breeding programme begun at East Malling in 1928 by H.M. Tydeman in collaboration with H.B. Crane of the John Innes Horticultural Institution at Merton, a new series of rootstocks was produced, the Malling-Merton (or MM.) types. They were originally bred for resistance to the woolly aphid, a problem on apple roots in warmer climates of the world. From nearly 4,000 seedlings, some 16 were short-listed and a selection of these were bulked up for planting trials on growers' farms and for release to nurseries.

By the late 1950s some of the MM. stocks proved to be superior to the older stocks of equivalent vigour: the semi-dwarfing 'MM.106' better than 'M.VII', the vigorous 'MM.111' better than 'M.II' and 'M.XXV' better than 'M.XVI'. Another stock, 'MM.104', which showed great potential proved to be susceptible to waterlogging on many trial sites.

In parallel with the MM. series, H.M. Tydeman was engaged in a series of crosses using the dwarf 'M.IX' as a parent. From one thousand seedlings, six stocks with a range of vigour extending from very dwarf to super vigorous were produced. One of this selection, the semi-dwarf 'M.26', was distributed in 1958 and was planted by both commercial and amateur growers. An eighteen-year-old tree of 'Ribston Pippin' on 'M.26' formed the subject of an exhibit at Chelsea in 1965. Two years before the Station had celebrated its Golden Jubilee by mounting a display at Chelsea entitled 'Fifty years of rootstock research'.

Another stock from the same stable was the very dwarf 'M.27', and this was distributed to nurserymen in 1975. This most dwarfing of all apple stocks, although of limited use to commercial growers in this country, has proved of value for planting on very fertile soils in continental Europe, while at home it is found to be an interesting stock for the amateur grower. This stock featured in exhibits of fruiting and ornamental cultivars at Chelsea in 1980 and some of the new columnar apples on 'M.27' were displayed in the Scientific Section of the Show in 1986. 'Step over' or single-tier espalier trees on this rootstock were featured in the Cotswold country garden of Highfield Nurseries, Whitminster, at Chelsea in 1988.

Pears on pear stock have a reputation for coming into bearing very slowly, a reputation summed up in the saying 'Plant pears for your heirs'. Seedling pear stocks were used for producing large pear trees well into the beginning of this century. The seed for stocks was obtained from perry pomace and dessert pears; sometimes hawthorn and mountain ash were used. Although quince stocks were known, they were not greatly used until Hatton had compared a number of vegetatively propagated quinces. He later recommended three main types from a wide collection at East Malling.

Thus, Malling 'Quince A', 'B' and 'C' were introduced to nurseries. 'Quince B' was very similar in appearance and vigour to 'A' and, although used widely in the 1930s, it is little used today. 'Quince C' proved to be the most dwarfing and Hatton recommended it for the shy cropping and vigorous varieties like 'Doyenne du Comice' and 'Beurré Hardy'.

Some pear cultivars failed to form a permanent and strong union with quince and these 'incompatible' cultivars were identified and listed. This bud or graft failure, or delayed incompatibility, at the union was a real problem for nurserymen and growers. In the hope of avoiding incompatibility problems, many pear stocks were examined for their vigour control

but most proved to be difficult to propagate. Techniques for 'double working' with an intermediate graft where a variety was incompatible with quince were introduced. Later in 1953 R. J. Garner developed a simpler method for overcoming incompatibility by double shield budding – placing a slip of an intermediate behind the bark.

Hatton mentioned that he was misled by the previous orthodox grouping of the Paradise and Free apple stocks being synonymous with dwarfing and vigorous growth. 'When, however, we approach the question of stocks for stone fruits,' he wrote in 1921, 'we find ourselves on the threshold of a field altogether more confused.' Some stocks were propagated by seed, others, for example, 'Pershore', rooted from suckers taken from orchard trees.

Between 1914 and 1916 Hatton invited nursery firms in Europe to send samples of plum stocks in use and these included Brompton, Brussel, Common Plum, Mussel, Myrobalan and St Julien. Some proved to be difficult to propagate, others were found to be incompatible with some cultivars. He demonstrated the importance of using the correct cultivar/rootstock combination and making this knowledge available. Clonal selections were made of those traditionally propagated by seed and from the collection of the main types orchard trials were planted in 1919 and 1921.

Eventually 'Myrobalan B' was recommended as a very vigorous stock though it did not induce early bearing and some cultivars did not form a sound graft union with it (they were incompatible). It had the advantage of ready multiplication by cuttings and this stock was extensively used by commercial growers but, because of its vigour, less so by gardeners. A second important plum stock, 'Brompton', slighty less vigorous than 'Myrobalan B' was introduced. This had the advantage of being compatible with all cultivars worked on it and, until recently, was widely used by commercial and amateur growers.

As stocks of intermediate vigour, 'Marianna' and 'Pershore', were examined and they cropped heavily for their tree size. 'Pershore', unlike 'Marianna', was compatible with all cultivars, though it was difficult to propagate. Both stocks were used for many years and a strong interest remained in the West Midlands for 'Pershore' until recently.

Following evaluation at East Malling, selections of the semi-dwarfing stocks Common Mussel, Common Plum and St Julien were all issued to nurseries. Because 'Common Mussel' was propagated by the laborious method of root cuttings and produced tree root suckers it gradually became obsolete. 'Common Plum' was widely used until the 1960s but eventually 'St Julien A' became the obvious first choice for all fruit growers.

A further development of importance to amateur growers resulted from research carried out by Dr A. Beryl Beakbane. In 1948 she visited the Orleans area of France to seek suitable parent plants for a new race of plum stocks and subsequently made a selection which included early fruit production on cultivars worked on it. This dwarfing St Julien was distributed by East Malling to nurseries in 1977 under the name 'Pixy'. Although not widely used by commercial growers it is now in strong demand by amateur growers.

Peach seedlings, unlike other fruits, often come into bearing quickly; in the past many peaches were not budded but were grown on their own roots. This helps to explain why there have as yet been no detailed investigations on stocks for peach.

Some stocks selected for plum proved disastrous for peaches through incompatibility between scion and stock, for example 'Common Plum', 'Marianna' and 'Myrobalan B'. Mussel stock and the selection 'Common Mussel' (Hatton wrote about its use for peaches) was extensively used by retail nurseries, despite difficulties with propagation, and it produced moderate sized peach trees but with a propensity to root suckering.

The vigorous 'Brompton' was compatible with all cultivars and produced medium to large peach trees. It was used widely until the semi-

The semi-dwarfing 'St Julian A' rootstock can be used for fan-trained plums, as in this example of the cultivar 'Opal' shown by Highfield Nurseries.

dwarfing 'St Julien A' virtually replaced it and the latter is now the only rootstock to be recommended for peaches in this country.

At the turn of the century most cherries were worked on seedling stocks collected from woodland, or perhaps on imported seedlings. The initial line of work at East Malling was an investigation into the so-called Mazzards, forms of *Prunus avium* raised as seedlings from the wild. Also studied, and subsequently discarded, were *P. cerasus* (Morello) and *P. mahaleb* (St Lucy cherry). N. H. Grubb, who undertook this study, found that the range of vigour in Mazzards was limited and only one, known as 'F12/1', was selected and distributed. 'F12/1' was a vigorous stock and, despite the laborious method of multiplication by layering, it became the sole cherry stock available: it was widely used in this country until the late 1970s, mainly for commercial plantings of sweet cherries. It was considered too vigorous for sweet cherries for the private garden though the sour cherry, 'Morello', made a suitable, moderate sized tree and was used for this purpose.

H. M. Tydeman and R. J. Garner started a systematic breeding programme at East Malling in 1953 using a number of *Prunus* species of apparent dwarfing habit. Crosses between one of Grubb's selected *Prunus avium* Mazzards and a *P. pseudocerasus* selection from China produced the most promising material. Following propagation and compatibility tests, the semi-dwarfing stock 'Colt' was sent to nurseries in 1976, leading to a transformation of the commercial cherry industry in the 1980s. For the first time moderate sized and relatively

closely planted trees could be considered. In contrast to 'F12/1', which can now be considered obsolete, 'Colt' can be multiplied easily and cheaply; it is an ideal subject for hardwood cuttings and can even produce roots at the bases of its shoots on nursery hedge plants.

Although perhaps not dwarf enough for sweet cherries in the small garden, 'Colt' has

For cherries the one rootstock is the semi-dwarfing 'Colt'. Chris Bowers & Sons of Whispering Trees Nurseries showed the cultivar 'Stella'.

These silhouettes show the effect of different rootstocks on the growth of a 10-year-old 'Cox's Orange Pippin' apple. From left to right: 'M. 27', 'M. 9', 'MM. 26', 'MM. 106' and 'MM. 111'.

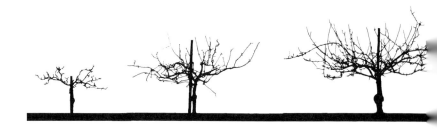

been extensively planted by amateurs for sweet and sour cultivars. The remarkable and compact tree of 'Morello' in the Royal Horticultural Society's Model Gardens at Wisley has encouraged many to plant this rewarding fruit in gardens. Perhaps the dividends of using 'Colt' for vigorous ornamental cherries have not yet been fully exploited. 'Colt', like so many of H. M. Tydeman's tree fruit crosses, achieved success after this modest man's death.

The outstanding achievement of Sir Ronald Hatton was to standardize the plant material available at the time. In the 1960s an important further development was the 're-selection' of all important stocks for freedom from systemic viruses, or virus-like diseases. Some stocks such as 'M.9' and 'Quince C' had to be heat-treated to inactivate virus, others were multiplied from fully indexed sources. Healthy and true-to-name tree fruit material was issued under the EMLA Scheme initially in 1969/70, the code letters EMLA representing the initials of East Malling and Long Ashton Research Stations. This major improvement and restandardization of fruit plants was principally undertaken by Dr A. F. Posnette (later Director of EMRS) and Dr R. Cropley at East Malling in close collaboration with Dr L. C. Luckwill and Dr A. I. Campbell of Long Ashton.

Trees exhibited by Chris Bowers, Whispering Trees Nurseries and Highfield Nurseries at the 1988 Chelsea Show gave a good idea of the range of rootstocks relevant to the amateur grower. Of Hatton's original apple selections, first described in 1917, only one rootstock still remains very popular, the dwarf 'M.9'. From those bred by H. M. Tydeman, the semi-dwarfing 'M.26' and 'MM.106' are still grown widely and the very dwarf 'M.27' by gardeners. After 75 years' work on quince and *Pyrus* stocks, the dwarf 'Quince C' and the semi-dwarfing 'Quince A' are still the main ones used.

When considering plum stocks, the two key ones are the dwarfing 'Pixy' and the semi-dwarfing 'St Julien A', with the latter as the only recommended stock for peaches. The position for cherries is that there is one stock, the semi-dwarfing 'Colt'.

What of the next 75 years? Nothing stands still, especially in the horticultural world. The former Ministry of Agriculture Chief Scientist (and former Director of EMRS), Sir Charles Pereira, linked the successes of the 'Green Revolution' with breeding temperate fruits, and said, at an international conference in 1976: 'I am convinced that the next battle must be won by the plant breeders.... I am very well aware of the differences between annual grasses and woody fruit bushes but I believe that the same principles apply, that the assembly of a large gene pool from the widest range of crop varieties and botanical relatives, the making of wide crosses, using very large numbers and rigorous selection, is as applicable to apples, plums and cherries as to wheat and rice.'

In the future we may have compact, self-supporting cultivars bred for ease of multiplication on their own roots. Should their vigour require checking, what will probably be used, instead of pruning, is an occasional watering with a growth supressing chemical.

Conservation-minded Gardening

Francesca Greenoak

Behind the splendour of the seventy-fifth anniversary at Chelsea lay complexity and contradiction. There were exotic displays of rare plants such as orchids and alpines from specialist nurseries. There were also urban and rural gardens built explicitly to attract and shelter wildlife, whatever the context, and displays by a wild-flower specialist. There were exhibits by groups involved with the protection of rare and threatened cultivars and there were large nurseries showing their top lines. In the garden sundries area were exhibits from ICI, Synchemicals, Chempak and Phostrogen but in the Scientific and Educational Section the Henry Doubleday Research Association from the National Centre for Organic Gardening was a lone voice in favour of a more sustainable system of horticulture. Nevertheless, there was scarcely an exhibit in the show not touched in some way by an awareness of the need for conservation in some aspect.

When the first Chelsea Flower Show was held in 1913, the word 'conservation' meant pretty well what it does now (preservation from destructive influences, natural decay or waste) but it was applied almost exclusively to abstract concepts such as order or power. The application to wildlife and nature is relatively recent. It is true that there were some who worried about animal wildlife and the flora of Britain and other countries but these as yet were severely in the minority and legislation on behalf of plants was intolerably slow in coming. Despite the fact that, while Prime Minister, Baldwin acknowledged the need for plant protection as early as 1925, the first legislation was the Wildlife and Countryside Act of 1981, over a century after the first Bird Protection Acts.

Organizations which promote positive conservation of wild life and

Water was an important element in the haven for wildlife – also a pleasant garden – created by the British Trust for Conservation Volunteers.

the environment are relatively recent. Gardening on the other hand has been vigorously pursued for millennia. Hardly any area of the world has been untapped by plant-hunters, who have hugely multiplied the variety and quantity of plants available to horticulture. Over the decades Chelsea has clearly reflected the subjects which specialist gardeners have energetically pursued, in particular orchids, alpines and bulbs. These are among the plants for which conservationists today feel real concern. One could argue that the concerns of gardeners and conservationists are at odds.

The stated objective of the RHS to promote excellence in horticulture enables it to stand aloof from the conservationists while not ignoring them. Indeed, such has been the public interest in wild flowers, wild-flower gardening and conserving rare cultivars in the last decade that the Society felt a responsibility to reflect what seemed to it the best practice in these areas. It is to the Society's credit that it made an approach to the seedsman John Chambers to see if he would like to submit a display at Chelsea. Nurseries and associations promoting unusual cultivars have also found a welcome.

There is, however, still a certain ambivalence among gardeners. The almost universal adulation of plant hunters is an example. Brave they may have been, but some did an awful lot of damage, the worst leaving the land behind them waste to ensure a monopoly in the rare species they collected. They also promoted a strongly entrepreneurial attitude to plants, which, even if growing in someone else's country, they regarded as their property. There are still, unfortunately, loopholes in national and international laws relating to plants. In this respect, the protection granted to a blackbird or wren as an independent living organism to be enjoyed by all does not extend to a daffodil or an orchid. In Britain, while it is illegal for people in general to dig up wild plants, a landowner or someone with the landowner's permission can dig them up at will. Further, in terms of international flora, agreements have been drawn up in an attempt to halt the sale of plants dug up from the wild, not only in Europe but outside it. However, as is well known,

Holland continues to import bulbs from Turkey and it is not illegal for British merchants to import from Holland.

John Chambers is well known as the man who almost single-handedly put wild-flower seeds on the commercial map and he has won awards every year since he first came to Chelsea seven years ago. In 1988, his wild-flower and grasses exhibit drew a Silver Flora award and his first outdoor enterprise, the honey-bee garden, won a well-deserved Gold award. In fact, the bee garden – pretty, busy, outstandingly well designed and planted – was even more of an achievement than the judges may have realized. Wild plants are, on the whole, more tricky to manage than cultivars and deeply resent being moved about, wilting at the drop of a hat. In the Chambers garden, Everything looked as if it had freshly opened out in a place it had been growing all season – foxgloves, ragged robin, columbines and cornflowers all at their best.

The garden was sponsored by Gales Honey (the first time a food company has sponsored a garden) and featured a path of honey-coloured stone leading to giant domed bee skeps with proportionately large model bees affixed to them. Originally, John Chambers had been asked to make a garden composed entirely of wild flowers but, on realizing it was a bee garden, had sensibly suggested a mixture of native species and cottage garden varieties. This rather homely cottage combination works exceptionally well and was echoed in many other of the 1988 model gardens – notably those of the Women's Institute and Ryl Nowell.

John Chambers has considerable expertise in turf and his choice of a mixture of meadow grasses, cut low as a lawn and allowed to rise at the periphery, enclosing the lawn area with a circlet of daisies and grass flower, is an idea which is being taken up in many real gardens. Well carried out, it looks neat but natural, with an interesting variety of textures – though it must have been very difficult to achieve in a model garden only made days before. In the beds taller plants such as monkshood, bronze fennel and majestic royal fern and rodgersia were well supported by slightly shorter flanking flowers such as Canterbury bells and dictamnus,

Giant bee skeps dominated the mixture of wild and
cultivated plants in the Gale's Honey Bee Garden. Some
of John Chambers' wild flowers brightened the verge.

with a medley of corn marigold, roses, alchemilla, corydalis, chamomile and *Veronica spicata*.

Continuing the planting outside the retaining wall was a winning touch. Here, the grass Yorkshire fog was a foil for blue columbine, rosebay and white dicentra, with ferns nestling into a rotting log and an escapee *Euphorbia griffithii* presiding over the extra-mural subjects. This garden was possibly the better for containing a combination of wild and cottage plants since it reminded visitors that it was a *garden* despite the number of native species inside it.

Many people who try to garden with wild flowers start with impossibly high expectations. Flower-filled hay meadows, woodlands and hedgebanks are ecological systems which have taken perhaps centuries to develop their range of species. It is folly to expect that we can achieve the same with a packet of wild-flower seed. This is after all why organizations such as the redoubtable RSNC (Royal Society for Nature Conservation) and other conservation bodies are buying areas of traditional land use and protecting them as nature reserves. The RSNC was present at Chelsea, closely associated with the bee garden. For them Chelsea 1988 marked the culmination of a national week in which there were efforts in every county in England to raise awareness of wild flowers. A co-ordinating body for the County Naturalists Trusts, they work at the heart of the matter, encouraging the protection by local people of the wild fauna and flora of their own region, urban as well as rural.

Another voluntary organization which at Chelsea bravely competes with the highly professional nurseries is the British Trust for Conservation Volunteers (BTCV). This body does vital work all over the country wherever help is required with any aspect of nature conservation. Volunteers undertake a range of environmentally positive activities such as planting, fencing, cutting back scrub and hedging. The BTCV garden was made entirely by a group of such volunteers and it is a tribute to them that it took a silver medal.

Their theme was a recycled garden but it had nothing in common with the make-do-and-mend school of conspicuous thrift. The result of their ingenious labours was as attractive and professional as gardens which had spent many times as much money. Their wildlife water garden was designed to show how even the smallest urban or suburban garden can attract and be a home for wild animals and plants. They managed to fit in pools and running water, a scented garden, alternative hedgerow, and a boardwalk from which you could sit and watch the wildlife. A pair of blue-tits started prospecting the nestbox in the BTCV's first wildlife garden at Chelsea in 1985, and within days of setting up their 1988 exhibit a frog was seen in the damp undergrowth, while birds sang in the alders.

BTCV made use of wild species and cultivars: dog rose and *Rosa* 'Fru Dagmar Hastrup', purple loosestrife and *Primula florindae*, sweet woodruff and hostas. Their trees were similarly varied, though they included several which would outgrow a small garden: Italian as well as English alder, the weeping form of ash, juniper, Spanish broom and a dwarf guelder rose (*Viburnum opulus* 'Nanum'). A thoughtful addition for an urban garden was a small *Pinus mugo*, the dwarf mountain pine, not especially common in Britain but used abroad in city plantings because of its resistance to exhaust fumes.

Visitors to the garden could take away a pack which explained the principles behind the different zones (planned to give as wide a range of habitats as possible within a small space) and how to make the features in the garden. A bold, slate-winged dragonfly sculpture added a flourish to this enterprise in creative conservation designed to be as attractive and interesting to its human as its wildlife inhabitants.

Wild-flower gardening as creating rather than preserving a wildlife habitat is a new and interesting phenomenon. As many of the gardens and exhibits at Chelsea in 1988 show without a doubt, some of the native wild flowers are as pretty as any cultivar and merit a place in the garden. Furthermore, these plants will attract more invertebrate and bird life than garden cultivars. However, gardeners serious about the conservation of plant species and working towards the ideal of a well-balanced habitat rich in wild flowers are breaking new ground. Even conservation bodies who have sown areas established over several years, are still gardening rather than managing them, as the constituent species vary from year to year before settling down into a stable system.

Nevertheless, many gardeners are enjoying a range of wild flowers which establish readily and self-seed in gardens. These are typically the flowers of wayside and old-fashioned arable farms; they include poppies, cornflowers, corn marigold, hearts-ease and corn cockle, ragged robin, red campion and dog daisy. Those prepared to work slightly harder will be able to establish primrose, cowslip, yellow rattle, even harebell or snakes-head fritillary in their grass. But these plants may be swamped by the surrounding vegetation and need a careful mowing regime, with a cut after they have flowered and seeded, to stop the grass getting clumpy and overwhelming them.

It is wise to use seeds from one of the well-known wild-plant dealers such as Chambers, Johnsons or Suffolk Seeds; you can be sure then of getting wild-flower seeds and not alien (and often rampant) agricultural forms. Customers can be sure the seeds were gathered under reasonably controlled conditions. Ironically, interest in wild-flower growing has created a trade in which collectors pay landowners a levy and then scour their woods, removing bluebell bulbs, snowdrops, aconites and wood anemones. Would-be wild-flower conservationists genuinely wanting to establish native plants in their gardens may unwittingly be sponsoring vandalism of the areas they are trying to emulate.

It is of course much easier and quicker to take a fully-grown plant from the wild than it is to grow one from seed, which is why so many wild places are already bare of primroses, orchids, the woodland mezereon and herb Paris. The same is true, of course, of the Turkish bulbs which still find their way to British suppliers not too fussy about the provenance of the stocks they buy in. As a general rule, if the bulbs you buy are shrivelled, misshapen and cheap they are more likely to have been imported from the wild. Those grown in nursery conditions are usually more uniform in shape and plumper. Quite apart from the ethical considerations, nursery-grown bulbs represent a better buy since they are far more likely to grow than the wild ones, and once grown to survive British conditions.

An EEC working party in Turkey in spring 1988 found warehouses full of bulbs awaiting export, testifying to the continuing trade, but there are signs of improvement. You can be virtually sure that all the crown imperials (*Fritillaria imperialis*) and the handsome purple *Fritillaria persica* at Chelsea and in shops have been raised in Dutch nurseries. Even the two kinds of plant still widely taken from the Turkish hillsides, wild snowdrops and cyclamen, are being more widely grown in nurseries, some in Turkey – in 1988 one nursery in Izmir was raising 300,000 *Cyclamen hederifolium* seedlings. Clearly, if the legitimate Turkish trade in bulbs can be increased this will benefit the cause of conservation, gardening and the economy of Turkey.

In the interim, however, it would be best for gardeners to steer clear of species snowdrop and cyclamen until completely assured of their being nursery raised, and to enquire about the provenance of any bulb which is a species rather than a hybrid. We may not be told the truth but, at the very least, it will impress on the bulb sellers that people are concerned about the subject and nudge them in the direction of reform.

A relatively new area of conservation relates to the saving of old garden cultivars from extinction. Two notable societies, the Hardy Plant Society and the National Council for the Conservation of Plants and Gardens (NCCPG), are concerned with protecting the rich variety of garden plants. As a result of the strength and popularity of the conservation movement there now appears to be more choice over a wider range of plants than ever before. This is not from the main seed and plant companies, who in general are trying to sell more of fewer items, but from a remarkable number of small nurseries and growers. Who grows what can be found in *The Plant Finder*, an excellent publication that is the brainchild of the Hardy Plant Society. The edition published just in time for the Chelsea Show lists 28,500 different plants and hundreds of nurseries and is absolutely indispensable for anyone wanting to track down an unusual or unfashionable variety of almost any hardy plant you can name.

The Hardy Plant Society came into existence in 1957 and members have been tracing, propagating and exchanging unusual cultivars regionally and nationally ever since. More specific in its interests than the NCCPG, it holds many of the National Collections and puts its expertise at their disposal. The first Hardy Plant exhibit at Chelsea dates from 1977 and the Society has exhibited several times, presenting its activities to a wider public. Plants for Chelsea and other shows are supplied by members, some of whom are nursery owners, but the majority are just people who love and enjoy plants. Sometimes, part of a National Collection is shown: at Chelsea 1988 there was a range of euphorbias and some handsome potgrown hostas, including 'Francee', with its attractive dark green leaves with dramatic white margins, 'Rippling Wave', 'Antioch' and 'Spinners'.

The Cambridge Group of the NCCPG (the national body is now in its tenth year) staged an exhibit in co-operation with the Cambridge University Botanic Garden and the Cambridge City Council showing plants especially associated with Cambridge. This joint presentation was no marriage of convenience; the three bodies work intimately together on plants, having built up a highly co-operative relationship between the botanical and the horticultural, professionals and amateurs. The Cambridge University Botanic Garden, for instance, holds the National Collection of geraniums but, being a botanical organization, concentrates on species while the City Council manages the collection of cultivars, greatly aided by experts from the Cambridge NCCPG. The same principle is applied also to bergenias. At Chelsea, among the plants of historical and regional interest was a geranium hybrid bred at the Botanic Garden, the elegant pink *Geranium × cantabrigiense,* as well as some interesting cultivars including the pretty 'Kashmir White' and the rarer 'Kashmir Purple'.

Garden plants as well as wild flowers are the subject of conservation measures. *Geranium* 'Kashmir White', from the Cambridgeshire National Collections, was exhibit by the Cambridgeshire Group of the National Council for Conservation of Plants and Gardens in co-operation with Cambridge University Botanic Garden and Cambridge City Parks Service.

A plant that caused considerable comment was *Polemonium carneum,* a perennial with pink and white flowers in sprays that is more compact than the common blue or white Jacob's ladder. It caught the Queen's eye as she was being escorted towards the red delphinium stand and she paused to ask about it. Another of the key exhibits on the stand was a new *Ceanothus*, grown at the Botanic Gardens from seed given to Lady Cynthia Postan and named after her. It has a dense conical shape and the flowers, instead of being light in colour, are a rich royal blue. There are plans to propagate and develop this shrub for the commercial market.

Of course, while giving credit to these organizations which specifically aim at conservation, one should not forget the trail-blazers such as Alan Bloom, who did so much to restore the popularity of hardy perennials and whose family nursery at Bressingham in Norfolk still stocks many interesting cultivars bred or introduced by him. The Bressingham exhibits at Chelsea contain a good range of perennials although they share the limelight now with heathers and conifers. An innovator, responsible for the re-introduction of many choice garden plants, not exhibiting at Chelsea 1988 but present in terms of her influence, is of course Beth Chatto. She has become such an established figure in the gardening world it seems absurd that her co-competitors at Chelsea used to scoff at 'Beth Chatto's unusual weeds' eleven years ago when she first started exhibiting. Peter Beales, who has made such strenuous and successful efforts to rehabilitate the classic old-fashioned roses, featured a new red rose 'William and Mary' as well as old favourites, such as the lovely climbing noisette 'Madame Alfred Carrière', with her fragrant white flowers. Another celebrated rose nurseryman, David Austin, included old-fashioned shrub roses in his gold-award winning exhibit.

The impression given by Chelsea 1988 is that gardeners seem to be more aware of conservation issues. There is increasing concern about birds, mammals, reptiles and invertebrates, and the effects of the use of inorganic herbicides, pesticides and fertilizers. There is also a move towards recreating fertile well-structured garden soils with compost and sympathetic management. Minor changes perhaps in our own small patch, but they lead to a better understanding of the complexity of the living world around us, and upon that, ultimately, our survival depends.

Greenhouse Improvements

George Sheard

'Winter gardens, sun lounges, conservatories, ranges, vineries, peach houses, orchid houses, carnation houses, forcing houses': such was the list offered by the Norwich-based company of Boulton and Paul Ltd in the 1914 Chelsea catalogue. It conjures up visions of opulent country-house living, with armies of gardeners producing luxury fruits, vegetables and flowers under glass, and a leisured society competing to fill conservatories with tropical exotics. As Chelsea 1988 showed, conservatories are back in fashion and many manufacturers are turning for their inspiration to the Victorian and Edwardian heyday.

Chelsea also showed that manufacturers are catering for the growing number of amateurs who are interested in greenhouse gardening. Market research has shown that already 1·7 million gardeners in the United Kingdom own a greenhouse. That means, roughly, a greenhouse for one household in every seven. Some of the credit for their popularity must go to the Association for Consumer Research. Since 1982 its investigations into amateur growing of plants under glass have been published in the magazine *Gardening from Which?* The typical greenhouse of readers of the magazine is aluminium framed (only about 15 per cent are made of wood, usually red cedar) and small, with a base measuring about 2·4 by 1·8 m (8 by 6 ft). Despite their modest size, these greenhouses significantly increase the range of ornamentals and crops that the amateur can grow with success.

The modern greenhouse owner still owes much to Victorian gardeners and inventors, notably to Sir Joseph Paxton, who designed the great greenhouse at Chatsworth, now sadly demolished, and later the buildings for the Great Exhibition of 1851. There have, of course, been technical

The ideal shape of a greenhouse for light transmission
is a hemisphere, as in the Solardome incorporated
in the Pershore College of Horticulture's exhibit.

improvements this century. Most of the advances made available to the amateur in recent years have come as spin-offs from research and development carried out since the last war for the benefit of commercial producers. The range of material at Chelsea 1988 gave a good opportunity to review the equipment available in the light of current research.

Lean-to and free-standing designs were represented at Chelsea. Free-standing greenhouses can be sited in any position within a garden, but the lean-to types require a high wall to which they can be fixed. The most important requirement of a greenhouse is that it should transmit the maximum amount of light, particularly in winter. In this respect lean-to houses are at a disadvantage as no light can enter through the opaque back wall. Light transmission is affected by roof geometry, orientation and the proportion of opaque structural material. The ideal shape is a hemisphere, but only one manufacturer, Rosedale Engineers, offers a house of this type, the Solardome. The next most suitable shape is a half cylinder, and the Clear Span designs offered by Clear Span Ltd approximate closely to this form. There is still, however, a general preference for rectangular greenhouses with span roofs, because they are more practicable for growing plants, easier to manufacture for the mass market and less costly than curvilinear designs. When greenhouses are longer than they are wide, light transmission is improved if the ridge is orientated east-west and the house has a steep south-facing side. If the base plan is near square, as in the most popular 2·4 by 1·8 m (8 by 6 ft) models, orientation makes little difference. Having the right slope for the roof can improve light transmission, a point demonstrated in the design exhibited by Serac, which incorporated refinements of roof geometry.

Though lean-to greenhouses are less well lit than span types they are less costly to heat and they may be connected to a house. The wall against which they are built acts as a storage radiator, absorbing heat from solar radiation during the day and releasing it to the greenhouse at night. Aspect is important in siting lean-to houses. A southerly aspect is to be preferred. East and west aspects are acceptable, with east being marginally better than west. A northerly aspect is least desirable, as such a greenhouse receives little direct sunlight and only about half of the total light received by a similar greenhouse facing south.

Over the last five years there have been considerable developments in the design of lean-to greenhouses. The standard of construction has been upgraded to provide conservatories and sun rooms which satisfy building regulations, incorporating acrylic-coated structural members, safety glass and, in some cases, eaves with a curved profile. A very wide range of styles is on offer from simple upgraded lean-to houses to designer productions in prices ranging from £600 to £7,500. Upgrading a basic design of a lean-to greenhouse to make a conservatory increases the price by about 50 per cent.

Glass, the traditional covering material for greenhouses, has no equal for light transmission, durability and cost effectiveness. However, plastics have advantages in toughness and safety, particularly for greenhouses attached to a house and in situations where vandalism is a problem. Acrylic and acrylic-coated polycarbonate are rigid plastics that can be used as direct alternatives to sheet glass. Both have optical properties similar to glass, and polycarbonate is available in the form of twin-walled sheets with the insulating properties of double glazing. Rigid plastics can also be formed to provide curved profiles for use in the eaves, eliminating the need for eaves guttering. The very tough film plastics Melinex and Tedlar can be manufactured in the form of stressed skin panels to make a cladding system. Such panels provide the basis of the design exhibited by Serac and are offered as an alternative to glass by Alitex. Melinex and Tedlar films must not be confused with polythene film, which does not have the same properties as these durable plastics. Polythene, however, has many greenhouse applications, mainly as a simple, low-cost, expendable covering, and not as a long-term alternative to glass.

Currently there is a lot of interest in 'mini-greenhouses', of which several models were shown at Chelsea. These are modern versions of Victorian 'wall cases' and, like them, need to be fixed to a solid structure. They stand between 1·2 and 2·1 m (4 to 7 ft) high, are about 60 cm (2 ft) deep and are clad in glass or polythene film. They make it possible to propagate and grow plants under protection in places where space is at a premium and where it is impossible to have a conventional greenhouse, but they have their limitations. They need to be tended from outside. More seriously, because of their large surface to volume ratio, they heat up quickly in summer, they are in

Very tough plastics, as used in a design by Serac, have useful applications but glass has no equal for light transmission, durability and cost effectiveness.

general poorly ventilated and difficult to keep cool in summer, and they provide poor frost protection.

Smallest in size in the range of 'greenhouses' are the free-standing propagators. These are designed for use in the house or within a greenhouse, but in principle they are very small greenhouses. The size and sophistication range from the small window-sill propagator exhibited by Ward to the thermostatically controlled and ventilated 'Supreme' propagator exhibited by Auto-Grow. They are most useful in the absence of a heated greenhouse for raising seedlings, rooting cuttings and, in the larger models, growing small plants in containers. Window-sill models sell at around £12, the more versatile thermostatically controlled models for about £30, and the larger sophisticated models with up to 3 sq m (10 sq ft) of growing area upward of £250. The latter approach the cost of a conventional greenhouse, and though they give accurate control of the environment the output of plants is limited.

To grow plants successfully in the greenhouse there must be good ventilation. It is needed to dissipate the heat energy in solar radiation, to control humidity and to maintain the ambient level of carbon dioxide. Natural ventilation may be provided by hinged ventilators in the roof and by hinged or louvred ventilators in the sides. Forced ventilation can be provided by electrically-driven fans.

Small greenhouses have a large surface area compared with their volume. This means that in summer and in sunny weather they heat up rapidly. As a whole, greenhouse manufacturers do not fit sufficient ventilators to give control over temperature rise. Rather than provide a proper basic standard they offer additional ventilation as an optional extra. The rule to follow when assessing the amount of ventilation necessary is simple: when the ventilators are in the fully open position, the total open area should be at least one fifth of the floor area of the greenhouse. This means that a greenhouse measuring 2·4 by 1·8 m (8 by 6 ft) needs a ventilator area of 3 sq m (10 sq ft). Frequent manual adjustment of ventilators to control greenhouse temperatures is rarely practicable.

Until very recently the only automatic controls available for fitting to small greenhouses were those based on the expansion of wax contained within a cylinder. Tests conducted by the Association for Consumer Research have shown that ventilator openers working on this principle have limitations. Although some makes performed better than others, all needed a large temperature differential to move ventilators from the closed to the fully open position. It was most encouraging to note exhibited at Chelsea 1988 the first electro-mechanical vent controller designed for use on small greenhouses, made by Electroflora and exhibited by Alitex. In speed and accuracy this kind of controller is a marked improvement on the wax expansion type but it is probably still too costly to be much used in the small greenhouse.

Fans give positive air movement and for small greenhouses they are the best system where fully automatic control is required. To give the correct performance fans should have a capacity of 2 cubic m ($7\frac{1}{2}$ cubic ft) per minute for each 0·3 sq m (1 sq ft) of floor area. Thus for a 2·4 by 1·8 m (8 by 6 ft) greenhouse the fan should have an output of 110 cubic m (360 cubic ft) per minute. The type of fan available will only perform satisfactorily against a low resistance and therefore the greenhouse must have an adequate air inlet. It needs to be the same size as the fan, it should be sited low down and must open when the fan is required to operate.

Heating a greenhouse, even slightly, increases the gardener's possibilities for growing and maintaining plants. Temperature rather than light is the limiting factor controlling plant growth in winter. Market research has yet to give an accurate idea of the number of amateur gardeners in Britain who heat their greenhouses, and by what means. The results of a survey carried out by the Association for Consumer Research within its membership suggest that less than half of those who owned greenhouses heated them in the winter.

For most situations there are three possible choices for the method of heating: electricity, direct-fired paraffin and direct-fired natural or bottled gas. With a lean-to greenhouse attached to a dwelling it may also be possible to tap into the domestic central heating. The use of paraffin is declining as many oil companies phase out the production of the premium-grade oils required for these burners. Small paraffin heaters cannot be thermostatically controlled. They burn at a constant pre-set rate and this can be wasteful. By way of contrast, gas and electrical heaters can be easily and accurately controlled. When direct-fired heaters burning either gas or paraffin are used, the greenhouse must be well ventilated, to reduce the risk of plant damage from pollutants and control excessive humidity from the water vapour produced in the combustion. The risk of damage increases as the temperature rises. Manufacturers do not sufficiently warn purchasers of gas burners of the risk of damage from nitrogen oxides and the procedures for minimising such risk. The cheapest source of heat is natural gas. Tests carried out by the Association for Consumer Research in 1987 showed that heating by electricity cost much less than by propane or paraffin. Though electricity has the highest cost per unit of energy it is more efficient, control of temperature is more accurate and no ventilation is needed when the heaters are operating. Electricity is particularly attractive when used on the Economy 7 off-peak tariff.

The cost of heating probably discourages a significant number of owners from making the most of their greenhouses. Good insulation can help reduce these costs, in some circumstances by up to 40 per cent with the use of an internal lining of bubble polythene. The cost of the lining must, of course, be set against these savings. Insulating linings also have disadvantages. Savings are not great when the temperature lift is small; the lining reduces light transmission and increases the problems of humidity and the risk of pollution damage if gas or paraffin heaters are used.

Heating the greenhouse space may not be the most efficient way of promoting plant growth. Plants suffer more from low root temperature than they do from low air temperature. It is therefore more advantageous, and also less costly, to heat the soil or growing medium than it is to maintain the greenhouse air temperature.

Solid or open benching can be used in the greenhouse and the choice will affect the management of the heating and watering systems available to the amateur.

Soil borders and benches can be heated easily and efficiently by electrical soil-warming cables. Recent work on the effect of temperature on plants suggests that plants respond to the mean diurnal temperature rather than to specific day or night temperatures. It is much less costly to raise temperature during the day and it is better to compensate for a low night temperature with a high day temperature to give the desired 24-hour mean. Solar gain can be exploited to advantage in this respect.

In many greenhouses container-grown plants are arranged on benching, the bench top being formed of open mesh or covered with solid sheet material. It is important to understand the effect of these covers on plant growth and management. Plants on an open bench can only be watered by hand or by drip nozzles. Plants on a solid bench may be watered by hand, drip nozzles or a capillary system. Plants on an open bench are subject to higher soil moisture stress, finding it harder to take up water than similar plants on a solid bench. This favours the open bench in winter and the solid bench in summer. Solid benches are cooler by night and warmer by day, but on sunny days the temperature rise can be excessive. In winter, solid benches are slow to warm up after a clear, cold night. Benches fitted with a capillary watering system are cooler by day than any other type of bench. Plants grown on capillary benches are subject to very low soil moisture tension and are therefore able to take up water easily. This is an advantage in summer when water loss is high, but it is a disadvantage in winter, when the low moisture tension promotes vegetative growth, excessive uptake of nitrogen and unbalanced growth, and delays flowering. The best balance of advantage is gained by using an open bench with drip watering in winter and a solid capillary bench in summer.

The amount of water needed by plants varies with the season and the weather. It is directly related to the amount of solar radiation entering the greenhouse. Provided there is a full leaf cover, water requirement is related to the floor area of the greenhouse and not to specific varieties of plant. All plants, whether they be tomatoes, cucumbers or lettuce, require the same amount of water per unit area of crop. As a guide, the water requirement on a clear June day will be of the order of 0·6 l per 0·3 sq m (1 pint per sq ft) floor area. In December it will be less than one tenth. In summer the popular 2·4 by 1·8 m (8 by 6 ft) greenhouse will need about 3·4 l (6 gallons) of water per day. Virtually all the water taken up by a plant is lost to the atmosphere in the process of transpiration.

This is a simple evaporative process which serves to dissipate some of the heat generated when solar radiation is absorbed by the plant tissue.

Hand-watering is time-consuming, and it is difficult to ensure that plants are kept adequately watered if attention is not available during the day. Automatic watering systems will overcome these problems to a varying degree, depending on the type of equipment installed. Plants grown in small to medium size containers on benches may be watered by a capillary system or by drip nozzles. Where the containers are small a capillary system is to be preferred on grounds of cost. Plants grown in the soil border, in modules or in large containers are best watered by drip nozzles.

The equipment available for supplying water by capillary action and by drip nozzles has changed little over the last ten years, but there have been marked developments in equipment to estimate need and control supply. Systems such as the Watermac (Geeco) and the Gardena Water Timer (Two Wests & Elliott) will apply predetermined quantities automatically, but

the quantity has to be estimated and may not be closely related to plant requirement. The introduction of the Camplex HD1500E automatic water controller and the virtually identical Access Autowaterer provides equipment which estimates demand and supplies the quantity of water needed. These systems use an evaporative wick which measures evaporation and triggers a solenoid valve when a pre-set deficit has built up. A further development of interest is the Gardena Water Computer (Two Wests & Elliott). This is a timer that can be programmed to allow six watering periods of any duration each day on all or any days of the week. This does not, as its name might suggest, compute the water requirement, but its versatility and the ease with which it can be programmed give it considerable advantages over earlier timing devices. The facility to program over a whole week makes it very useful for dealing with periods of absence.

The growing of crops such as tomato and cucumber in the soil border of a greenhouse presents difficulties for the amateur. After a few seasons the soil becomes 'sick' and yields

Although the modern greenhouse owes much to 19th-century engineers, recent developments have reduced costs and made watering and maintenance less time-consuming.

decline. The amateur does not have the means available to the commercial grower to sterilize the soil and restore fertility. The advent of peat modules and 'Gro-Bags' has changed this situation, and the gardener can now have a fresh, clean growing medium each season. The volume of peat in a module is relatively small, and it does not have the capacity to hold enough water for a day's supply in the height of summer, when modules need to be watered at least twice each day if the weather is clear and sunny.

The John Innes seed and potting composts were devised in the mid 1930s. These were loam-based and over a period of thirty years they provided a very reliable, standard and predictable growing medium. Increasing demand for potting composts and difficulties in obtaining supplies of loam of the right quality have led to their replacement by loamless composts based on peat. Peat may be used alone or in mixture with sand, grit, pulverized bark, vermiculite or perlite. Such mixtures now form the bulk of the seed and potting composts used both by the amateur and by the commercial grower. As with most developments there are advantages and disadvantages. Peat-based composts can be made from readily available, standardized bulk components without sterilization. However, in contrast to loam-based composts they have a much lower buffering capacity, control of the pH (the compost's acidity or alkalinity) and nutrition is more difficult, minor elements need to be supplied, phosphate is readily leached and they need constant feeding or the addition of slow-release fertilizers.

If there is any slackening of interest in greenhouse gardening it certainly was not evident at Chelsea 1988. It seems reasonable to expect that more and more amateurs will extend the scope of their gardening by acquiring greenhouses, with interest focusing on those of small size that can incorporate a number of automatic features. Amateurs will probably continue to benefit from technical developments first applied in commercial greenhouse gardening. These developments will be something to look out for at future Chelsea shows.

Pleasing the Public

Deborah Kellaway

'Look at this – look at this!'

'Incredible!'

'It is superb!'

'Remarkable . . . splendid . . .'

We were all smiling and gasping and many people were taking photographs. It was Stephenson's Rocket, momentarily at rest in a flower-fringed railway cutting deep in the country. We had a thrilling close-up view of the engine driver in his top hat and frock coat, and of the fireman standing in his tender, wearing a humbler jacket and peaked cap. Behind a little fence two children were watching too – the railway children, the little boy with his hand on his sister's shoulder. She had one hand on the wire of the fence, with the other she was waving. The fireman was waving back. It seemed a timeless tableau, but on the far side of the cutting, out of sight unless we changed our viewpoint, something more sinister was happening. A fox was stealing across the line, and the tableau seemed about to dissolve into movement. The scene invited a return to childhood worlds of dolls' houses and fairy tales except that these people were life-size and, as this was the Chelsea Show, 1988, the whole thing was made from living plants. The catalogue entry read simply:

Torbay, Borough of Parks & Recreation Dept., *Carpet Bedding*.

It is six years since Torbay won their first Gold Medal for a model cottage, thatched in heather, standing in a cottage garden. Since then they have enchanted crowds (and judges) with a mounted guardsman outside his sentry box, a London street scene complete with double-decker bus and penny-farthing perambulator, and a mock-up of the Pied Piper of Hamlin and the Old Woman who lived in a Shoe. These

The carpet-bedded tableau created by the Parks and
Recreation Department of the Borough of Torbay
featured Stephenson's Rocket in a railway cutting.

creations have been made out of small plants pushed through a steel-meshed framework to root in the tight-packed peat inside. This year, the dapper, silver-grey trousers of the engine driver were *Arabis caucasica* 'Variegata' (all its white flowers cut off as soon as they appeared to leave a trimly tailored texture). The fox was a mixture of alternanthera and *Sedum spathulifolium* 'Capa Blanca', the panelling on the tender was *Pyrethrum* 'Golden Feather', and the lettuce green of the fireman's jacket was *Sedum acre*, as was the mop of curls on the little boy's head. The round flowers on the little girl's full, three-quarter-length skirt were the round rosettes of echeveria; more variegated arabis made the lace frill round her hem; she wore pantaloons of alternanthera. The railway children's clothes were copied from a pattern book of 1829, the year when Stephenson produced The Rocket; a plan of The Rocket itself was supplied by York Railway Museum. John Carnell, the man behind these scenes, is a stickler for detail.

But he is also an artist; he believes in his creations, and loving attention to detail made sure that a few weeds grew through the bolt holes of the old railway sleepers that edged the scene, while grass grew beside the loose metal along the track and a few tall flowers seemed to have seeded themselves beyond the neat beds of white alyssum and pelargoniums tended, perhaps, by some imaginary gardener who lived near the railway line. In one corner, past a small plantation of silver birches, there grew a semi-wild mixture of daisies, marigolds and poppies. All these flowers were a joyous frame for the central figures in their subtly shaded greens and garnets. A few bits of the blacksmith's work had been allowed to show. The railway lines were metal; there was a real copper pipe on The Rocket's side; and every alternate spoke of its wheels was ochre-painted steel piping. The judgement of when *not* to use plants in the creation of this illusion was as flawless as the use of the plants themselves.

'I must say I'd much rather see a lovely garden with flowers in their *right places* ...' came a fastidious voice from the crowd. There will always be people who are not amused, who refuse the invitation to smile at Torbay's adorable absurdities, while spoilsports mumble about the cost. What price can be put on pleasure? Torbay's Chelsea exhibit returned to Torbay when the show was over to enhance holidays on the sea front until September.

I had marked seven displays for scrutiny this year. Torbay happened to come first. My brief was to write about 'gardening for the public' from the viewpoint of someone who gardens on a domestic scale, for pleasure. We private gardeners throng Chelsea with pencils at the ready, as we have always done. In the 1980s we particularly like old-fashioned roses, herb gardens, herbaceous mixtures of hardy plants, wild flowers and small flowers. We zoom in on specific plants; mass effects do not engage us.

But mass effects, I assumed, are what 'gardening for the public' is all about. There must be carrying-power in the displays of the public parks, big blocks of colour, preferably bright. Thousands of bedding plants raised in municipal nurseries under glass and polythene are bedded out each year. John Carnell of Torbay even describes his floral sculptures as 'three-dimensional bedding'.

For real bedding, carpet bedding, there was the City of Birmingham's highly stylized and professional exhibit mounted by its Department of Recreation and Community Services. On one side of the stand was a steeply raked crescent of blooms; one half white, touched with blue (creamy stocks, huge white mop-headed hydrangeas, violet blue cinerarias), the other half deepest strawberry, wine and crimson. The line between the two blocks of colour was not abrupt, but oblique, and all along the edge of this high crescent a row of green ferns and white impatiens gave unity. In front, in the newly laid lawn, were two roughly triangular beds of streptocarpus: one pink and white, the other blue and white. In the middle was a stroke of theatre: an old cast-iron signpost, newly painted black and gold, pointed to Birmingham in one direction, London in the other. And London meant: Chelsea.

For this was Birmingham's reminder to London, via Chelsea, that it is not just a concrete wasteland on the motorway. 'There's

A racing car among massed foliage and flowering plants in the City of Birmingham's exhibit was a reminder of the Super Prix event in August.

more to it than that,' said one of the gardeners manning the display.

There was certainly more to it than anyone could suspect who saw the old signpost amongst the dazzling blooms. This stand had been designed to look quite different from every angle, and when you walked round to the other side you found – a bright blue Formula 3 racing car, a real one (not made of flowers). There was a simulated road spanned by an arch hung with pennants, and a black-and-white chequered flag lay on the ground. Birmingham mounts a Super Prix on its streets each August Bank Holiday; this was a preview. Beyond, the banks of brilliant flowers resumed: orange zinnias, brick-red kalanchoe; the names of varieties signalled the colour scheme: the marigolds were 'Orange Fireworks', the celosia 'Century Yellow', the impatiens 'Accent Orange'. This, it emerged, was autumn; the white had been winter, the red summer, the pink and blue – spring. Colour ruled; individual flowers counted for less than total effect, perfect though each bloom was. Hardy and half-hardy annuals mingled with tropical foliage plants. Above the banks of flame

towered three handsome specimens of *Pandanus baptistii* – one, with pale variegations, thought to be unique. In the midst of the gardening spectacular, the racing car looked crude. It may have been a winner, but it could not compete with flowers.

There have always been flamboyant displays of bedding plants at Chelsea, but until the 1970s they were primarily supplied by the great seed houses. From 1913 onwards, accounts of the Chelsea Show repeatedly praise Carters, Suttons and Webbs for 'mounds' – the word recurs in the descriptions – of calceolarias and cinerarias, gloxinias, petunias and stocks. In the blurred black-and-white photographs of the old *Gardener's Chronicle*, these banks of bloom were topped by fashionable fronds of palm. Nor were they always merely banks; in 1913 Messrs Sutton and Son staged a series of scalloped beds, while Messrs Carter and Co showed 'a large central circle, surrounded by a series of smaller circles, linked by triangles and squares; the last-named were filled with seedling grasses closely clipped as on small lawns ...' (*Gardener's Chronicle*, 24 May 1913). It is said that

Pyramids of schizanthus, 'the poor man's orchid', in shades from red to violet, were staged by Slough Corporation Works Department.

when rising costs obliged the seed houses to retire from Chelsea in the 1970s, the boroughs took their place. Of course, the boroughs had started to exhibit some years before Suttons and Carters stopped. As early as 1960, the City of Liverpool Parks Department won a Gold Medal for a display of tropical plants with a fruiting pineapple in the middle. And today there are two seed houses back in the Great Marquee; Marshalls of Wisbech have been exhibiting since 1982 – admittedly their 'mounds' are of shining vegetables, not annual flowers; and this year Colegrave Seeds (wholesale suppliers of seed to the trade) presented their second Chelsea spectacle, a pointed pink pavilion of busy lizzies and geraniums mounted on pink silk skirts; it came with a hand-out about 'colour theming'. Colour theming seems to mean playing variations on a single colour – matching rather than contrasting. 'Think pink' was the caption for their 1988 display.

Slough Corporation Works Department were thinking pink too – pink shading to red at one end of the spectrum and to violet at the other. The whole display depended on different varieties, both short and tall, of a single flower: schizanthus, the very flower with which Slough has dazzled Chelsea crowds before. For 1988 they built four exquisitely pretty pyramids of varying heights, informally arranged on Bradstone paving; the second tallest was topped with Canterbury bells; they were like spreading crinolines made from the finest Liberty prints. The print effect came from the delicate nature of the schizanthus itself: it is called 'the poor man's orchid', perhaps because its touching pansy-face is lightly speckled in close-up. From a distance, and *en masse*, it is a stunning gold-medallist. In a useful hand-out, Slough explained to the public how it achieved such perfection, and sought to persuade us that we, too, could grow these ravishing flowers with a little care and a cool greenhouse. Slough is ready to supply bedding plants to other local authorities, and opens its nurseries to the public on selected days. Its Chelsea displays are sponsored by Hurst Seeds, an instance of a happy marriage between a seed house and a borough council. The 1988 display represented another happy marriage: lavish exuberance was wedded to simplicity.

The Royal Borough of Kensington and Chelsea called its 1988 exhibit 'The Garden of Paradise'. Paradise in this case must be a tropic clime, or a painting by Henri Rousseau, where richly dark foliage shines and an occasional scarlet flower of *Cordyline terminalis* glows amongst dark green leaves. A magnificent specimen of *Ficus benjamina* concealed the tent pole which rose from the middle of this site, flanked on either side by towering palms. Water splashed; a demure white sculptured maiden seemed to study a little dish in her hands. The greens were interspersed with mahogany reds and ice-cool greeny-whites (*Neoregelia carolinea* beside *Syngonium* 'White Butterfly'). despite the tropical and sub-tropical origin of the plants, the colours were the colours of the English Christmas – deep green and scarlet, silver and chestnut. These were plants for civic decoration, mayoral receptions, not for public gardens. The display supplied what Chelsea lost when Rochfords ceased to exhibit – superb examples of indoor plants.

The Royal Borough of Kensington and Chelsea staged a paradise garden of tropical plants, with palms and a large specimen of *Ficus benjamina*.

Superb outdoor plants, woodland plants, were shown by Southampton City Council. This exhibit was called 'A Hampshire Garden', the sort of thing, said one of its staff, that anyone with a garden on the fringes of the New Forest might have. It was refreshingly natural, un-selfconscious. Was it really 'public gardening'? Yes, for Southampton City Council has a large woodland garden at Mayfield Park, where the public can wander along walkways between trees and flowering shrubs – rhododendrons, azaleas, magnolias and, later in the year, hydrangeas. It was a sample of this sort of wood-land that they brought to Chelsea; beneath larch and birch, Japanese maple and pine, the azaleas and rhododendrons bloomed in apricot, scarlet, orange and pink, with the pretty little cream-coloured Dunwich rose carpeting the ground between, and healthy hostas along the edges. Bedding, it was fast emerging, is by no means the whole story of 'gardening for the public'.

Indeed, the final two exhibits by parks departments to be seen at Chelsea this year showed not only half-hardy annuals but also herbaceous plants. First there was the Metropolitan Borough of Wigan; its Leisure Department is responsible for large parks in and around Wigan, with rose beds and herbaceous borders as well as 'bedding out'. They found themselves landed with a small and narrow site in the marquee. They made a virtue out of limitation with a strong design: a straight gravel path ran down the middle of the stand under three simple black metal arches from which dangled cream and cherry fuchsias in hanging baskets. At the end of the path water from a fountain fell into a round pond, and behind this, to close the vista so cunningly contrived, mixed larkspurs rose through Japanese maples. The feeling of the garden was of twin herbaceous borders – that classic recipe for success. In fact the herbaceous plants on either side of the path, the lupins and anchusas and striped grasses, were interspersed with annuals – mixed nicotiana and pink geraniums, fibrous-rooted begonias and standard fuchsias – bedding plants used in a non-bedding way. The men who jointly designed this garden were simply hoping to show the public what can be done with a very small plot. They accentuated its length by repeated clumps of misty anthemis amongst the stronger flowers. 'Make it *float*,' one said. It did float. It became a small dream garden, romantic, enclosed and pretty.

We private gardeners are told to aim for mystery in our gardens – a private garden should not reveal the whole of itself at once. I had thought that here lay another difference between private and public gardening: the public garden should *not* have secret places – all should be wide open to the view. But Wigan's garden felt secret; if you could have stepped over the white rope, tall flowers would soon have hidden you from sight. And when at last I reached the Royal Parks display, I recognized the sort of planting to which, in all my own gardening for pleasure, I have aspired.

'You've got to make them walk round,' Bob Wadey, the apprentice master, had told the final-year apprentices who constructed the exhibit. 'They mustn't be able to see it all at once and say, "That's it."'

There was no danger of seeing it all at once, nor even of walking quickly round it, let alone of saying, 'That's it.' Wherever you stood, you wanted to stay and gaze, close-up, at these plants mixed by a master hand. And yet they were simple things: foxgloves, astrantias, irises, verbascums, columbines. The colours were pastel on the side where I stood first – a beautifully shaded palette of pink and lemon, lavender and white. I tried to frame any sensible question about such apparently effortless beauty.

'The usual thing,' said one of the staff in a throw-away fashion, 'heights and dips.'

On the highest point of the gently sloping display, the spires of *Digitalis* Excelsior Hybrids towered; then came the beautiful *Verbascum* 'Gainsborough'; lower down the slope, *Crambe cordifolia* foamed over a shorter foxglove, the perennial *Digitalis × mertonensis*; there were peaks, too, of rodgersia, and two strong silver heads of the great cardoon, *Cynara cardunculus*. In the 'dips' flowered a mass of lilac-coloured sweet rocket, *Hesperis matronalis* 'Mauve'; lychnis, *Dictamnus fraxinella* (the burning bush) and then there was the substantial softness of hosta leaves.

'Form views wherever you go,' the member of staff was saying. 'Wherever you stand, you want to go further.'

I did go further. The far side of the stand had a lime-green corner, all alchemilla, euphorbia, tiarella and heuchera; this melted into more intense colours, with an edging of *Heuchera micrantha* 'Palace Purple' and *Geum rivale*; and almost imperceptibly this merged into a warm sunset corner with *Helenium hoopesii*, *Geum chiloense* 'Rubin', *Verbascum* 'Cotswold Queen'. I went further still and at last discovered that the whole thing was arranged round a little stream, trickling over three stone slabs until it fell into a pool fringed with *Lysimachia nummularia*, and thickly planted with moisture-loving plants: primulas, mimulus, aruncus. In an attempt to capture the secret of this planting, I had been scribbling names, but there is no magic in a list of plants. There were 200 varieties on this small site, yet the effect was harmony. The exhibit was simply called: 'Woodland and Herbaceous Plants'.

The Royal Parks can rise to royal heights of formality when occasion demands, witness the spectacular crown mounted on the purple velvet of African violets with which they celebrated the Queen's Silver Jubilee, or the Prince of Wales feathers which marked the royal wedding in 1981. More and more, however, they like to show informal gardening carried to its perfection. It was Tom Hay, superintendent of the Central Royal Parks Group during the 1930s, who filled beds in London's parks with meconopsis and thousands of primulas to the delighted astonishment of passers-by. Today, in Regent's Park and Greenwich we, the public, can enjoy informal herbaceous borders. At Chelsea, as I turned the page to take notes for my own use, I felt the distinction between public and private gardening crumble.

'How did you design this border?' I asked Bob Wadey.

'Let's not beat about the bush,' he said. 'It's all trial and error.'

The men and women who garden in the public parks experiment, hesitate and ponder. They are intuitive, not doctrinaire. Things sometimes go wrong for them, and they have to improvise. At Chelsea in 1988, however, things went right. When I returned to the show on Thursday, each of the seven public parks exhibits had won a medal: two were silver, one was silver-gilt, and four were gold.

The 'Hampshire garden' exhibited by the Southampton City Council was partly inspired by the Council's own woodland garden at Mayfield Park.

WESTMINSTER
and
REGIONAL
SHOWS

The glamour and excitement of Chelsea make it an important date in the calendar for many who may start out with only a slight interest in the real business of gardening. The Great Spring Show has a way, however, of making converts. Those with a newly acquired enthusiasm will find, as committed gardeners do, that attending other horticultural shows is a highly enjoyable way of sustaining and enlarging their interest.

Some who regularly attend the Society's shows at its halls in Westminster look back at their first visits as a kind of graduation from Chelsea, marking the beginning of a grown-up attitude to plants and gardening. This should not put the novice off, for there is much to please the eye. On a murky winter's day the light scent and starry beauty of early flowers exhibited in the New Hall would focus, for a moment at least, the attention of the most frivolous Chelsea socialite. Among the advantages of this building, opened sixty years ago, is that from the dais you get an overall view of exhibits, ranged below you as a magic indoor garden.

The Old Hall, built to mark the Society's centenary in 1904 (largely through the efforts and generosity of Baron Sir Henry Schröder, one of the Society's greatest benefactors), is brought into use for the larger shows. Some will remember it most for tables loaded with the aromatic gold and russet fruits of autumn. For others its main association will be with orchids or alpines.

At Chelsea one feels, all seasons come together, with summer-flowering roses and ripe tomatoes as conspicuous as spring bulbs. To some extent the impression is misleading, for the glories of

Iris unguicularis lazica, a painting exhibited by
Jenny Jowett at Westminster in 1988. There are four
Westminster shows at which paintings are exhibited.

autumn – coloured foliage, berries and fruit – are absent. In contrast to Chelsea, the eleven Westminster shows of the year (formerly they were held fortnightly), unmistakably take their cue from the seasons.

Setting the seasonal tone is the programme of competitions organized by the Society and by kindred societies in association with it. No early planning can take fully into account vagaries of weather but, as far as possible, competitions are scheduled to coincide with the seasonal performance of plants. In 1987–88 there were, to take a few examples, a Summer Fruit and Vegetable Competition in July, Gladiolus and Heather Competitions in August, The Late Apple and Pear Competition in November, the Early Camellia Competition in March and in May the Daffodil and Main Rhododendron Competitions.

As Marigold Assinder makes clear in her article, those who show competitively are not members of an exclusive inner circle. She and others who get a keen pleasure from the rivalry of the show bench would welcome even more competition and joining them is not complicated. Arrangements for all the Society's competitions are spelt out in schedules that are available from the Secretary, RHS, Vincent Square, London SW1P 2PE.

Nursery exhibitors also show plants according to their seasonal interest, a few exhibiting throughout the year but others selectively, according to the plants which are their specialities. In a year of show going you get a real sense from their exhibits of the surge of spring and summer growth, the ripeness of autumn and the relative quietness of winter, with brave flowers and steadfast evergreens.

As space on stands is limited, the emphasis is on new introductions and less common plants, for there are many knowledgeable gardeners scrutinizing exhibits who would be disappointed to go away without making a fresh discovery. Exhibitors are allowed to sell and there are few plant enthusiasts who can resist purchasing an old favourite or something promising but unknown. Although stands are often busy, there is not the hurly-burly of Chelsea so generally it is possible to ask exhibitors their advice on the requirements of plants and their likely performance in the conditions your garden can offer. There can be few better opportunities for getting information direct from experienced nurserymen, a complement to the service available from the Advisory Bureau, which the Society mans at all the Westminster shows.

The articles that follow pick up themes that emerged from exhibits staged between June 1987 and May 1988. Although they give the flavour of the year between two Chelsea Shows, there are, inevitably, large gaps, not fully compensated for by the listing of exhibitors and the awards they received. Subsequent issues will take up different themes so that, in the medium term, it will be possible for readers to get a sense of the range of exhibits staged at Westminster.

There are many exhibits from the last year that warrant special mention: cacti and succulents shown by Mr and Mrs W. L. Tjaden and also by Mr T. J. Earles; dahlias from Aylett Nurseries Ltd and Tom Bebbington Dahlias, Ladygate Nurseries; autumn-flowering gentians and alpines from Edrom Nurseries; hostas from Goldbrook Plants; trees, shrubs and other ornamentals from Burncoose and Southdown Nurseries; carnations, pinks and alstroemerias from Steven Bailey Ltd; pleiones from Butterfield Nursery; stovehouse plants shown by Anmore Exotics; and daffodils from, among other nurseries, two in Northern Ireland, Carncairn Daffodils and Rathowen Daffodils. This is just a selection, and a very personal one, of exhibits that have left a deep impression but it may help to give an idea of the range of plants not necessarily covered in the articles that have been shown in the year.

Equally memorable was the effortless demonstration of flower arranging at the February show by Doris Wellham, with an introduction by Tom Gough of Longmans. On the first day of shows there is generally a lecture or demonstration and lectures have proved so popular that entry is only by free ticket. Application should be made to the Secretary (London Lecture Tickets), RHS, Vincent Square, quoting membership number and enclosing a first-class s.a.e. The application should reach Vincent Square not later than the Thursday before the show.

The illustration that opens the introduction to this section is a reminder that at Westminster there is an opportunity to exhibit and see exhibits of plant paintings and botanical illustrations during October, November, January and February shows. Regular displays of items from the Lindley Library help to set the work of modern artists in an historical perspective, the Library holding a magnificent collection of botanical books.

The Society's activities and facilities have in the past favoured those living in the south-east of the country, though by no means all regular visitors – and exhibitors – at Westminster shows are from London or the surrounding counties. The Society's Council has recognized the need to share the benefits of membership more widely and one way to do this is through the Society participating in regional flower shows. At the Malvern Spring Gardening Show in early May there was, as a modest beginning, a mobile bookshop and a team of gardening experts from Wisley.

It is certain that the Society's regional activities are bound to increase though the pace of change and precise direction are still under review. Future issues of *The Chelsea Year* will give regional shows more prominence as the Society's participation develops.

Friendly Competition

Marigold Assinder

In 1988 the Royal Horticultural Society celebrated the 75th anniversary of the Chelsea Flower Show, but a case could be put forward for the celebration of a hundred years of holding large yearly shows. The first of such shows took place on 17 and 18 May 1888, in the gardens of the Inner Temple on the Embankment, only two months after the Society had moved into new offices in Victoria Street. Although there was heavy rain on both days and they suffered a loss of £91, the show was considered a success – the result of superb organization and gardening skill. An even more significant event earlier in the same year was the holding of the first of a continuous series of fortnightly meetings only two days after the move to Westminster. These fortnightly meetings eventually became the Fortnightly Shows after a further move to Vincent Square in 1904.

The Fortnightly Shows have seen some changes in the hundred years since they started. Nowadays they are held monthly, except December, when there is no show. To anyone who lives within an easy distance of London – and even further afield – they represent great value, even if you are not a member of the Society. They are infinitely preferable to the Chelsea Show in so many ways – although of course they lack the 'designer' gardens and huge range of garden tools, accessories, conservatories and so forth to be seen there. But the crowds are smaller and the stands are equally good from the plantsman's point of view. You do not see the excesses you get at Chelsea – the plants are shown in their season and not held back or forced on. You may buy plants immediately from the stands and not have to wait until the end of the show as at Chelsea, and these plants are often very difficult to obtain from the ordinary garden centre, being sold by specialist growers, and are usually very, very much cheaper. I hesitate to give examples, but this year

Among the most colourful competitive classes late in the year are those for trees and shrubs grown in the open with autumnal fruits or foliage.

at an early show blue and white *Clematis alpina* were being sold for £2 a well-grown plant on one stand. Above all, these shows are beautiful – to gaze down the length of the hall from the raised platform is an experience not offered at Chelsea.

These Vincent Square shows, except for the Great Autumn Show in September, have another element missing at Chelsea – competitive classes which anyone can enter, whether members of the Society or not, without paying any sort of fee. Each month there are classes for flowering trees and shrubs and herbaceous plants; for example, in March and April for camellias, and in March and May for rhododendrons. In July and October there are classes for fruit and vegetables and in November there is a Late Apple and Pear Competition. The succession of competitions throughout the year covers most categories of garden plants, some classes, such as orchids, fuchsias and carnations, being organized by specialist societies. The classes for berried plants and leaf colour in the autumn produce some of the most stunning exhibits of the year from great gardens, including those of the National Trust, such as Nymans, Sheffield Park, Windsor, Borde Hill and Bodnant. However, you must not be intimidated from showing by the presence of these giants – long though it took me to realize that. I think it was the huge quantity of plant material, and its rarity, that the great gardeners put into their vases that made me feel a town or suburban garden was not able to compete. How wrongly, I was to find out.

Although I started gardening in our smallish garden in Putney – back garden about 7·5 by 42·5 m (25 by 139 ft), front garden 7·5 by 7·7 m (25 by 25 ft) – in 1957 it wasn't until 1981 that I summoned up the courage to start showing at Vincent Square. The seeds had been sown the previous year when my brother had come up from Chyverton, his garden in Cornwall, with a quantity of camellias, mostly reticulata, for the main Camellia Competition, one of the prize-winning raids he makes every so often when he has something particularly good to show. I watched as he set up his exhibits. It

was about eight o'clock in the morning and there were several other 'grand' gardeners there, setting up and standing around gossiping – and some not so grand. One turned to me and whispered apologetically, metaphorically pulling his forelock, 'You know, my garden's only a third of an acre.' In that moment I realized I had a goal, and it was to show that small gardens can produce prize-winning camellias.

At that point I only had four camellias in the garden. The first one I planted in 1959 was one not grown at Chyverton, as if I wanted to break away from the influence of that lovely garden. My mother and I went up from Cornwall to the Garden House at Buckland Monachorum to choose a camellia from Lionel Fortescue, that splendid plantsman, who always had the best form of everything. We chose a large plant of what was then called 'Nigra', had before been called 'Old Port', and now is known as 'Kouron Jura', and asked the price. 'Five guineas,' he said. I have never forgotten the stunned look on my mother's face. She was giving the plant to me and it was a simply outrageous price – I don't dare try to translate it into modern money. Some people did not earn that in a week. But she bought it and I have blessed her ever since as it has paid its rent, as they say, for nearly thirty years and has won prize after prize.

So at the beginning of 1981 I sent for a Show Schedule from the RHS and entered two classes in the Camellia Show in April. Feeling ridiculously nervous I took the two blooms to the hall early on the day of the show to set them up – the hours for this being 2 to 9.45 pm on the Monday and 7 to 9.45 am on the Tuesday of the show.

The first thing you have to do is to find your show cards. These are usually left on top of one of the stands and for the sake of the nervous new exhibitor I could wish them easier to find. Until 1988 camellia blooms were placed in sunken vases surrounded by moss; now, sadly, the 'vases' are white plastic cups, easily knocked over – small-flowered camellias just disappear into their depths. I am glad I did not have to cope with them when I first started showing. By a lucky chance I had cut the blooms – of

'Kouron Jura' and 'Contessa Lavinia Maggi' – with leaves as I was so green that I did not know that each flower had to have an attached perfect leaf. The moral of that is, of course, read the rules in the schedule. Looking back it is difficult to know why I felt so nervous, but this con-

tinued for a year or so – aggravated into panic one year by all the vases being put away early on the show morning, before I had set up, leaving me racing round the hall lifting the hessian skirts of the stands trying to find them. To return to that first show – I came back later

There are two main fruit and vegetable competitions in the year, the summer competition in July and an autumn competition in October.

that morning after the judging to find first prize stickers on both my show cards. I have been reasonably successful in the intervening years but nothing, *nothing* since has stunned me with such joy and amazement. A kind man told me he had never seen a better 'Contessa Lavinia Maggi', no, not even in Devon, and my cup was full. I was hooked.

Since those day the number of camellias in my garden has gone up alarmingly; now, instead of only four there are nearly eighty. When I reached twenty-seven I wrote in a gardening diary I kept briefly: 'I have reached the limit; there is no room for any more camellias.' But of course there always is room for just one more – a driving obsession can make you very ingenious. I find the camellia shows increasingly enjoyable as I get to know other people who show, and joining the International Camellia Society widened my horizons – it is not expensive and the yearly journal is excellent. Although, as I said earlier, I shall probably never know again the pure pleasure of that first show I still get a thrill when plants from my garden win prizes. However, this thrill has become increasingly diluted because of the decrease in entries in the classes. In 1983 John Gallacher wrote in the *Rhododendrons with Magnolias and Camellias Year Book*: 'Seeing [as I do] many camellia shows in America where enthusiasm is quite infectious it does seem strange that so few camellia lovers exhibit their flowers in London.' In some respect this decline is because of a run of late, difficult springs when the camellias are not ready for the show but also, I think, there are two other factors. Gardeners with small gardens simply do not realize that their plants have any chance against the 'big boys' and the mechanics of entering and showing in classes are not given sufficient prominence in *The Garden* – not enough encouragement comes from the RHS.

After a few years just showing camellias was not sufficient. I began to realize that other plants in the garden might also be worth showing. Anyway, the whole process was so easy that it was worth a try. My father had given me a *Magnolia campbellii* var. *mollicomata* from Caerhays in 1957. I had to wait for over

twenty years before it flowered but by 1987 it was flowering prolifically. I showed it in the Magnolia Classes in March and in, inevitably, a small class it won first prize. It was so difficult cutting a branch off a fastigiate tree that I vowed never to do it again and it is now retired, having won its laurels. One disadvantage of a small garden is the impossibility of adding to your collection of plants with modern improvements – the new large magnolias are so thrilling but I know, really know, there is no room for one.

Competitions organized in co-operation with the RHS by kindred societies, such as the Delphinium Society, are held regularly at Westminster shows.

As I gained experience I discovered that some plants just are not show material – *Cotoneaster lacteus*, for one. It is never successful, even though covered in berries. It could be that there are more entries in the autumn. One year *Prunus* 'Tai Haku' was out at the same time as the April Show. I put in a vase of it but did not read the schedule carefully. It was over the required height and so was disqualified – but then so was the only other entrant, who had also ignored the rules!

Again and again we come back to the dearth of exhibitors – only two entries in the Prunus class when all London is covered in glorious cherry blossom. Without the 'grand' exhibitors

like Lord Abcrconway and the National Trust and other great gardens like theirs the shows at the RHS would hardly be viable and the situation seems to be getting worse. In May this year I showed two plants in the Tree or Shrub other than a Rhododendron Class and got first and second – only one other entry. In June I got first in the Tree or Shrub shown for its Ornamental Foliage – no other entry. And this is typical. I spoke to an official at the RHS after the June show and expressed my concern. Was there anything to be done to improve matters? Perhaps the great gale of last autumn had made it difficult for some competitors in the Tree and Shrub classes this year? I felt this could hardly be the whole explanation as Alan Hardy, of Sanderling Park in Kent, which had been badly damaged by the Great Gale, was still exhibiting generously.

So come on now, you dedicated gardeners in Chelsea and Fulham and Putney and Kensington – and all the rest of London and the south-east. You at least live close to Vincent Square and I have seen wonderful plants in your gardens. You are proud of your plants – try exhibiting them in 1989. Write to The Secretary, The Royal Horticultural Society, PO Box 313, Vincent Square, London SW1P 2PE for your Show Schedule in January and plan your showing year. When you get used to the routine you will find it very trouble-free. I usually go up to the hall on the Monday evening, having remembered to put my entries in a week before (they are getting rather fussy about prompt entries). The traffic is minimal and there are no problems with parking. Take your secateurs and possibly some moss or oasis so that your exhibit is securely anchored. Having removed all obvious imperfections, dead leaves, faded flowers etc. set up the best-looking vase you can – and good luck! You will not find the prize money an inducement – although it can add up; my garden has won over £60 already this year, which will pay for quite a lot of peat – but you will find great interest and stimulation in showing. If you enter I will win less but I yearn for the challenge of larger and more interesting classes – so do not hesitate!

See you in the New Hall . . .

Bulbs for Four Seasons

Jack Elliott

Bulbs are featured at all the RHS shows throughout the year and reach a climax in March, April and May. In addition to all the popular cultivars of narcissus, tulips, lilies, gladioli etc. which contribute much of the impact of bulb exhibits, there are always some species bulbs to be seen. These seem to many gardeners to have a more delicate charm than their 'bigger and better' progeny, especially in the case of the dwarf bulbs which, in spite of their small size, flower profusely and can create as much colour in the garden as the more popular large varieties.

In considering some of the more interesting bulbs exhibited during the year the accent will be on these species and on a few first and second generation hybrids, which seem not to have lost the charm of their wild progenitors.

The shows of June, July and August are undoubtedly the quiet season for bulbs, especially for the dwarf species so conspicuous in spring and autumn, their place taken mainly by lilies and gladioli, with a few taller alliums and other small genera. The only exhibitor solely of bulbous plants in June was Jacques Amand, but many of those flowering in the garden in June and July had been seen at Chelsea on the stands of other exhibitors, for example Avon Bulbs, Broadleigh Gardens and Van Tubergen.

Alliums seem to be becoming increasingly popular as border plants, and several excellent species were shown by these exhibitors. *Allium aflatunense* is a well-known species with stems 75 cm (30 in) tall surmounted by dense globular heads of small rosy-purple flowers. 'Purple Sensation' is a newcomer similar in height, but with much darker purple flowers. *Allium christophii* (*A. albopilosum*) also has dense heads of flowers

The species tulips, in the wild often remarkably variable in size, shape and colour, and the numerous hybrids include some of the showiest spring bulbs.

but these are paler and the stems a little shorter. *Allium giganteum* again is similar but with even larger heads up to 15 cm (6 in) in diameter. All are easily grown and suitable for the herbaceous border or amongst shrubs. *Allium pulchellum* differs in having a loose head of drooping pink flowers (occasionally white), 30 to 45 cm (12 to 18 in) tall stems, seeding itself freely in the garden. Among the smaller alliums, *A. unifolium* was one of the best exhibited, an American species with flat heads of a dozen or more comparatively large clear pale pink flowers on stems standing 15 to 20 cm (6 to 8 in) high.

Gladiolus to most gardeners conjures up a picture of tall, stiff-stemmed plants for cutting or maybe for the border, needing replanting every year. These were well shown by Jacques Amand and other exhibitors from Chelsea onwards. In nature, gladiolus is a large and widespread genus which includes several species that are reasonably hardy, and which have given rise to some smaller hybrids well worth planting permanently in gardens in the south. Some of these were shown by Jacques Amand, as well as by Broadleigh Gardens and

Many of the ornamental onions are easy plants for sunny well-drained positions. The heads of *Allium christophii* can be dried for winter decoration.

Rupert Bowlby. *Gladiolus primulinus* is a dainty pale yellow species which will survive mild winters outside and is the parent of a range of named small hybrids that are more easily obtained. *Gladiolus* 'The Bride' has beautiful white flowers, their whiteness enhanced by green markings towards the base of the petals. Several other small hybrids were shown as cultivars of *G. nanus*, mainly in pink and red.

Lilies were exhibited at all the summer shows, the climax being the magnificent ones shown by the Lily Group of the RHS at the July show, an exhibit which also included hostas and some other liliaceous plants flowering at that time. Although most of the lilies exhibited were hybrids, there were impressive spikes of some species, including the rare *Lilium nepalense* with extraordinary large flowers, yellowish-green with a conspicuous deep chocolate-coloured central blotch. It is a difficult species for pot cultivation, its creeping stolons resenting constriction, but is a little tender for the average garden. Many of the lilies shown were also available from exhibiting nurserymen, for example, the ever-popular *L. regale*, probably the easiest garden lily, with fine white trumpets shaded yellow at the throat. *Lilium speciosum* is evidently easy to force as it appeared on many exhibits from May onwards, although not flowering in the garden until August or September. It can be grown in acid woodland conditions and has exceptionally large white Turk's-cap flowers heavily blotched with deep pink in the form usually exhibited. *Lilium auratum* needs similar conditions in the garden and has up to ten even larger, heavily-scented flowers to a spike. These are white with a broad central deep yellow band and numerous purple spots. Largest of all lilies, shown by the Lily Group, is *Cardiocrinum giganteum*, with mammoth spikes of violet-centred white trumpet flowers on stems up to 2·4 m (8 ft) high, requiring deep rich acid woodland soil in the garden. *Lilium chalcedonicum* was shown by Jacques Amand and Rupert Bowlby at Chelsea and in June. It is one of the best garden species for a sunny place with brilliant orange-red Turk's-cap flowers on stems that are 60 to 90 cm (2 to 3 ft) tall.

One of the easiest and loveliest lilies, *Lilium regale*,
was collected in China by E. H. Wilson, the first
bulbs being sent to England in 1904.

In August some *Eucomis* and *Hedychium* species were shown by Rupert Bowlby. These genera have always been considered on the borderline of hardiness, but recently have been increasingly planted in the open garden in sheltered positions, preferably in front of a south wall. The *Eucomis* species have a conspicuous ruff of green bracts at the top of the flower spikes, hence the common name 'pineapple plants'. *Eucomis bicolor* is the most frequently seen in gardens, with greenish-white flowers bordered with purple on spikes 30 to 45 cm (12 to 18 in) high. *Eucomis comosa* is generally a little more robust and has white flowers with a pinkish tinge and a central purple eye. Both species have the merit of producing a long-lasting succession of flowers on each spike.

The hedychiums have tuberous roots which can be treated like dahlias and lifted for the winter or left in the ground, with a reasonable chance of success in the south. The commonest available are *H. aurantiacum* and *H. densiflorum* 'Assam Orange', with striking spikes 90 to 120 cm (3 to 4 ft) high of orange flowers, and *H. gardnerianum* with yellow flowers with conspicuous red anthers. All the species flower in August or September.

At the Great Autumn Show in September many of the plants already mentioned were exhibited, especially lilies, but in addition there were some excellent exhibits of the early autumn-flowering hardy bulbs, notably cyclamen and colchicum. The Cyclamen Society and Peter Moore both staged comprehensive exhibits of cyclamen species. On both exhibits the most striking feature was the wonderful range of leaf shape and leaf markings of *Cyclamen graecum*, *C. hederifolium* and *C. africanum*. In the case of *C. graecum* flowering is unreliable, possibly varying from clone to clone, but the plant is worth growing for the velvet-textured leaves alone. The pale pink flowers, when they are produced, are among the largest of any species but the plant, like *C. africanum*, requires the protection of a cold greenhouse or frame. *Cyclamen africanum* resembles *C. hederifolium* but in most forms has considerably larger leaves. *Cyclamen cilicium* and *C. intaminatum* were also shown, the former with pale pink flowers, the latter with small pure white flowers and usually unmarked rounded leaves. Both of these are sufficiently hardy to be grown in the open. Two other pink-flowered species were seen, *C. cyprium* and *C. mirabile*, the former needing some protection whereas the latter can be grown in the open garden.

Particular genera of plants seem to enjoy waves of popularity, and colchicums are very much in vogue at present, particularly the large autumn-flowering species which are suitable for the garden. Many different species and varieties were exhibited in September and at the later shows by Jacques Amand and the Rev. R. J. Blakeway-Phillips, with a few from other exhibitors. The most striking must surely be

In a sheltered position *Eucomis bicolor*, a species from southern Africa, produces its curious flower spike topped with a tuft of green bracts.

The current popularity of the autumn-flowering colchicums takes in the species and several hybrids, including the double *Colchicum* 'Water Lily'.

Colchicum speciosum album, with its very large white goblets. Although still expensive, it is good value for the garden, each bulb producing a succession of flowers and increasing gradually to a sizeable clump. *Colchicum speciosum* itself has deep pink flowers with a white throat. *Colchicum autumnale* and its white form have much smaller flowers, but they increase more freely and are excellent garden plants. Under the name *C. giganteum* a deep rose-purple species with the largest flowers of all was exhibited. In many species the flowers are heavily chequered, a feature particularly well marked in *C. agrippinum* which has dark medium-sized flowers with white tessellation. Double flowers may not appeal to all gardeners, especially in bulbous plants, but the strange *C.* 'Water Lily' was seen on several exhibits, with a multiplicity of narrow rose-coloured segments.

Several autumn-flowering crocus species were exhibited at these late shows by Jacques Amand and by the alpine specialists Potterton and Martin. One of the best and most unusual was *Crocus banaticus*, once known as *C. iridiflorus* because the shape of flowers resembles that of an iris, with small inner segments and large flaring outer segments, a delicate pale lavender in colour with a conspicuous boss of frilly white stamens. Among those of more orthodox shape was *C. nudiflorus*, with very deep purple flowers appearing before the leaves, and *C. goulimyi*, an exquisite plant with more globular lavender flowers on exceptionally long tubes, usually appearing with the leaves. All these are good open garden plants, *C. banaticus* favouring moister, partially-shaded conditions.

Potterton and Martin also showed the rare *Sternbergia clusiana*, with very large crocus-like deep yellow flowers appearing before the leaves. Unfortunately this probably needs a good summer baking in a frame to flower well.

The show season begins in January with a surprisingly colourful collection of exhibits, including the earliest flowering bulbs. Snowdrops make an outstanding start to the year and were beautifully exhibited at the early shows, particularly by Avon Bulbs and Jacques Amand and by Foxgrove Plants, who specialize in the genus. For the snowdrop enthusiast there was a remarkable range of species and cultivars to be seen differing not only in the subtle arrangements of green markings on the flowers, but in the size and colour of the leaves. Among the most distinct were the very robust *Galanthus caucasicus* and *G. elwesii*, with very broad, very glaucous grey-green leaves, contrasting with the glossy green leaves of two subspecies of *G. ikariae*, *G. i. ikariae* and *G. i. latifolius*. Much of the variation is in the markings on the inner segments, but only *G. nivalis* 'Viridapicis' has green tips to the outer segments also. Different again is *G. lutescens*, a very uncommon form in which all the normally green parts of the flower are yellow.

Cyclamen were as much a feature of the early shows as of the late, the Cyclamen Society staging a good exhibit in February. Again the beautiful leaf markings must have impressed visitors, particularly in the Pewter Group of *Cyclamen coum*, in which the whole leaf, apart from a narrow border, is silver-grey in colour. These plants breed true from seed and are becoming more freely available. This and other alpine plant exhibits showed the great variety of flower in *C. coum*, the colour varying from pure white, through pink to deepest magenta, always with a dark blotch at the mouth. *Cyclamen trochopteranthum* differs from *C. coum* in having curiously twisted petals, giving the flower a striking 'propeller' shape. The largest-flowered species, *C. libanoticum*, was also exhibited, with its delicate pale pink flowers with dark markings at the mouth. This has proved much hardier in the garden than many authorities have suggested in the past! Very different from *C. libanoticum* is the diminutive *C. parviflorum* which has only rarely been exhibited and is one of the more difficult species to grow,

resenting drought at any time. The flowers resemble those of a very small *C. coum*, pink with the usual dark blotch.

Even in January some of the earlier-flowering narcissi were to be seen, the number increasing in February and March, with Broadleigh Gardens joining Avon Bulbs and Jacques Amand. *Narcissus romieuxii* and 'Nylon' were shown in January. These are usually the earliest to flower in the garden, often before Christmas. 'Nylon' has pale cream flowers of 'hoop petticoat' shape, whereas *N. romieuxii* is pale yellow with a very prominent boss of stamens. Various forms of *N. bulbocodium*, the commonest hoop petticoat narcissus, were to be seen later, with the exquisite *N. asturiensis*, which is the smallest of the trumpet daffodils, with stems under 15 cm (6 in) high. At all these early shows an excellent range of miniature hybrid narcissi were to be seen, especially on the stands of Broadleigh Gardens and Avon Bulbs, in addition to the larger varieties shown superbly by Michael Jefferson-Brown.

Dwarf iris species were exhibited in February

Cyclamen coum, a winter-flowering species, shows interesting variations in the leaf markings. Flower colour varies from white, through pink to deep magenta.

by the British Iris Society as well as on several of the trade stands mentioned previously, and by some of the alpine specialists like W. E. Th. Ingwersen and Holden Clough. *Iris histrioides* 'Major' was one of the most striking with very large deep blue flowers on short stems. Until recently this species as supplied by nurseries seemed constant, but now considerable variation is seen in the depth of colour and the lip markings, even within one nursery's stock. In the garden the flowers are very weather-resistant and soon build up to give an early splash of colour in January and February.

Iris danfordiae always appears at the early shows. Evidently raised very easily in Holland, it seldom makes a good garden plant, flowering well the first year and then tending to split into small bulbils. To enjoy its dumpy yellow flowers it must either be replanted frequently, or planted much deeper than usual. No such problems afflict *I. reticulata* and its various cultivars, all excellent garden plants, which were shown by several of the nurseries mentioned. One of the most unusual is 'Clairette' with pale blue standards and deeper blue falls, flecked and striped with white, rather than the usual yellow markings.

From February onwards an exciting range of fritillaries was to be seen. This genus has rapidly increased in popularity recently and, in addition to the common species, some rarer plants of more recent introduction have been exhibited, notably by Cambridge Bulbs, who also included uncommon irises on their small but fascinating stands in February and March and April. Among the most interesting fritillaries were an exceptionally large-flowered form of *Fritillaria aurea*, always one of the earliest to flower, with very large dangling deep-yellow bells, an easy and freely-increasing plant for the cold house or bulb frame. They also had a very good form of *F. caucasica* which usually has rather narrow reddish-brown flowers with segments incurving towards the tips, but on these plants were much larger and more open bells. One of their rarest plants was a yellow-flowered variety of *F. hermonis* ssp *amana*, usually green with brown markings and a plant which is proving easy outside.

The dwarf irises that flower early in the year include *Iris reticulata*. The cultivar 'Clairette' is unusual in having white markings on the falls.

Fritillaria pallidiflora, a member of a genus that is enjoying great popularity, is a beautiful and undemanding plant for cultivation in the open.

Anemone species were a feature of Edrom Nurseries, and Potterton and Martin's stands in March and April; both had areas devoted to shade-loving plants, in which they had included erythroniums and trilliums. Among the anemones were *Anemone ranunculoides*, a freely-increasing woodlander with small yellow flowers, its double form, and its hybrid with *A. nemorosa*, *A. × seemannii*, similar to its parents but with pale yellow flowers. A very similar coloured plant was exhibited by Edrom Nurseries as *A. ranunculoides* 'Pallida'. Several cultivars of *A. nemorosa* were to be seen, for example blue forms such as 'Royal Blue' and 'Robinsoniana', together with double and single whites. Edrom Nurseries also showed the extraordinary *A. nemorosa* 'Virescens', in which the flowers consist of broad heads of frilly green 'leaves' or bracts. To a lesser degree *A. nemorosa* 'Bracteata' is similar, with a normal white centre surrounded by a frilly ruff of green. One of the rarest anemones, *A. petiolulosa*, was shown by Potterton and Martin. This is a beautiful Asiatic species 10 cm (4 in) high, with clear yellow flowers. It will probably require a cold house or bulb-frame treatment rather than woodland conditions.

Anemone nemorosa 'Robinsoniana' is a fine blue form of the common wood anemone.

It is not just at Westminster that you get a chance to see good displays of bulbs. At the Harrogate Spring Show in late April there many excellent exhibits combining alpine plants and bulbs. Potterton and Martin were awarded a Large Gold Medal for an exhibit which included some of the later-flowering bulbs, among them a fine group of *Fritillaria pallidiflora*, one of the best species for the garden with very large pale cream flowers on stems 25 to 30 cm (10 to 12 in) high and conspicuous glaucous grey-green leaves. They also exhibited trilliums, as did Jacques Amand, with groups of *Trillium sessile* with large upright reddish-brown flowers stemless on the leaves, and of *T. erectum* with dark-centred white flowers carried above the leaves. Both these exhibitors showed the first *Rhodohypoxis* of the season, mixed colours, pink, white and red, from Potterton and Martin, and the large-flowered named 'Tetra Pink' and 'Tetra White' from Jacques Amand. Although only an inch high, they produce a long succession of flowers and can make a fine splash of colour in the garden. Jacques Amand also had several remarkable groups of fritillaries, including the somewhat difficult Asiatic species, *F. liliacea*, with several white flowers above glaucous leaves, and the pure green *F. alfredae* ssp *glaucoviridis*.

Among the excellent range of bulbs from Avon Bulbs was the beautiful yellow *Arum creticum* and the unusual *Scilla peruviana*, which has large pyramidal heads of purple flowers with long green tassels (bracts) among them towards the tips. They also showed *Tulipa* 'Bronze Charm', a good dwarf hybrid between the red *T. linifolia* and pale yellow *T. batalinii*, with large flowers in a delicate shade of apricot.

Chelsea Show gave gardeners the opportunity to see again most of the bulbs exhibited at earlier shows and many of those mentioned at later shows. Cold storage has evidently become a fine art, and in judicious combination with gentle forcing, has made it possible for our leading bulb exhibitors, such as Avon Bulbs, Walter Blom, Broadleigh Gardens, Jacques Amand, Michael Jefferson-Brown and Van Tubergen to contribute stunning exhibits with a vast range of narcissi, crocuses and fritillaries,

in combination with the later flowering tulips, alliums and gladioli. In addition to these both Potterton and Martin and Jacques Amand, on their Gold Medal exhibits, showed broad groups of their rhodohypoxis first seen at Harrogate, and of *Arisaema sikokiana*, a dramatic aroid suitable for peat conditions, with a large spathe striped green and brown within, and a pure white spadix.

Among the fritillaries were some fine groups of easier species which will thrive in the open garden. Apart from forms of the incomparable snakeshead *F. meleagris*, there were *F. pontica*, 15 to 20 cm (6 to 8 in) tall, with pale green bells with a light shading of orange-brown, and the considerably taller *F. acmopetala*, the flowers of which were green with a slightly narrow waist and dark brown edge to the segments. *Fritillaria verticullata* also grows to about 30 cm (12 in) but has whorled leaves and heads of several pale straw-coloured flowers. Although having a reputation for being shy-flowering, it seems to settle down a year or two after planting and then flowers regularly.

The dark flowers and mottled foliage of *Trillium sessile* give this woodland plant a sinister beauty.

Rhodohypoxis flower over a long period, making a good splash of colour despite their small size.

Evergreen Choice

Kenneth A. Beckett

Good evergreens are valuable throughout the year and especially during the dull chill days of winter, when it can be such a pleasure to look out on a garden which is cheerfully green. Such a garden need not be left to wishful thinking. The range of plants available makes it easy to achieve. Indeed, owners of small gardens will find that they are spoilt for choice.

At every one of the Society's Westminster shows there are exhibits that include a wide variety of evergreen shrubs and perennials. For the future, it is worth bearing in mind that at the February show, the first of the new year, a number of exhibitors make a point of showing foliage plants of interest in winter. This year, for example, Goldbrook Plants and West Country Plants, as well as the long-established Hillier Nurseries, were among several exhibitors who presented good selections of evergreens.

Although the plants are seldom exhibited to show each other off, as they might be in a garden, it is often possible to get ideas for pleasing associations by browsing among the stands. When choosing evergreens for the small garden, one must be highly selective. Every plant should be hardy in your area, pleasing in habit and foliage throughout the year and have no soil fads you can't satisfy. Getting accurate information on a plant's qualities and requirements can make all the difference between success and failure; the shows give a splendid opportunity to get the advice of knowledgeable nurserymen.

In a year of regular visits to Westminster shows I have been reminded of a number of evergreens that have proved their worth over a period of twelve years in my own garden in East Anglia. More often than not, seeing the plant itself has refreshed my memory, but sometimes the

The sword fern (*Polystichum munitum*), a North American evergreen species, flourishes in moist shady positions, forming a dense clump.

showing of a species or cultivar has called to mind close relatives that are well worth growing. In retrospect I have not found it easy to attribute plants to specific exhibitors but all the evergreens I mention are available. Should any readers have difficulties getting the plants they want, I would be happy to point them in the right direction.

No garden in which evergreens are a feature should be without a holly or two, and as there are 400 species and many more cultivars in existence there is no lack of choice. For the small garden, some of the forms of *Ilex crenata* can be recommended. These have the advantage of being unarmed, but they are essentially foliage plants, for their berries are black. Among the finest is *I.c.* 'Convexa', seldom seen at shows but worthy of greater recognition. It forms a rounded bush generally wider than high, densely set with glossy, elliptic, convex leaves. 'Golden Gem' forms a very different, spreading, flat-topped bush with yellow leaves which are especially bright in winter. Just as different again is 'Mariesii', eventually a gnarled bonsai-like shrublet densely set with tiny round dark green leaves. It is an ideal rock garden shrub seldom exceeding a growth increment of 2 cm ($\frac{3}{4}$ in) per year. All the *I. crenata* cultivars seem to thrive best in neutral to acid soil.

For those to whom a holly is not a holly unless its leaves bear spines *I. pernyi* should be given a try. Of neat columnar habit, it has erect slender stems and crowded oval, five-spined dark leaves which seldom exceed 2·5 cm (1 in) in length. Unlike most hollies, which are either male or female and need both sexes to be present if fruiting is to occur, single specimens of *I. pernyi* produce their red berries regularly.

This holly associates nicely with the lighter leaves of hebes and contrasts totally with the lustrous paddles of bergenias. These evergreen perennials provide bold foliage and good flowers and thrive in a variety of soils. Not to be despised are the commonly seen *Bergenia cordifolia*, *B. crassifolia* and *B. × schmidtii* (*B. crassifolia × cilata*). All these and *B. purpurascens* plus the many hybrid cultivars such as 'Abendglut', 'Silberlicht', 'Ballawley' and 'Sunningdale' are splendid dual-purpose plants. In addition, some sorts, notably 'Sunningdale', turn red or purple in winter.

Rather more spiny than hollies are several evergreen kinds of barberry or *Berberis*. Nevertheless, some of the dwarf evergreen species are first-class shrubs which look good all the year and are excellent items where evergreens are appreciated. Rarely above 1 m (40 in) in height and spread and fairly slow growing is *B. candidula*. This dense rounded shrub has arching bright brown stems and narrowly elliptic leaves with rolled-under margins which are a rich polished green above and intense blue-white beneath. Ultimately twice as tall, but slow growing is *B. verruculosa*, with broader leaves having a few spiny teeth. Like *B. candidula* each leaf is a deep lustrous green above and blue-white beneath. There is a hybrid between these two barberries known as *B. × frikartii*. It much resembles a large growing *B. candidula* and is confused with it in cultivation. Anyone seeking the genuine small *B. candidula* in a garden centre should be aware of this as the hybrid can, in less than ten years, exceed 1·5 m (5 ft) in height.

Most daphnes, although they have quite pleasant evergreen foliage, are grown for their fragrant flowers. *Daphne odora*, however, is very much a dual-purpose shrub of quality. In time it forms a hummock to 1·2 m (48 in) tall and half again as wide. Its bright green glossy leaves are narrowly oval and 4 to 9 cm ($1\frac{1}{2}$ to $3\frac{1}{2}$ in) long. In the best known form, *D.o.* 'Aureomarginata', which was shown by several nurseries this spring, the leaves are narrowly edged with creamy-yellow. Extremely sweet-scented flowers, which are red-purple in bud and open almost white, appear in terminal and axillary clusters from late winter to spring. It needs a sheltered corner and makes a fine specimen to plant beneath a window or by a door. Having similar but darker leaves is *D. laureola*, a splendid plant for shade and tolerating dryish chalky to wettish clay soils. In winter it produces somewhat hidden clusters of lime-green flowers which exhale a sweet scent on damp mild evenings. A close ally, *D. pontica*, is sometimes seen at the Society's shows.

Bergenias are among the best evergreen herbaceous
perennials for ground cover. 'Silberlicht', raised
about 50 years ago, is a fine white-flowered hybrid.

These last two daphnes combine nicely with the winter-flowering sweet boxes, *Sarcococca*, a very amenable genus of modest charm (and for that reason, perhaps, not so commonly brought to Westminster), which will not only grow in the shade of trees, but also in totally sunless north-facing sites. *Sarcococca confusa* and *S. ruscifolia* var. *chinensis* are among the best. Both have small oval to elliptic deep green, fairly glossy leaves and form bushes to 1·2 m (48 in) or more in height. During mild days in mid- to late winter tiny but fragrant flowers appear. Although these have no petals, the four fat white stamens which comprise each bloom are surprisingly conspicuous. *Sarcococca ruscifolia* produces red berries, while those of *S. confusa* are black. Having longer, willow-like leaves and an erect suckering mode of growth is *S. hookeriana*. In time it can attain 1·8 m (6 ft)

Like other sweet boxes, *Sarcococca hookeriana* var. *digyna* tolerates shade. It is valuable in winter for its glossy leaves and sweetly scented flowers.

in height and is a little large for the smaller garden. Shorter and more compact is *S.h.* var. *digyna* with cream-stamened flowers, but most desirable of all is *S.h.* var. *humilis*, rarely above 1 m (40 in) tall and with pink-tinted stamens. A quietly effective planting scheme can be achieved by using sarcococcas surrounded by the evergreen fern *Polystichum setiferum* 'Acutilobum', or the totally hardy maidenhair *Adiantum venustum*. This fern, which is rhizomatous and can form large colonies, is evergreen in mild winters but turns rusty-fawn after severe frost, persisting until the bronzy-red tinted young fronds push through in spring.

Ferns add elegance and variety to any garden scene and the evergreen sorts maintain this value throughout the winter. Fibrex Nurseries, for example, has several times shown fine displays. Strikingly attractive is *Polystichum munitum*, a densely clump-forming species from western North America, where it is known as sword fern. In rich moist soil it can exceed 1 m (40 in) in height but is usually smaller. The lance-shaped fronds are divided in ladder fashion into numerous slender, leathery, rich green pinnae (leaflets), each one with a thumb-like basal lobe. This is a specimen fern *par excellence* and deserves a position where it can be seen in its entirety. Less majestic but very welcome in the garden in winter is *Asplenium scolopendrium*, still often listed as *Phyllitis scolopendrium*. Familiarly and aptly known as hart's tongue fern, its strap-shaped leathery, glossy green fronds are best in shade. Several cultivars are known, but none better than the one sold variously as 'Crispum' or 'Undulatum', with the leaf margins beautifully and deeply waved. Very much smaller is the southern hemisphere hard fern, *Blechnum penna-marina*. The commercially available form spreads by slender rhizomes and can make a pleasing ground cover of small, deeply lobed, narrow fronds which are a charming bronzy-red when young. It thrives most exuberantly in moistish peaty conditions but is not really fussy in its soil requirements. Certainly this little fern makes an attractive foil for the small rhododendrons and other members of the heather family.

The finest display of rhododendron exhibits coincided with the Main Rhododendron Competition in early May. For those lucky enough to garden on acid soil or who are prepared to make even a small peat bed, there are many small rhododendrons of the highest garden value. Among these species with good evergreen foliage and beautiful flowers (and which have proved totally hardy in East Anglia) the following can be recommended. *Rhododendron radicans* forms dense slow-growing mats of deep green glossy leaves above which perch large, solitary, almost saucer-shaped flowers of rose-purple with darker spotting. It is closely allied to the more hummock-forming, broader-leaved *R. keleticum*. Both are native to open stony moorland in Tibetan mountains. Somewhat larger is *R. calostrotum*, which slowly builds into a rounded bush 60 to 100 cm (24 to 40 in) in height. Its small aromatic leaves are sage-green above and white to buff beneath. The almost flat flowers are even larger than those of *R. radicans* and a brighter, lighter, shade of rose-purple. Superior is the cultivar *R.c.* 'Gigha', which has claret-red blooms. A species that is essentially a foliage plant is *R. lepidostylum*. Its small leaves, which are pale blue-green above and paler beneath, seem to glow with a phosphorescent luminosity. The flowers are a pale to greenish yellow. A nice contrast can be had by planting this rhododendron beside the somewhat larger deep green hummocks of *R. williamsianum*. The latter has much to offer in its own right with its neat heart-shaped leaves on red stalks. In winter the prominent buds glow redly and in spring the whole bush lights up with exquisite, nodding pink bells.

Rhododendron calostrotum is a dwarf species,
conspicuous in flower and attractive throughout the
year on account of its aromatic sage-green foliage.

To add variety to the rhododendrons there is much to be said for using some of their less frequently seen allies, notably *Andromeda*, *Phyllodoce* and *Cassiope*, all heath-like plants of quality for a cool site in lime-free soil. Easiest to accommodate is *Andromeda polifolia*, the so-called bog rosemary, from moist moorland and bogs around the northern hemisphere. It forms suckering clumps of very narrow leaves which are blue-white beneath. In early summer, globular icing-pink bells garland every stem tip and present a charming sight. Particularly good is *A.p.* 'Macrophylla' with broader, dark leaves and freely borne flowers. *Cassiope* has a reputation for being difficult in the warmer drier areas, and there is some truth in this. However, some of the man-made hybrids are more amenable, and of these 'Edinburgh' is an outstanding success. Forming a twiggy bushlet to 30 cm (12 in) or more in height, its slender stems are covered with overlapping deep-green scale leaves. In spring every shoot is covered with quite large white bells and the plant becomes an eye-catcher of distinction. It flowers best in a sunny site and stands warm dry spells with equanimity. Distinctly heath-like in foliage are the six to seven species of *Phyllodoce*. They have a similar reputation to that of *Cassiope*, but are well worth trying in a peaty soil. Easiest is *P. empetriformis*, a low hummock former with red-purple bells of substance. Its hybrid is perhaps even more rewarding. This is *P. ×intermedia*, a more vigorous plant, which produces many light purple bells in spring and a lesser display on and off until the autumn. They are wider than those of *P. empetriformis*.

Thriving in a wide range of soils, from acid to alkaline, are the New Zealand hebes, a large genus which steadily rises in popularity and now even has a society devoted to its interest. Many hebes are regularly shown at Westminster, especially by that enthusiast for New Zealand plants Graham Hutchins of County Park Nursery. Despite their popularity, it has to be said that more than 50 per cent of all known hebes are either tender or unreliably hardy away from warm sheltered areas. However, this still leaves us plenty of choice, and at least twenty different sorts have survived the

RIGHT Despite their reputation for tenderness, some of the New Zealand hebes have stood up to a succession of cold winters. *Hebe rakaiensis*, which has proved hardy, produces white flowers early to mid-summer.

BELOW Most cassiopes, natives of peaty moorland conditions, are not easy to grow satisfactorily, but the hybrid 'Edinburgh' is an accommodating garden plant.

past ten years in north Norfolk. Best known and among the finest is *Hebe rakaiensis*, still often listed and shown erroneously as *H. subalpina*, a very different species. *Hebe rakaiensis* forms a dense round bush of small, bright, almost yellow-green elliptic leaves, which in ten years can attain a width of 1·8 m (6 ft) and a height of 75 cm (30 in). After about five or six years it starts to produce spikes of glistening white flowers, sparsely at first but in greater abundance each successive summer. By ten years of age it bears a dense wig of bloom across the dome of foliage. It makes a fine specimen plant and combines especially well with forget-me-nots, which not only provide spring colour but have winter green foliage. Smaller-growing but with larger grey leaves is *H. albicans*. It is less neat in outline than *H. rakaiensis* and the flower spikes, which have purple stamens, are more evenly disposed and squatter. *Hebe a.* 'Prostrata' has a carpeting mode of growth, very useful as ground cover around more erect species. *Hebe odora*, syn. *H. buxifolia* is a variable species, several different clones of which are exhibited from time to time, sometimes wrongly as *H. buxifolia*. It has richer green,

smaller leaves and like *II. rakaiensis* only blooms freely when several years old. Among the forms stocked by Graham Hutchins is *H.o.* 'New Zealand Gold', which I collected in New Zealand's South Island, at Arthur's Pass, in 1972. In most gardens it has yellow shoot tips for much of the year. Some growers complain that the yellow variegation disappears when grown in their soil and it now seems certain that the coloured leaves are the result of a nutritional disorder, probably lack of sufficient magnesium, a common feature of soils in the British Isles. All the hebes can be planted together and make a very satisfactory association with their varied foliage hues. Once they have grown together, few weeds survive beneath their dense shade.

Hebes also combine well with some of the smaller junipers, another genus of increasing popularity and with a great range of habit, foliage type and colour. Although their fruits are semi-fleshy and almost berry-like, junipers are conifers, another group of plants very much on an upsurge of popularity and of inestimable value in the smaller garden. Several nurserymen display them regularly; they are frequently used to give weight to displays of alpines and rock garden plants. Justifiably popular is *Juniperus squamata* 'Blue Star', an irregularly hummock-forming cultivar, with intense steely-blue foliage composed of innumerable tiny awl-shaped leaves. More vigorous, less intensely blue and spreading horizontally to 1·5 m (5 ft) or so, is *J.s.* 'Blue Carpet', a splendid plant for clothing a bank, especially in company with a plant of similar habit, *J. communis* 'Green Carpet', or the taller *J.c.* 'Depressa Aurea'. The latter turns bronze in winter and then changes dramatically in spring, when the young shoots are a butter-yellow. The cone and column shapes of many conifers make fine accent plants for the smaller garden. A broad cone which gradually turns into a sturdy blue-grey column to 2 m (80 in) or more in height is *J. chinensis* 'Pyramidalis'. This can add substance to a small bed of winter heaths or spring bulbs, or can grace the edge of a tiny lawn. If yellow foliage is preferred then *J. communis* 'Gold Cone' is worth considering.

Not all the best smaller conifers are junipers. Cypresses, firs, hemlocks, pines and spruces all provide small versions in a variety of foliage shades. Lawson cypress, *Chamaecyparis lawsoniana* is a prolific parent of many garden-worthy cultivars. Of compact and rounded habit is *C.l.* 'Gimbornii', which takes some years to attain 60 cm (2 ft). Its soft blue-green leaves combine well with the taller, yellow-tinted columns of 'Ellwoods Gold' and the rich green shell-like sprays of *C. obtusa* 'Nana Gracilis'. Very different is the tiny hemlock, *Tsuga canadensis* 'Jeddeloh', which forms a spreading bush to 40 cm high by 60 cm (16 by 24 in) or more wide, nicely set with light green almost pendulous shoot tips. Among the spruces, *Picea omorika* 'Nana' forms a pyramid of light green shot with blue to 1 m (40 in) or more in height, and *P. abies* 'Nidiformis' is flat-topped and dark green. No planting of evergreens would be complete without one or two of the pygmy pines which contrast so well with other conifers and broad-leaved shrubs. *Pinus mugo* is a naturally bushy pine from the mountains of central Europe, but though small as pines go it can in time attain 3 m (10 ft) or more. Naturally very variable, it has given rise to prostrate and very condensed forms. *P.m.* 'Mops' is one of the most reliable and useful cultivars, forming rounded bushlets of grey-green needles to 40 cm (16 in) or more in height, greater in spread. *Pinus m.* 'Ophir' is of similar size and shape, with gold-tipped needles which turn completely yellow in winter. The Scots pine, *P. sylvestris*, has also provided some first-rate dwarfs, notably the long cultivated 'Beauvronensis'. This very slow-growing cultivar is believed to have been raised from a witch's broom in France and has been in commerce for almost a century. After many years it can attain 1 m in height and 1·5 m in spread (40 by 60 in). Eventually somewhat larger is *P.s.* 'Hibernica', a dense bush with more strongly blue-tinted needles, while 'Fastigiata' is narrowly columnar, a unique habit in pines. The latter makes a fine accent plant especially when rising above a grouping of mat and hummock-forming broad-leaved evergreens.

Among the broad-leaved evergreens, and a hummock-former of distinction, is *Cotoneaster congestus* from the high Himalaya. In fifteen years, a rooted cutting can attain 1 m in height and 1·5 m in spread (40 by 60 in), creating during that time a remarkable density of rich reddish-brown stems and tiny oval leaves of bright matt-green. Curiously enough flowering and fruiting seems to be rare in cultivation, but it hardly matters. Closely related is *C. microphylla*, a looser, more rangy grower but with very dark glossy leaves and quite large matt-crimson berries which glow in a most satisfying way when struck by the low rays of winter sunlight. This, with other species carrying berries, was shown in the autumn. Completely mat-forming is *C. dammeri*, a comparatively fast-growing species from central China. Its oval leaves, 2 to 3 cm (approx 1 in) long, are dark and fairly glossy, providing a pleasing ground-cover. Unlike other cotoneasters, its white flowers are borne singly or in pairs and make little impact. They are followed by coral-red berries which, when carried in sufficient numbers, enhance the foliage in winter. This shrub is seen to best effect when clothing a steep bank or hanging over a retaining wall. On the flat it provides a nice contrast to such grey-leaved plants as *Hebe albicans* and the yellow *Juniperus communis* 'Gold Cone'.

No garden should be without a few climbers, and even the smallest plot usually has a good expanse of wall to utilize. Indeed, climbing plants provide a linking element, especially when growing up a house wall from among shrubs and other plants at the base. Unfortunately, hardy decorative evergreen climbers are a rather select band of plants, and they are not so commonly seen at Westminster shows.

Happily, one of the finest is commercially available, *Clematis armandii*. This vigorous plant bears trifoliate leaves composed of lustrous green, lance-shaped leaflets which are bronzy when young and can reach 15 cm (6 in) in length. In spring a profusion of six-petalled white flowers appear which, for a few weeks, totally eclipse the foliage. There is a charming pink-tinted cultivar known aptly as 'Apple Blossom'. Very different is the so-called fern-leaved clematis, *C. cirrhosa* (from southern Europe to western Turkey). It has elegantly dissected leaves and nodding, bell-shaped creamy-white flowers in winter and spring. *Clematis c.* var. *balearica* (*C. calycina*) has even more ferny leaves and flowers that are reddish in bud and spotted red within. Despite its homeland, this smallish clematis is surprisingly hardy but deserves a sheltered sunny wall.

Among the roses are two that are almost ever-green, the closely allied *Rosa wichuraiana* and *R. luciae*. They produce neat, polished rich green leaves and trusses of small, fragrant white flowers in late summer. Having a greater floral impact is the semi-evergreen rose 'Alberic Bar-bier', a child of *R. wichuraiana*, and the small yellow tea rose 'Shirley Hibberd', raised in

1900. It has fragrant double flowers which are yellow in bud and expand creamy-white.

Well worth trying on a sheltered wall is the star jasmine *Trachelospermum asiaticum* which can clothe a wall ivy-fashion with a little help. It has dark, glossy oval leaves and in late summer trusses of fragrant white flowers 2 cm ($\frac{3}{4}$ in) wide which age to a dull yellow. It needs summer warmth to flower freely but the leaves are always cheerful.

There are many more evergreens of all kinds to be seen at the Society's shows or which are at least stocked by exhibitors, but this very random and personalized account does, I hope, show that a garden in winter need never lack the enlivening greens of summer.

The dark glossy leaves of *Cotoneaster microphylla* show off the large crimson berries of this very tough species.

Starting with Orchids

Phillip Cribb and Joyce Stewart

Many myths and misconceptions about orchids are still prevalent. They are rumoured to be difficult to grow, extremely expensive to buy, parasitic and even poisonous. Ian Fleming, no less, in his James Bond novel *Moonraker*, had his villain Blofeld extracting a deadly poison from a black-flowered orchid in his mission to rule the world! Let us set your mind at rest immediately. No orchid is at all poisonous to our knowledge. Indeed, the pods of *Vanilla* are commonly used as a flavouring, and the Chinese herbalists use over 140 species in traditional medicine. Neither are orchids parasites, despite the habit of many plants in the tropics, which grow on the bark of trees, and the undoubtedly bizarre and even grotesque flowers of some of these. Many of the widely held beliefs about orchids are simply not borne out by the facts.

The majority of tropical orchids are easy to grow. They are quite tolerant of the whims, eccentricities and holidays of owners who understand their growing requirements, and many, in fact, are hard to kill. We recently had two New Guinea orchids destined for Kew that quite happily survived six months in a box in the corner of a warehouse at Heathrow airport. Orchids are also relatively less expensive than they have ever been. The wonders of modern micropropagation techniques, such as tissue culture, have enabled prize cultivars to be multiplied by the thousand. The unit cost has been reduced to a level that makes orchids no more expensive than a plant such as a magnolia or rhododendron from your local garden centre.

The cultivation of tropical orchids was a truly British invention. It gradually came to the fore in private horticulture in the last century, at least partly as a result of the increasing affluence and leisure of the

The Eric Young Orchid Foundation was awarded a
Certificate of Cultural Commendation in January 1988 for
this specimen of *Miltoniopsis* Hannover 'Mont Millais'.

Victorians following the Industrial Revolution and accompanying the expansion of the British Empire. The latter, in particular, gave the early British orchid growers access to plants from the tropics of both the old world and the new. The Royal Horticultural Society played a leading role in this new development, with special greenhouses in its garden at Chiswick for experiments in growing techniques. The Society's Orchid Committee will celebrate its centenary in 1989. However, it was the discovery in the 1850s that orchids could be hybridized easily that was responsible for the amazing development of orchid growing as a hobby that is now worldwide. Orchid growers need never tire of their wards, because, to the 25,000 or more wild species of orchids, tens of thousands of man-made hybrids can now be added.

Orchids feature prominently, today, at the RHS's shows at Westminster and also at Chelsea. At the latter, orchid displays have occupied the Monument site in the main marquee twice in the past four years, a tribute to both the strength of orchid growing in this country and to the continuing popularity of these plants. The magnificent stands of white, pink, red, green and gold *Cymbidium* hybrids, and the dazzling elegance of the arching sprays of pink or white moth orchids, the *Phalaenopsis*, can be breathtaking. However, it is often on the smaller stands that the range of orchids can be best appreciated. Here, species orchids and their hybrids are displayed in mixed groups of almost bewildering variety.

For the beginner who wants an introduction to orchids and their cultivation, there are two shows in the calendar that demand attendance, one in the late autumn, the other in March. At the end of November every year, the Orchid Society of Great Britain holds its Autumn Competition in conjunction with a regular RHS show. High-quality orchids are always on display, many of them grown by amateurs in small greenhouses. The show is supported by commercial exhibits, ensuring that potential customers have plenty of choice. In 1987 the orchid that caught everyone's fancy was a neat plant from Ecuador that was covered with a cascade of cream and gold flowers. *Masdevallia*

strobelii, 'Muriel' which received an RHS Award of Merit, was a great delight to the public and to its owner, Jack Whitehouse of Solihull, who was exhibiting at Westminster for the first time and who received a Certificate of Cultural Commendation for this plant.

Other tropical species have received awards for fine form and good culture throughout the year. In June 1987 there were spectacular contrasts between the red lined *Catasetum pileatum* var. *imperiale* 'Pierre Couret', the unruly loop of deep brownish-red flowers of *Oncidium orgyale* 'Loja' and the exquisite pink spikes of the tiny terrestrial *Stenoglottis woodii* 'Kew Delight', which everyone can grow, even on a windowsill. In July a very large number of wild species received awards. Amateur growers from Bournemouth shared the honours with others from Littlehampton, West Yorkshire and Bristol. A superb specimen of the scarlet *Laelia milleri* 'Rosemary', a metre across, was displayed next to a splendid spike of *Eriopsis biloba* 'Highcliffe Castle', also from Brazil. Immaculate plants of *Epidendrum prismatocarpum* 'Bromesberrow Place' and *Aerangis distincta* 'Kew Elegance' were also noteworthy for their cultivation and many flower sprays. In August it was the turn of a grower from Lancashire to see his plant of *Promenaea xanthina* 'Alfreda Lancs' gain for him a Certificate of Cultural Commendation; six months later it was featured on the cover of the *Orchid Review*. In September we saw the plant with the smallest flowers and also the greatest number among all that were displayed during the year. The 'golden chain orchid', *Dendrobium filiforme* 'Bromesberrow Place' had fifty-one flower spikes each carrying over a hundred minute, golden-yellow flowers. And so the list could go on. Every month there is something of interest; old and new, large and small, gaudy or subtle in colouring, round or spidery in shape, there is something for everyone's taste and pocket.

The term 'tropical orchids' that is so often used to refer to the exotic species of horticulture can be quite misleading for the inexperienced grower. In the tropics the majority of orchids grow in the mountainous regions. Places such as the Andes of Venezuela, Colombia, Ecuador and Peru are particularly rich in orchid diversity. It is thought that as many as 5,000 species grow in Colombia alone, while on the other side of the world New Guinea can boast 2,500 species. It is a reflection of how little is known of these regions that such figures are at best 'guesstimates'. Since most of the orchids are found on the mountains, it follows that truly 'tropical' temperatures are unnecessary if these species are to be successfully cultivated. Many of the Andean *Odontoglossum* and *Masdevallia* species grow at altitudes up to 3,000 m (10,000 ft) elevation, where night temperatures drop to only a few degrees above freezing.

The odontoglossums, and many colourful intergeneric hybrids bred from them, remain one of the most popular kinds of orchid for the beginner to grow. Enthusiasts had a unique opportunity to appreciate the great variety, in size, colour and shape, that is now available in this group when the British Orchid Growers' Association held their annual show combined with the first meeting of the International Odontoglossum Alliance to be held outside North America, at Westminster in March 1988. The Old Hall was full of orchids, and every exhibit featured lovely species and hybrids of this undemanding group of plants. The most outstanding gold-medal group was brought over from Jersey and staged by the Eric Young Orchid Foundation. In design and content it eclipsed all the others. Bright red pansy orchid hybrids (*Miltoniopsis*) showered from trees and contrasted with the orange-flowered *Ada aurantiaca* below and yellow and white odontiodas.

The slipper orchids from tropical Asia, species and hybrids of the genus *Paphiopedilum*, form another easy group of orchids for the beginner. With a carefully selected small collection of these it is possible to have plants in flower throughout the year, and many people do. There have been paphiopedilums in flower at every show during the last year, either in the trade and Orchid Society exhibits or on the dais of the New Hall among the plants submitted to RHS committees for awards. Their popularity stems both from their long-lasting, distinctive flowers and from their ease of culture. Being terrestrial plants from shady forests and rocky hillsides, they are easy for a new orchid grower to understand. They need a well-drained compost, not unlike that of many other pot plants, and to be kept moist throughout the year. The wild species, of which about sixty have now been recognized, continue in popularity, but there are also several distinctive kinds of hybrids which have been spectacular this year. The best known are the round, saucer-shaped blooms in a wide range of colours which appeal to many admirers on account of their polished and glossy symmetry. The kinds which we find more appealing are the stately plants with tall sprays of several striped flowers that have been bred from *Paphiopedilum rothschildianum* and a range of other species. The pink *P*. Delrosi 'Roydon' (× *P. delenatii*) was a favourite in September. In October we saw *P*. Mrs Rehder (× *P. argus*) and *P*. Transvaal (× *P. chamberlainianum*) and in May a really superb *P*. St Swithin (× *P. philippinense*). All of these are handsome, and the easiest to grow and flower is probably Transvaal. The elegant flowers of the Maudiae-type hybrids are always a great delight. They are borne on long stems and their shades of lime green and white or dark red and white ensure that their popularity never fades. The originals were crosses of the albino forms of *P. lawrenceanum* and *P. callosum*, but other species and colour forms have also been incorporated in the breeding lines. Recently some very dark-coloured forms, with intriguing names like Vintner's Treasure, Dragon's Blood and Masupi, have become available, and these are just as easy to grow as the older varieties. An added bonus that these plants offer is their attractively mottled leaves.

Among the really showy orchids pleiones must rank as one of the easiest to grow and they are greatly in demand in spring, early summer and autumn. Despite their origins in India and China, pleiones are hardy enough to be judged by the Rock Garden Plant Committee of the RHS rather than the Orchid Committee. The display of pleiones by Butterfield's Nursery has been a regular gold-medal winner at spring shows for the past few years and at Chelsea since 1986. Their popular name of windowsill

These four hybrids, painted for the Society's Orchid Committee by Cherry-Anne Lavrih, received Awards of Merit in 1988: two cymbidiums of the same parentage (Strathmore × Caithness Ice), 'Cooksbridge Delight', and 'Cooksbridge Green Gem', *Paphiopedilum* Dinah Albright 'Bromesberrow Place' and *Odontioda* Becky Falls 'Dipper'.

orchid indicates just how easy they are to grow; several are hardy enough to survive outside in the garden throughout the year. Their current popularity owes much to the wide range of colours now available, from white and primrose yellow to pink and rose-purple, and also to the expanded flowering season, both resulting from the introduction to the breeding lines of new species in recent years. You can now flower pleiones from October through until June if you grow the right cultivars and keep them completely dry during the resting stage. More species and cultivars are available than ever before. *Pleione formosana* comes in a variety of shades, from the pure white 'Clare' to the large-flowered 'Oriental Splendour', with purple sepals and petals and a white lip spotted with orange. *P. bulbocodioides* will provide the true orchid purple that is almost too rich for the eye. The rare Chinese *P. forrestii*, with rich bright yellow flowers and red spotting on the lip, is now more readily available but perhaps rather expensive. For our money the best hybrid of all is *P.* Shantung. It is vigorous, flowers well,

often with two blooms on the spike, and ranges in colour from white to primrose yellow, always with orange-red spotting on the lip.

A precious few orchids are suitable for the garden. A few of these can be seen at shows in May, June and July, but usually among the exhibits of bulbs and alpines rather than among the orchids. One or two specialist growers are bringing in dormant tubers from the Netherlands and exhibiting rather small plants for sale as they come into flower. These are unlikely to transplant well. Sprouting rhizomes of *Epipactis gigantea* that we purchased at Westminster earlier in the year, from a Scottish grower, have settled well in a moist woodland garden and will flower in late summer. Despite their charm, the lady's-slipper orchids (*Cypripedium*) are not plants to buy. They are at best short-lived in the garden and most of those on sale have been dug up from the wild. They are best appreciated in their natural habitats, though many are, sadly, declining in numbers.

By far the best orchids for the garden are some of the dactylorhizas, variously called marsh orchids or spotted orchids. Several species are available in the trade, usually sold by alpine garden specialists. The native species *Dactylorhiza maculata*, with spotted leaves and pink flowers, and *D. praetermissa*, with plain leaves and purple flowers, have both been shown in June and July. They will thrive in a peaty border, forming clumps that reach 45 cm

(18 in) in height in ideal sites. Their hybrid is occasionally seen in cultivation and grows much more vigorously. However, the best of the marsh orchids are the giants of the genus, *D. foliosa* from Madeira and *D. elata* from South-West Europe and North Africa, both with unspotted leaves. They will grow 60 to 90 cm (2 to 3 ft) tall in cultivation, forming large clumps if left in place for a few years. They are often confused in the trade, but *D. foliosa* usually has flowers in which the lip is broadly three-lobed and relatively unspotted, while *D. elata* has a narrower, purple-spotted lip with reflexed side lobes.

The last year has been an outstanding one for British orchid growers. It started in Tokyo, in the spring of 1987, with the joint exhibit of the Eric Young Orchid Foundation of Victoria Village in Jersey and McBeans Orchids of Cooksbridge, Lewes, Sussex, capturing more awards than any other exhibitor at the spectacular 12th World Orchid Conference Show. At the same event it was announced that the honour of hosting the 14th World Orchid Conference, in 1993, had been awarded to the Scottish Orchid Society, and it will be held in Glasgow. Later in the year there were two events that demonstrated the continuing strength of the British orchid scene, both on the professional front and at the amateur level. The British Orchid Council's Show in March, opened by Princess Michael of Kent in Chel-

tenham, was widely considered to be one of the best ever; it filled the capacious and beautiful town hall with a myriad of scented blooms. The combined efforts of McBeans, Burnham Nurseries and Wyld Court Orchids with Anmore Exotics produced a memorable imitation of a New Guinea rain forest around the obelisk at Chelsea. In truth, no rain forest ever looked so exotic, because this mammoth display, with its wealth of spectacular flowers, demonstrated the advances produced by over one hundred years of orchid breeding.

Throughout the long history of flower shows at Westminster, orchids have had a prominent and much appreciated place, but there have been changes. The large collections of wealthy private growers have disappeared, to be replaced by carefully nurtured and highly prized plants from the small greenhouses and conservatories of a much greater number of ordinary people. Today, great emphasis is placed on good cultivation, and the award of a Certificate of Cultural Commendation to the grower of an excellent, well-flowered plant is, for many amateurs, the ultimate accolade. Throughout the country, and indeed the world, the interest in orchid growing is increasing, with new recruits to this most absorbing branch of gardening every year. Thanks to modern technology, exotic orchids are now available to everyone, at a reasonable price, in greater variety than ever before.

A Storm to Remember October 1987

Arthur Hellyer

The day after the great storm of 15–16 October 1987 the myths and the misconceptions began to be created, and it is probable that they will never be completely dispelled. This was a hurricane, it was said, the most severe that had occurred in Britain since the Spanish Armada was providentially blown away three centuries ago. The damage to trees was unprecedented and much of the south-east of England had been devastated.

The truth was different but just as strange. It was not a hurricane that had struck, for these are a special kind of storm occurring mainly in the tropics and sub-tropics with mean wind speeds of 64 knots (roughly 73 mph) or more. In many places our visitation was no more than a force 10 storm with mean wind speeds below 56 knots, but in places it rose to 62 knots, which made it officially a violent storm, force 11. In Jersey the mean wind speed was 55 knots but at Gatwick Airport it was no more than 34 knots (say 40 mph) which, put in that way, does not sound very terrible. Yet at Nymans, the National Trust garden at Handcross, West Sussex, only 7 miles away, 80 per cent of the trees were blown down or severely damaged, and it was probably the most severely damaged of all the famous gardens in the path of the storm. At Leonardslee, the great woodland garden created by Sir Edmund Loder at Lower Beeding, West Sussex, 10 miles as the crow flies from Gatwick, 90 per cent of the trees in the pinetum were destroyed and a vast amount of damage was done in the garden, though much of it is in a valley.

Wakehurst Place at Ardingly, 8 miles from Gatwick, which belongs to the National Trust but is leased to the Royal Botanic Gardens, Kew, was another famous garden which suffered a high degree of damage.

Nymans after the Storm, by Cherryl Fountain, commissioned by The National Trust's Foundation for Art to illustrate the aftermath of the October 1987 storm.

Early accounts tended to play this down, comparing it with the damage in Kew Gardens themselves, 22 miles from Gatwick in the opposite, north-westerly, direction, but this appears to have been because attention at Wakehurst Place first concentrated on the 10 acres or so of garden around the house. Only later did aerial observations reveal the full scale of the destruction in the valley below.

In fact it was not the sustained or mean speed of this gale that was unique, nor did it account for the huge amount of damage to trees. It was the violence of the gusts, their concentration in particular places and the rather peculiar way in which they behaved among trees that explains the scale of the devastation. In Jersey gusts were recorded up to 85 knots, at Gatwick 86 knots and at Hurstmonceaux, near Eastbourne, said to be right in the centre of the storm, the top figure was 90 knots or around 103 mph. A more detailed, hour-by-hour, picture emerges from records made at the Institute of Horticultural Research, East Malling, Kent. Here the storm arrived at 1.30 am, with a wind speed of 38 knots (44 mph). The highest mean speed reached for any ten minutes was between 3.05 and 3.15 am at around 48 knots (55 mph) but at 3.15 am and again at 5.00 am there were gusts of 74 knots (85 mph).

The gusts also caused excessive turbulence, which seemed to be worst where trees were fairly closely packed. One example of this was at Sheffield Park, near Uckfield, East Sussex, another famous National Trust garden. Here 50 per cent of the trees in the pinetum were destroyed, but a much smaller percentage around the four large lakes, where the wind had more chance to pursue its way and was not thrown into all manner of cross-currents and miniature whirlwinds. It was very noticeable in my own garden that big, multi-stemmed conifers, including some tall Leyland cypresses and a couple of incense cedars (*Calocedrus*, formerly *Libocedrus*), lost trunks on the leeward, not the windward, side, as though they had been sucked rather than blown out. One big *Prunus sargentii* had its branches spreadeagled all around as though by a bomb. At Chanctonbury Ring, the great circular plantation of beech

trees on the South Downs above Steyning, most of the damage was to the interior trees and so was not very apparent from a distance.

Because it was the high speed gusts that did the damage and these were concentrated on quite narrow fronts, sometimes as little as 45 to 55 m (50 to 60 yds) wide, there was enormous variation in what happened even within the same garden or in a garden and the surrounding countryside. Thus the beautiful nineteenth-century picturesque landscape at Scotney Castle, Lamberhurst, Kent, was largely swept away, and it took six men, working almost around the clock, three days to clear the drive of over a hundred fallen trees, yet driving to Scotney it was impossible to guess such a disaster had occurred until one actually turned into the drive. Three miles to the east the Bedgebury National Pinetum suffered far less severely and, when all the fallen timber has been cleared away, it will once again be a fine spectacle, but it will take at least twenty years to restore Scotney to its former glory.

The destruction was all the greater because trees were still in full leaf and the soil was excessively wet. So maximum pressure was brought to bear on the trees and the soil offered minimum support to enable them to resist it. It is certain that no previous storm has ever damaged so many important gardens in England, and probably not anywhere else. The reason for this is not any unique violence in the gale itself but in the route it took over that part of England in which fine gardens are most densely congregated. It crossed north-eastern France, reached the Channel Islands about midnight and was crossing the south coast, roughly between Southampton and Dover, about 2 am. It continued over Hampshire, West and East Sussex, Kent and some parts of Surrey to reach London and then continued over Essex, Suffolk, eastern Cambridgeshire, reaching Norfolk by about 4 am and then moving out into the North Sea.

A list of the well-known gardens and parks it crossed reads like a roll call of the great. It included, in Hampshire: Exbury, the Manor of Cadlam, Hinton Ampner and The Vyne; in West Sussex: West Dean, the famous National

Trust beechwood at Slindon, Cowdray Park, Petworth Park, Highdown, Parham, Uppark, Leonardslee, the High Beeches, Nymans, Standen, Gravetye Manor, Wakehurst Place, Stonehurst, Heaselands and Borde Hill; in East Sussex: Sheffield Park, Stanmer Park, Bodiam Castle, Batemans, Wych Cross and other parts of Ashdown Forest and also Wych Cross Gate (a fine example of Thomas Mawson's work), and Great Dixter; in Kent: Hall Place, Penshurst Place, Hever Castle, Chartwell, Emmetts, Chevening, Knole, Scotney Castle, Sissinghurst Castle, Sandling Park, Leeds Castle and Port Lympne; in Surrey: Sutton Place, the Royal Horticultural Society's garden at Wisley, Claremont Landscape Garden, Winkworth Arboretum and Polesden Lacey; in the London area: Kew Gardens, Hampton Court and the Waterhouse Plantations in Bushy Park, Richmond Park including the Isabella Plantation, Chelsea Physic Garden and all the Royal parks; in Berkshire: the Savill Garden and the Valley Gardens in Windsor Great Park; in Hertfordshire: Ashridge and Hatfield House; in Essex: Hyde Hall and Hatfield Forest; in Suffolk: Helmingham Hall, Ickworth, Saling Hall and Somerleyton Hall; in Cambridgeshire: Anglesey Abbey; and in Norfolk: Blickling Hall, Talbot Manor, Sheringham (mercifully little damaged), Raveningham Hall and Holkham Hall.

Some commentators thought the roots that came right out of the ground were often not very extensive and suggested that many of these trees were either starved or diseased. This I believe to be a misconception, a failure to appreciate that it was only the strongest anchor roots that came up; the smaller feeding roots, which spread much more widely, were left in the soil. No doubt trees damaged by honey fungus and other root diseases were among the first to go but I saw a great many trees blown down that appeared to be in excellent health. In general it was big trees that suffered most, presumably because they offered much more resistance to the wind.

It was this same resilience of young trees that enabled most tree nurseries to escape fairly lightly. Nor did orchards fare too badly, if the trees were in good condition and on strong rooting stocks, but apple trees on 'M.9' root-stock suffered badly. At the Horticultural Research Institute, East Malling, the extensive orchards escaped quite lightly.

It was an altogether different story with glasshouse nurseries, which suffered severely, especially in the Channel Islands. Of course, old houses that were in poor condition suffered most and polythene tunnels tended to be completely destroyed, but it would not be possible to conclude that safety lies with the latest techniques. The glasshouses of the much admired Eric Young Orchid Foundation in Jersey were only erected in 1985 but they are wood-framed houses of traditional design, glazed with old-fashioned panes of glass, curved top and bottom to speed the downflow of rain, and these houses, very exposed at one of the highest parts of the island, were only slightly damaged. Many modern metal-framed houses fared much worse. Mr Nigel Spilman, chairman of the British Commercial Glasshouse Manufacturers' Association, concluded that, in general, pre-1980 structures suffered more glass damage but slightly less structural damage than those erected since that date. He compared damage of glasshouses built to the British Standard (BS5502) with those built to the Dutch Standard (NEN3859) and concluded that, on balance, the British Standard houses survived best, especially structurally. This standard allows for wind loading to be calculated according to the part of Britain in which the house is to be erected, based on a map showing maximum wind speeds to be expected. For the south-east corner of England over which the October gale blew, this would be for survival of gusts up to 48 m per second or about 94 mph, just about adequate for what was actually experienced on that October night. For glasshouses in the north of Scotland the requirement is for survival of gusts of 50 m per second, or nearly 112 mph, which highlights the considerable difference between wind expectations in the north and south of Britain.

Returning to the gardens and landscapes, it is instructive to note some remarkable differences in the way species of trees reacted to the storm. Wellingtonias and redwoods (*Sequoia-dendron* and *Sequoia*) were highly resistant. Even the very exposed wellingtonia on top of the hill at Emmetts remained virtually unscathed when so much else was devastated and there were also good reports of these trees from many other places. The dawn redwood (*Metasequoia glyptostroboides*) came through this first serious test of its stability well, and the swamp cypress (*Taxodium distichum*), with similar shape and leaf style, was another success. The western hemlock (*Tsuga heterophylla*) was yet another conifer that stood well. Tulip trees (*Liriodendron*), usually so brittle, seem to have come through far better than could have been expected. At Sandling Park, near Hythe, which lost over 200 trees and was considered to have been one of the most severely damaged privately owned gardens, tulip trees, Monterey pines (*Pinus radiata*) and wellingtonias were among the survivors. I should add, though, that this was one of the gardens in which the very concentrated character of the gusts was noted, so it would be difficult to say which trees were subjected to the greatest pressures.

In general Scots pine (*Pinus sylvestris*) seems to have suffered badly but more, I think, by being shattered than by being blown over, but the Monterey pine usually survived as, I suppose, one might expect of trees which evolved on the Pacific coast. Yet Douglas firs (*Pseudotsuga menziesii*), also from western North America, proved vulnerable and shelter belts of them in both the Savill Garden, Windsor Great Park, and Wakehurst Place proved no protection from this gale since they all collapsed. Cedars (*Cedrus*) and incense cedars also fared badly and it was the loss of both at Scotney Castle as well as of the 'Erecta' variety of Lawson cypress (*Chamaecyparis lawsoniana*) that deprived that skilfully contrived setpiece of its principal actors, leaving only a jumble of the supporting cast. Here there has been a suggestion that, in replanting, some fast-growing Leyland cypresses (× *Cupressocyparis leylandii*) may be included as temporary fillers until the slower starters are ready to take over. Monkey puzzles (*Araucaria araucana*) were

easy victims of the storm and at Nymans a large specimen, unique because it bore both male and female flowers, fell and grazed the wall of the ruined house but without causing any further damage. Indeed, it was remarkable how little damage was done to garden buildings; at Nymans even the rather fragile temple at the head of the pinetum still stands, though nearly all the trees around it have disappeared.

Beeches suffered terribly, bringing up great rafts of root as they tumbled over. Oaks rather disappointingly tended to shatter and larches toppled like ninepins. Magnolias on the whole did rather well but some of the big tree kinds such as *Magnolia campbellii*, toppled; in March I saw one remarkable specimen at High Beeches, Handcross, just across the valley from Nymans, that was almost flat on the ground but still had many of its roots in the soil and was in full and magnificent flower. It was hoped that later on it could be winched back into an upright position and made secure. My own experience with much smaller trees is that this is very difficult, since the wind has shifted the roots, quite often in the opposite direction from that in which they fell, so that, when pushed or pulled up, they resolutely refuse to return to their former holes. I think a great deal of excavation will be required to get the roots back into the soil.

All estimates of the damage must be largely guesswork, because so many of the trees lie in dense woodland where it is physically impossible to make an accurate count. Figures such as eight million broad-leaved trees destroyed plus seven million conifers convey some mental picture of the scale of the damage but seem to me to be too favourable to the conifers. Certainly where broad-leaved and coniferous trees were growing close together it was the conifers that almost always appeared to have come off worst.

Almost immediately after the storm the Department of the Environment allocated a grant of £2.75 million to the Countryside Commission to help with the restoration of the landscape. The Ministry of Agriculture, Fisheries and Food (MAFF) allocated £1 million for restoration of environmental damage under a

As these before and after photographs show, the grounds of
Scotney Castle, an outstanding example of a 19th-century
picturesque landscape, were devastated by the storm.

Storm Recovery Scheme and a further £2 per tree to fruit growers for replacement of apples, pears, plums, cherries and nut bushes destroyed or seriously damaged by the gale. The House of Commons Agricultural Committee examined these matters in considerable detail and elicited the further information that 'serious damage' would include trees with significant root damage or other damage likely to impair future cropping. It concluded that this would include salt damage, which in many places was severe. Leaves of all trees in my own small orchard became black a couple of days after the storm, though it is 22 miles from the coast, with the South Downs intervening. After visiting Sussex, the House of Commons committee concluded that environmental damage was far more severe than MAFF had originally supposed and that the overall allocation was entirely inadequate. There was no government-funded compensation for glasshouses but, under the Agricultural Improvement Scheme, the existing ceiling of £50,000 for the replacement of heated glass was increased to £74,000.

Many landowners found it difficult to dispose of fallen timber because of the great glut caused by the storm, but some did quite well, especially those, such as Kew and Nymans, with rare timber trees to offer and contacts with timber merchants who had outlets to cabinet makers and others able to make good use of such uncommon wood.

By January the work of replanting was well under way in some places, especially in the London parks and in the Chelsea Physic Garden. Many suggestions have been made, some amusing, some very practical. Mr Patrick Tompset, writing in the *Sunday Telegraph* on 8 November 1987, pleaded that monkey puzzles be excluded from all replanting plans because, he said, 'a more objectionable, unattractive and unnatural occupant of the English landscape I cannot imagine'. The following day, in *The Times*, Lord Aberconway hoped that *Ginkgo biloba* may be planted in London parks and squares in place of planes because it is 'a splendid town tree as those well know who are acquainted with New York where it is extensively planted along streets and in open places'.

The ginkgo or maidenhair tree, at any rate in America, seems to survive well when transplanted at a considerable size and it was one of the notable survivors of the October gale. No doubt this suggestion will be as repugnant to some as the araucaria is to Mr Tompset, because the maidenhair tree is not a native. But nor is the London plane (*Platanus × hispanicus*), despite its name, and at least the ginkgo is a genuine species and an extremely ancient one, whereas the London plane is probably a fairly modern hybrid, though there is argument about this.

I mention these matters in the hope that it will make tree planters a little resistant to the protests of some of those who call themselves conservationists without being well informed. Our native flora is relatively small because much of it was destroyed by the last Ice Age and re-colonization from Europe was curtailed by the interposition of the sea. To deny ourselves the use of all European plants suitable for our climate would seem about as sensible as to prevent, on grounds of conservation, the use of surgery to restore the features of a person seriously injured in an accident. Taking an even longer view, there was a time when all the land masses in the northern hemisphere were united, so we share an ancient heritage with the whole of this vast area. Clearly one does not want to clutter the landscape with alien shapes and foliage, but the situation is different in an urban setting and even more different in gardens created in many instances for the express purpose of cultivating exotic plants. Of course, the guardians of the great plant collections will need no such exhortations and are already busy trying to replace the lost treasures at Kew, Wakehurst Place, Sheffield Park, Nymans and many more such gardens. It is those in charge of the landscape gardens who may need a little support in using whatever trees will most rapidly restore the gardens to the image intended by their creators, even if they are not always precisely those that were there before the gale.

At Emmetts special problems of restoration must arise because of the scale of the destruction and because its creator, Fred Lubbock, was

Two National Trust properties that suffered heavy damage in the storm, Nymans and Sheffield Park, staged gold-winning exhibits of conifers at the Westminster show of 24–25 November 1987. Both exhibits (that from Nymans is shown here) were grim but fascinating displays of material from fallen or damaged trees, including a number of uncommon species.

more interested in plants than in design. Its situation, overlooking the Kentish weald and the Bough Beech reservoir, is one of the most spectacular in Kent. Should the National Trust, which now owns the place, seek to replant it exactly as it was when it took possession, or would it be better to adopt an entirely new design, using similar plants but disposing them in a way better calculated to make full use of the magnificent panorama? I would choose the second option.

Those faced with the task of clearing up the mess had many very different experiences. At Nymans thieves broke in during the first week and stole all the chain saws and other tree surgery equipment. At Leonardslee a group of expert Dutch woodsmen offered their assistance because they had heard of the disaster and remembered the garden as one that had given them great pleasure. It was gladly accepted. At Chevening garden historians had a field day when a falling tree broke the drainage plug in the large landscape lake and revealed a much older, more formal sheet of water beneath it. At Sheffield Park a would-be visitor, a day or so after the storm, refused admission because of the danger from half-fallen trees, wrote an

angry letter to the National Trust saying that it was for him, not the head gardener, to decide whether he should take the risk. The gardeners at both Sheffield Park and Nymans took advantage of the fallen trees and torn branches to stage at the Society's Westminster show 24–25 November two of the finest exhibits of conifer growth and cones seen for many years.

Yet for all the smiles and tears, in all the important gardens the work of clearance and restoration went ahead apace. By mid-January Nymans was clear and ready to receive a press party to see the miracle that had been achieved by five men and the head gardener. When I questioned Sir Giles Loder about Leonardslee he replied that the gale had opened up many attractive new vistas, that most of the rhododendrons, azaleas and camellias had survived and, as most of them were big bushes, they would provide their own shade to the roots and would flower all the more freely as a result of the extra light. Mr and Mrs Alan Hardy at Sandling Park engaged the very clever garden designer and plantsman Jim Russell to come and help them make their garden even better than it had been before.

The optimism was infectious.

Roses in the Autumn

Michael Gibson

Looking round the Great Autumn Show, with the colourful splashes of the rose nurserymen's stands catching the eye, it is perhaps worth reflecting on how it was pure chance that made all this possible. Before about 1820, only a Chinese author could have written an article of more than one or two paragraphs about roses in the autumn, for varieties that flowered other than at midsummer were practically unknown in the West. Only *R. × damascena bifera*, also known as Rose des Quatre Saisons or the Autumn Damask, made a fitful attempt to produce a few autumn blooms in Western gardens, but for reasons which as far as I know are still unexplained, roses from the Far East were fully recurrent.

Roses from China first began to arrive in the West late in the eighteenth century, but for a good many years they made little impact. They were considered, erroneously in some cases, to be too delicate for our climate and, in contrast to the currently fashionable Damasks, Centifolias, Albas and the rest, to be poor, puny things. They were comparatively light and airy in their habit compared with what had gone before, and many of them made quite small bushes, so perhaps it is understandable that they were ignored by gardeners used to other standards. However, that their potential as breeding stock should have been missed seems difficult nowadays to comprehend until it is remembered that the deliberate crossing of one plant with another – planned hybridization – was by no means generally understood or practised at the time.

So here, sitting in the gardens of a few connoisseurs of unusual plants, was a bank of material with the potential for revolutionizing the rose world of the West, and probably some botanist would have woken up to its possibilities in due course. However, it was pure chance that was

'Zéphirine Drouhin', an almost thornless Bourbon
rose that is a true climber, flowers over a long season
but does need spraying against mildew.

137

to bring about a cross between the Autumn Damask and a China rose, and it took place, not in Europe, but on the French Île du Bourbon, right in the middle of the Indian Ocean. This island is to be found on maps nowadays under the name Réunion, and in the days of sail it was an important staging post for trade between East and West. It was there that a Damask rose, almost certainly the Autumn Damask, and a China rose, almost certainly what we now call 'Old Blush', were planted together in a hedge. Here bees or the wind did what man had so conspicuously failed to do and hybrid seedlings were the result. These were seen by a botanist by the name of Bréon, who realized their potential and sent seeds back to France in 1819. There in due course they flowered and a new race of roses was born which combined the vigour of growth and toughness of the Damasks with the recurrence of the Chinas, and which had bigger and more sumptuous blooms than either. The first of the Bourbon roses had arrived, known at the time as *R. borboniana*.

At much the same time, late in the eighteenth or at the very beginning of the nineteenth century, another chance cross came about, this time probably between the Autumn Damask and a Gallica rose, possibly *R. gallica officinalis*. It occurred in Italy but when the roses reached England – it is said by the courtesy of André Dupont, whose name will always be associated with the gardens of the Empress Josephine at her Villa Malmaison near Paris – they were named Portland roses after the then Duchess of Portland. They were also sometimes called Perpetual Damasks as they, like the Bourbons, were repeat flowering, but good as they were they never achieved the eminence of the latter. They were not easy to breed from and they did not have the might of the French nursery industry behind them as the Bourbons did in their early days, a factor not to be ignored. This was a pity for they were (and are) first-rate roses, more remontant than many of the Bourbons and much more manageable in a small garden as they do not get so big.

There are comparatively few Portlands left in commerce now, but the Peter Beales Nursery had two of them in particularly fine form at the 1988 Autumn Show. These were 'Jacques Cartier' and 'Comte de Chambord', both with full, rich pink flowers, sweetly scented, and there are several others on the Beales list, including the original 'Portland Rose' (sometimes known as 'Duchess of Portland'), with semi-double, deep cerise-pink flowers, and varieties like 'Rose de Rescht', 'Rose du Roi', 'Marbré' and 'Mme Knorr', the parentage of which is less certainly Portland.

Bourbons on the Beales' stand were represented by, amongst others, 'Mme Isaac Pereire', which is about the most richly perfumed rose there is and has huge, very double deep pink blooms that are probably rather better in the autumn than in midsummer; often a number of the first flush are malformed.

In the early days of repeat-flowering roses it was actually recommended that they should be disbudded in spring if they were to put on a really spectacular show later in the year, William Paul, in his *The Rose Garden* of 1848, gives this advice, and his variety descriptions are divided into two sections under the headings 'Summer Roses' and 'Autumnal Roses'. The latter section contains over fifty Bourbon varieties, but much more remarkably 549 Hybrid Perpetuals. These were the roses that followed the Bourbons and became enormously popular in Victorian times, though it could not be said, despite the implications of their name, that all of them were reliably remontant. They tended, too, to be rather tall and leggy, their long canes blowing every which way in the wind with their big double blooms clinging for dear life to their tips. Pegging down was the only answer; the canes were bent over and their ends tied to pegs in the ground, which caused flowering shoots to break into growth along their entire length. Varieties which are good in the autumn, and which are not generally so tall as to need this drastic treatment, are 'Mrs John Laing', 'Georg Arends', 'Frau Karl Druschki' and the wonderful 'Général Jacqueminot', a scarlet variety that was to become the ancestor of most of our best modern red roses. Also in Paul's list under the 'Autumnal Roses' was 'La France', now generally considered to have been the first of the Hybrid Teas. He classed it as a Hybrid

Perpetual, which illustrates as well as anything that new plant families do not emerge overnight. It was some years after Paul's book was published that it was realized that the old Hybrid Perpetuals were changing, particularly after the introduction of Tea roses from China into the breeding lines, and that a new class was emerging. Then it was a case of looking back to find the first of the new roses that could be said to have been distinctly different and the vote went, by no means unanimously, to 'La France'.

Other late-flowering roses of the period also to be seen at the Great Autumn Show were some of the so-called Perpetual Moss roses like 'Alfred de Dalmas' and 'Salet' which do, when in the mood, produce some autumn flowers, and the one and only recurrent Scotch rose, the lovely 'Stanwell Perpetual'. This is of spreading growth, thorny of course, as all Scotch roses are, and with a constant succession throughout the summer and autumn of the most enchanting blush-pink double flowers, sweetly scented. The purplish mottling of the leaves which is sometimes evident is a natural phenomenon and should not be mistaken for black spot.

The Rugosa 'Roseraie de l'Hay' was outstanding in the display by Harkness Nurseries and is one of the best of hedging roses, bushy to ground level and with the healthiest of foliage. The flowers are loosely double, wine red, and come with great freedom, but they are not followed by decorative hips as would have been the case with Rugosas with single or semi-double flowers. Rosy magenta 'Scabrosa', pale pink 'Fru Dagmar Hastrup' and Rugosas 'Alba' and 'Rubra' (well featured on the Mattock stand) are four that do have the most enormous, tomato-shaped hips following the flowers. As they bloom right through the summer and into the autumn, this often means that both flowers and hips will be displayed at the same time, but so prolific are they that they really do not need dead-heading after the first flush of bloom. Most of the family are well scented, too, though not the Grootendorst branch – 'Pink Grootendorst', 'F. J. Grootendorst' and the rest – which to some extent make up for this deficiency by having the most enchanting clus-

ters of quite small flowers which have the petal edges frilled like a carnation. They are also the best of the group to use for cut flowers as the others do not last too well.

Mention of the Rugosas has brought up the subject of hips. With these roses hips are a bonus provided by a group which also flowers in the autumn; hips are also an attraction late in the year provided by midsummer-flowering species. This was well demonstrated on the John Mattock stand, where of course the Rugosas were also to be seen.

Of the Moyesii family, which has some of the best hips of all – bright orange-red, bottle-shaped and each about 5 cm (2 in) long – Mattocks were showing the variety 'Geranium', its seedling 'Highdownensis' (which was raised by Sir Frederick Stern at Highdown in Sussex and which has the brightest scarlet-crimson flowers in early summer), *R. sweginzowii* (which, being more bushy would probably be preferable to *R. moyesii* if it were not so infernally prickly), and *R. glauca* (*R. rubrifolia*). The latter is grown mainly for its blue-grey foliage rather than for its flowers, and for its autumn show of bright red rounded hips. They seem much too big to have come from the very small and fleeting pink flowers.

Rosa macrophylla was another hip-bearing species that Mattocks were showing. This makes a very large shrub indeed, with single pink flowers and flagon-shaped orange hips to follow, lighting it up like the candles on an old-fashioned Christmas tree. This and the other roses already mentioned are some of the best of the hip bearers, but of course there are many more from which a choice can be made, with hips ranging from the brightest scarlet to pale coral pink. Those of the Pimpinellifolia group are black.

A family of roses with a reputation for continuous flowering that is not entirely merited is the Hybrid Musks. Two of them, 'Prosperity' and 'Felicia', were outstanding on Peter Beales' stand at the Autumn Show, but I wonder how much dead-heading had to be done after the first always spectacular summer flush to achieve such results. Quite a lot, I would say, to judge from my own experience of these roses.

ABOVE 'Comte de Chambord', which appeared in 1860, is one of the few Portlands still available. It gives a good second flush in autumn.

LEFT The sweetly scented flowers of 'Stanwell Perpetual' are produced recurrently, making it an exception among the Scotch roses.

ABOVE 'Fru Dagmar Hastrup' is one of the best Rugosas for the small garden, flowering well late in the season and producing handsome hips.

The Hybrid Musks comprise a big group of autumn-flowering roses, largely developed around the turn of the century by a clergyman-cum-nurseryman called Joseph Pemberton, who ran the nursery with the aid of his sister from a small village in Essex. They used to raise plants to give to their friends, but the demand became so great that the nursery was started and the whole thing put on a commercial basis. They concentrated on introducing their own hybrids, largely derived from the German rose 'Trier', raised by Peter Lambert in 1904, which the Pembertons crossed with Hybrid Teas and other roses. 'Trier' was a shrub rose growing to about 1·5 m (5 ft) with clusters of small white flowers, and the Pemberton varieties inherited quite a lot of its characteristics, including its scent. Their link with the true Musk Rose is tenuous to say the least; it was their scent that was the cause of them being dubbed Hybrid Musks by the then Secretary of the National Rose Society.

Creamy-peach flowered 'Penelope' is perhaps the best known of the Pemberton roses, but there have been numerous additions to the line over the years, from the German breeder Wilhelm Kordes with 'Wilhelm' and others and from America 'Bishop Darlington' and many more. After Pemberton's death his head gardener, Bentall, who had inherited the nursery, continued to work on a number of the old breeding lines, resulting in such varieties as 'Buff Beauty' and the completely different, Polyantha-type roses 'The Fairy' and 'Ballerina', the latter being one of the outstanding roses on the Harkness stand at the show. It is a low-growing shrub with huge heads of flowers resembling nothing so much as apple blossom.

Finally among the older roses performing well in the autumn months the group that started it all should not be forgotten, the Chinas. 'Old Blush', which was mentioned earlier, is reputed to be The Last Rose of Summer of the old song, a reputation it probably gained from the fact that it will, in the right season, stay in bloom to Christmas and beyond. Then there is 'Cramoisi Supérieur', which is the true deep crimson that was introduced into Western breeding lines by 'Slater's

Crimson China', and the very low-growing 'Miss Lowe', which is crimson, too. 'Hermosa' takes us back to pink and a much fuller flower, while 'Comtesse du Cayla' introduces the flame colours to be found also in that chameleon of a rose, 'Mutabilis', with changing tones.

It is a mistake to think that roses are worth growing only for their flowers. Foliage can be an important asset and the hips of a number of species and cultivars make a colourful show in the autumn. Those of *Rosa moyesii* are flask-like and are carried in great profusion.

For many years the breeding of climbing roses was sadly neglected, presumably because they were only bought in very small numbers when compared with the kinds of rose used for bedding. It was not worth a breeder's time to spend the many years necessary to put a new rose on the market if he could only expect to sell a very few of them at the end of it all. So the same climbers appeared in the nursery lists year after year and among these were some that repeated well in the autumn, roses like 'Mme Alfred Carrière' and 'Mermaid', and also many climbing sports of variable reliability. It is only in comparatively recent times that breeders, following the example of Sam McGredy and a few others, have given their attention once more to this indispensable group of roses. Crosses made with recurrent bush roses have resulted in a stream of new varieties that produce a very good second crop of blooms. Kordes' 'Dort-mund' and 'Leverkusen' are examples; others include the Bay series from Sam McGredy himself and his 'Handel' and 'Swan Lake', 'Rosy Mantle' and 'White Cockade' from Cocker and, the sweetly scented peach-pink 'Compassion' from Jack Harkness.

A feature of many of these new roses is that they are not so rampant as many from the past. Vigorous growers, they will not, however, go much above 2·7 to 3 m (9 to 10 ft), making them much more suitable for modern gardens and modern houses. There are still climbing sports on the market and some of them, like 'Climbing Iceberg', are very good and repeat well. Others, though coming as sports from fully recurrent bush roses, will repeat only fitfully, if at all, so make careful enquiries before you buy.

Many modern bedding roses showed up well at the Autumn Show. On Rosemary Roses' stand the creamy pink 'Fleur Cowles' made one wonder why it is not more widely available, while C. and K. Jones had 'Lincoln Cathedral' in particularly fine form. So too was the yellow shrub rose 'Graham Thomas', 'Sweet Magic', the dwarf, cluster-flowered 'Regensberg', which is one of the McGredy 'hand-painted' varieties, and 'Sexy Rexy' from the same breeder. Among their miniatures, 'Apricot Sunblaze' caught the eye.

'Sweet Magic' was again outstanding on the Mattock stand, together with that prince of yellow cluster-flowered varieties, 'Korresia', and the king of the reds, 'The Times'. 'Congratulations' was also proving that it liked the airs of late summer, and 'Loving Memory', too.

The fact, which I have noticed over the years, that roses with yellow or orange tones seem to do particularly well in the autumn, was well borne out on the Harkness stand. Here at their best were creamy-yellow 'Peaudouce', bright yellow 'Freedom', orange-salmon 'Rosemary Harkness' and buff-orange 'Anne Harkness'.

Modern roses in the yellow and orange range, such as 'Peaudouce', do particularly well late in the season.

The latter is a particularly good rose for late in the season, for it does not start to flower until well into July and comes again later than most in consequence. It is a marvellous rose with huge heads of flowers tightly packed with petals, and will last and last if picked for the house. It can, however, get rather too tall and top-heavy in the garden and may need the help of a stake. White 'Margaret Merril' and warm rose-pink cluster-flowered 'Radox Bouquet' were other roses doing well for Harkness.

There were, of course, other varieties on the stands of all the rose exhibitors which were a joy to see, for the modern bedding rose can be relied on to repeat well. It is just that the cooler airs of the end of the year suit some roses better than others. With all of them it brings a greater intensity of colour. The yellows and oranges fairly glow in an autumn twilight.

My own experience will add something to the lists above, for I have found that pinky-orange 'Just Joey', yellow 'Dutch Gold', peach pink 'Silver Jubilee' and 'Paul Shirville', the ever-faithful 'Peace', coppery 'Fragrant Delight', deep scarlet 'Invincible' and the climbers 'Aloha', 'Golden Showers' and 'Zéphirine Drouhin' are all outstanding. Oh, and 'Piccadilly'.

I have said that modern bedding roses repeat well, but what can be done to improve their later performance? Quite a lot, for the natural sequence of growth in a rose – and any other plant – is to produce leaves and then flowers, which are pollinated so that hips or seed pods are formed, which lead to the next generation. If the seed heads are allowed to develop, the rose will not produce so many new flowers, and in fact may not produce a second crop at all. Thus dead-heading becomes necessary; the removal of the spent flowers before they can form hips will cause the rose to try again by producing more flowers. If you want even a third flush of bloom, and some roses will oblige, dead-heading must be carried out yet again, but do not simply cut off the dead blooms. Cut as if pruning to a bud 10 to 15 cm (4 to 6 in) down the stem, which will produce a good strong new shoot, bearing much larger flowers, and you will not be left with unsightly flower stalks

'Golden Showers' has proved one of the best modern climbing roses, not too vigorous for the small garden and flowering freely in late autumn.

dying back and disfiguring your bushes.

Feeding the roses will help too. A spring feed should be followed by a small handful of a proprietary rose fertilizer scattered round each plant not later than the end of July and lightly hoed in. Applied any later it will result in soft, sappy growth coming so late that it cannot ripen before being destroyed by the frosts or cold winds of winter. Keep suckers at bay, if necessary scraping away a little soil to find the spot from which they are growing so that you can be sure that what you are looking at is not a new shoot of the rose. If they come from below the budding union they will be suckers. Do not cut them, which would be the equivalent of pruning to encourage fresh growth: pull them off if you possibly can, though this may be difficult or impossible if they come from right under the plant. It is better to cut than to risk pulling the rose right out of the ground.

Finally there will be the routine of spraying, for there is little point in having roses in the autumn if they are defaced with disease. With modern sprays they need not be. They can be every bit as glorious as they were in June and July. Better, sometimes.

The coppery tones of 'Just Joey', one of the most successful introductions of the 1970s, take on an extra depth late in the season.

PERSPECTIVE
1987–1988

Among the most interesting plants to keep an eye open for at Chelsea and Westminster shows are those submitted for awards. The award system is an important way of drawing the attention of members to new species and improved cultivars deserving a place in the garden. A century ago this year the scale of awards was revised, with the Award of Merit replacing the Second Class Certificate, which, as it praised too faintly, had been underused. In the present scale the most prestigious award is the First Class Certificate (FCC), followed by the Award of Merit (AM) and the Certificate of Preliminary Commendation, the latter recognizing promising new plants. A Botanical Certificate may be awarded to a plant of exceptional botanical interest. Awards are made on the recommendation of panels of impressively experienced and knowledgeable gardeners, the members of the Society's Standing and Joint Committees (a Joint Committee consists of representatives from the Society and an associated society or societies).

The illustrations on pp. 146 and 148 to 150 and those of orchids on pp. 126 and 127 show a small selection of the many good plants that have received awards in the period June 1987 to May 1988.

The Society also recognizes the achievements and contributions to horticulture of individuals by awarding cups, trophies, medals and prizes. Many of these record distinguished names from the past. The Engleheart Cup, for example, founded by the Society in 1913, honours a distinguished daffodil breeder, the Rev. G. H. Engleheart.

The award that stands above all others is the Victoria Medal of Honour in Horticulture. It was instituted in 1897, to mark the sixtieth anniversary of Queen Victoria's accession to the throne, the number of recipients at any one time being restricted to sixty. On the Queen's death the number of recipients was increased to sixty-three, corresponding to the total years of her reign.

In December 1987 Mr W. L. Banks, the Society's Treasurer, and Mrs Beth Chatto were added to the distinguished group who have received this honour. We congratulate them and all recipients of awards in the year under review.

Paeonia 'Phylis Moore' received an Award of Merit
as a hardy flowering shrub when shown at Chelsea
1988 by Miss Valerie Finnis.

ABOVE The heavy-cropping raspberry cultivar 'Autumn Bliss', raised by East Malling Research Station, was given an Award of Merit in August 1987 when exhibited by the Director, National Fruit Trials, Brogdale.

ABOVE *Liquidamber styraciflua* 'Worplesdon' (Award of Merit October 1987 when shown by Starborough Nursery) was selected by Roland Jackman, of the nursery family, for consistently good autumn colour on lime-free soil.

RIGHT *Clematis viticella* 'Purpurea Plena Elegans' (First Class Certificate August 1987 when shown by Graham Stuart Thomas) is probably the double clematis described by Parkinson in 1629.

RIGHT A *Camellia japonica* cultivar, 'Miss Charleston', shown in May 1988 by Mrs A. Hooton, received an Award of Merit.

BELOW *Zantedeschia aethiopica* 'Green Goddess', for a temperate greenhouse, Award of Merit May 1988, shown by the Director, RHS Gardens, Wisley.

BELOW 'Leonard Messel', a compact *Sorbus*, received a First Class Certificate when shown by the Hillier Arboretum in September 1987.

RIGHT *Rhododendron* 'Hesperides', from the Rothschild collection of azaleas, rhododendrons and magnolias at Exbury Gardens, received an Award of Merit when shown at Chelsea in 1988 by Edmund de Rothschild.

BOTTOM LEFT 'Badbury Rings', a Division 3 daffodil cultivar suitable for showing, received an Award of Merit when exhibited by its raiser, Mr J.W. Blanchard, in April 1988.

BOTTOM RIGHT The Queensland wattle, *Acacia podalyriifolia*, received a First Class Certificate as a flowering and foliage plant for the cool greenhouse when shown by Dr J.A. Smart in January 1988.

Beth Chatto

David Joyce

Although Mrs Chatto has received a string of Golds at Chelsea and, in 1987, the Lawrence Medal for the best exhibit of the year and the highest award the society can bestow, the Victoria Medal of Honour, she still remembers with special relish the pure delight of her first Silver. Her nursery was little known and she had never exhibited with the Society before when, in January 1975, she took a collection of plants, gathered directly from the garden, to a Westminster show. Nothing had been forced or cossetted; a run of mild weather ensured that plants were advanced and in good condition. Her winter collection drew admiring attention; it marked the arrival at the Society's shows of a discerning gardener of exceptional artistic flair.

The inspiration of this and later exhibits and of the books that have helped to make Mrs Chatto a name to be reckoned with wherever ornamental plants are taken seriously is the garden that she and her husband began creating in 1960. They had already been gardening in Essex for seventeen years – on chalky boulder clay – when they set about making a new home and breaking in a piece of waste farmland at Elmstead Market, near Colchester, in one of the driest areas of Britain. On the face of it the land was no more suitable for a garden than it was for a farm. And yet, as those who visit the Beth Chatto Gardens now can see, it could be made into something of magical beauty.

Simple hard work achieved a great deal, with the clearing of scrub, the laying of paths and steps and the constant addition of leaf mould and other organic material to give body to the hungry soil of the gravel areas. Their success with plants lay in choosing those suited to the growing conditions available. In this the life-long ecological interests of Mr Chatto and the artistic gifts of Mrs Chatto were well matched. The 'unusual plants' they grew and which, from 1967, Mrs Chatto began to sell through her nursery were not freakish monstrosities. Quite the contrary, in fact, for good forms of species were favoured over showy hybrids.

What made Mrs Chatto's plants so refresh-ingly unusual was her way of looking at them. They were valued not simply for their flowering potential but as whole plants, with interesting shapes, forms, textures and foliage colour, the beauty of their flowers, often fleeting, being counted a bonus. When it came to placing them in the garden, or in an exhibit, Mrs Chatto's sure eye for a simple and harmonious com-position made the most telling use of each plant's qualities. Perhaps one should detect in this the underlying principles of Japanese flower arranging, which, Mrs Chatto says, influenced her greatly.

The hot dry beds were planted first, with stately verbascums, jagged eryngiums, bleach-ed artemisias and the like. Under the oaks there were good conditions for woodland plants, and when the ponds had been formed there was scope for lush-growing plants such as bamboo-like miscanthus and the giant parasol-leaved gunnera. The Chattos did not set out to make a teaching garden but the accommodation of so many plants differing widely in their requirements makes their creation an invalu-able source of ideas for all gardeners.

Many visitors to Chelsea in 1988 accustomed to make a pilgrimage to the green oasis of Mrs Chatto's stand were disappointed to find that she had not staged an exhibit this year. For the moment, Mrs Chatto feels, other activities must be given priority over preparing for Chelsea. She does not want to see the standard of the garden slipping as a result of the long and con-centrated work needed to stage an exhibit at the Great Spring Show. She is well aware of the responsibility of maintaining the nursery as a viable business, with well-trained staff who enjoy what they do. As a passionate propagator all her life, she wants to see that rare and difficu-lt plants are maintained in cultivation and dis-tributed widely. The decision against showing at Chelsea in 1988 signals no loss of direction but rather a concentration of her efforts to show how good plants can be used to best effect.

RECIPIENTS OF CUPS, TROPHIES, MEDALS AND PRIZES

A. J. WALEY MEDAL
To a working gardener who has helped the cultivation of rhododendrons. *December 1987*
Mr O. R. Staples
Head Gardener, Heaselands, Haywards Heath, Sussex

AFFILIATED SOCIETIES' CLASS PRIZE, DAFFODIL SHOW
For twelve daffodil cultivars from division 1 to 4. *12 April 1988*
Norfolk & Norwich Horticultural Society
c/o Barn End, Grimmer La, Cantley, Norwich, Norfolk

AFFILIATED SOCIETIES' CUP, AUTUMN FRUIT AND VEGETABLE COMPETITION
For a collection of fruit shown by an Affiliated Society (apples and pears). *6 October 1987*
Eastcote Horticultural Society
c/o 11 Boldmer Rd, Eastcote, Pinner, Middx

ASSOCIATESHIP OF HONOUR
Conferred on persons of British nationality who have rendered distinguished service to horticulture in the course of their employment. *December 1987*
Mr H. A. Baker
The Lilacs, Wisley, Woking, Surrey

Mr P. Blake
County Advisor for Horticulture & Rural Studies, County Hall, Station Rd, Truro

Mrs W. V. Bowie
Thomas Carlile (Loddon Nurseries) Ltd, Carlile's Corner, Twyford, Reading, Berks

Mr S. Coutts
Four Oaks Nurseries Ltd, Farm La, Lower Withington, Nr Macclesfield, E Sussex

Mr A. V. Skinner
Sheffield Park Garden, Sheffield Park, Uckfield, E Sussex

BLANCHARD PRIZE
For the greatest number of first prize points awarded in Section XII at the Daffodil Show. *12 April 1988*
Mr P. J. Applegate
Penn House, Lewes Rd, Ringmer, E Sussex

BOWLES CUP
For fifteen daffodil cultivars, representing not fewer than four divisions, shown by an amateur. *12 April 1988*
Mr C. Gilman
86 Mousehold Ave, Norwich, Norfolk

CROSFIELD CUP
For the best exhibit of six *Rhododendron* hybrids raised by or in the garden of the exhibitor, shown in Class 66 at the Main Rhododendron Competition. *4 May 1988*
Exbury Gardens
Exbury, Southampton, Hants

DEVONSHIRE TROPHY
For twelve daffodil cultivars, representing not fewer than three divisions, shown at the Daffodil Show. *4 May 1988*
Mr F. C. Postles
The Old Cottage, Purshall Green, Elmbridge, Droitwich, Worcs

E. H. TROPHY
For the best exhibit in which carnations or pinks predominate shown to the Society during 1987 (garden pinks, Chelsea 1987). *December 1987*
Three Counties Nurseries
Marshwood, Bridport, Dorset

ENGLEHEART CUP
For twelve daffodil cultivars, bred and raised by the exhibitor, shown at the Daffodil Show. *12 April 1988*
Mr F. C. Postles
The Old Cottage, Purshall Green, Elmbridge, Droitwich, Worcs

FARRER TROPHY
For the best exhibit of plants suitable for the rock garden or alpine house staged during 1987 at one of the Society's shows other than Chelsea (autumn-flowering gentians and related alpine plants, 6 October 1987). *December 1987*
Edrom Nurseries
Coldingham, Eyemouth, Berwickshire

FOREMARKE CUP
For twelve cultivars of gladioli, one spike of each. *11 August 1987*
Mr S. Moorhouse
33 Northumberland Ave, Wanstead, London E12

GEORGE MONRO MEMORIAL CUP
For the best collection of vegetables shown by an affiliated society or individual at the Vegetable Show. *Not awarded*

GEORGE MOORE MEDAL
For the new *Paphiopedilum* which shows the greatest improvement on those of the same or similar parentage and which has been submitted to the Society during 1987. *December 1987*
Mr F. R. Haynes
Esseburne, 272 Broadway, Derby

GORDON LENNOX CUP
For the best exhibit of fruit or vegetables staged during 1987 at one of the Society's shows other than Chelsea (vegetables, 15 September 1987). *December 1987*
W. Robinson & Sons Ltd
Sunny Bank, Forton, Preston

GUY WILSON MEMORIAL VASE
For six white daffodil cultivars,
representing any or all of Division 1
to 3, shown at the Daffodil Show.
12 April 1988
Mr F. C. Postles
The Old Cottage, Purshall Green,
Elmbridge, Droitwich, Worcs

HOLFORD MEDAL
For the best exhibit of plants and/or
flowers (fruit and vegetables excluded)
shown by an amateur during 1987 at
one of the Society's shows other than
Chelsea (mesembryanthemums, 6
October 1987). *December 1987*
Mrs E. Tjaden
85 Welling Way, Welling, Kent

JONES-BATEMAN CUP
For original research in fruit culture
(awarded triennially). *December 1987*
Dr F. H. Alston
Fruit Breeding & Genetics Dept,
Institute of Horticultural Research,
East Malling, Maidstone, Kent

KNIGHTIAN SILVER MEDAL
For the most meritorious exhibit in
the single dish classes for vegetables.
6 October 1987
Mr J. Dean
120 Frimley Rd, Chessington, Surrey

LAWRENCE MEDAL
For the best exhibit shown to the
Society during 1987 (Chelsea exhibit).
December 1987
Mrs B. Chatto
White Barn House, Elmstead Market,
Colchester, Essex

LEONARDSLEE BOWL
For twelve *Camellia* cultivars, one
bloom of each, shown at the Main
Camellia Show. *12 April 1988*
Mrs A. M. Hooton
Paddock Farm, Plaistow Rd,
Loxwood, W Sussex

LIONEL DE ROTHSCHILD CUP
For the best exhibit of eight species of
Rhododendron, one truss of each,
shown in Class 1 at the Main
Rhododendron Competition.
4 May 1988
Swansea City Council
Development Dept, Guildhall,
Swansea

LODER CUP
For the best exhibit of any hybrid
Rhododendron, one truss shown in
Class 64 at the Main Rhododendron
Competition. *4 May 1988*
Mr R. J. Gilbert
Lancarffe, Bodmin, Cornwall

LODER RHODODENDRON CUP
For work in connection with
rhododendrons. *December 1987*
Mr E. Millais
Crosswater Farm, Churt, Farnham,
Surrey

LYTTEL LILY CUP
For work in connection with *Lilium,
Nomocharis* & *Fritillaria*.
14 July 1987.
Mr B. Mathew
Royal Botanic Gardens,
Kew, Richmond, Surrey

McLAREN CUP
For the best exhibit of any species of
Rhododendron, one truss shown in
Class 3 at the Main Rhododendron
Competition. *4 May 1988*
Swansea City Council
Development Dept, Guildhall,
Swansea

MRS F. E. RIVIS PRIZE
To the employee responsible for the
cultivation of the exhibit for which the
Williams Memorial Medal is
awarded. *December 1987*
Mr M. Clare
Michael Jefferson-Brown Ltd,
Broadgate, Weston Hills, Spalding,
Lincs

PETER BARR MEMORIAL CUP
For work in connection with daffodils.
12 April 1988
Mr J. Gerritsen
P.O. Box 86, 2250 AB Voorschoten,
Holland

REGINALD CORY MEMORIAL CUP
To the raiser of a hardy hybrid which
is either the result of a deliberate cross
which, as far as is known, has not been
made before or a new and distinct
cultivar resulting from the deliberate
repetition of a previously made cross
(*Primula* × *loiseleurii* 'Lismore
Yellow', 14 March 1987).
December 1987
Mrs J. A. Burrow
'Lismore Alpines', Low Bentham
Road, High Bentham, N Yorks

RHS VEGETABLE CUP
For the highest number of place
points in classes for vegetables at the
Vegetable competition 6 to 7 October
1987. *6 October 1987*
Mr C. F. Richardson
108 Felbridge Ave, Stanmore, Middx

RICHARDSON TROPHY
For twelve daffodil cultivars,
representing each of divisions 1 to 4,
shown by an amateur at the Daffodil
Show. *12 April 1988*
Mr N. A. Burr
Popes Hall Cottage, Limes Lane,
Buxted, Uckfield, Sussex

RIDDELL TROPHY
For a collection of nine kinds of
vegetables shown at the Fruit and
Vegetable Show on 6 and 7 October
1987. *6 October 1987*
Mr C. F. Richardson
108 Felbridge Ave, Stanmore, Middx

ROSSE CUP
For three conifers shown for foliage,
Class 8, at the November Ornamental
Plant Competition. *24 November 1987*
**Anne Countess of Rosse and The
National Trust**
Nymans Gardens, Handcross, Sussex

ROZA STEPHENSON CUP
for the best exhibit of one spray of a
Rhododendron species, Class 64,
shown at the Late Rhododendron
Competition. *4 May 1988*
Exbury Gardens
Exbury, Southampton, Hants

SEWELL MEDAL
For exhibits of plants suitable for the
rock garden or alpine house. *Not
awarded*

SIMMONDS MEDAL
For the best bloom at the April
Daffodil Show (seedling 'Easter
Moon' × 'Fair Prospect').
12 April 1988
Mr E. Jarman
Cobbles, Church Rd, Ramsden
Bellhouse, Billericay, Essex

For the third highest points in the
open classes for single blooms at the
April Daffodil Show. *12 April 1988*

For the best bloom at the May
Daffodil Competition ('Dudley
Hall'). *4 May 1988*

For the third highest place points in the open classes for single blooms in the May Daffodil Competition. *4 May 1988*
Mr F. C. Postles
The Old Cottage, Purshall Green, Elmbridge, Droitwich, Worcs

For the champion spike size 500 or 400 at the August Gladiolus Competition ('Amsterdam'). *11 August 1988*
Mr T. N. Fawcett
197 Ashton Clinton Rd, Aylesbury, Bucks

For the champion spike size 300 or less at the August Gladiolus Competition ('Red Bantam'). *11 August 1988*
Mr J. E. Sudell
8 Guildford Rd, Canterbury, Kent

SIMMONDS SILVER-GILT MEDAL
For the highest place points in the open classes for single blooms at the April Daffodil Show. *12 April 1988*
Rathowen Daffodils
Knowehead, Dergmoney, Omagh, Co Tyrone, N Ireland

For the highest place points in the open classes for single blooms at the May Daffodil Competition. *4 May 1988*
M. Harwood
Hope Cottage, Halebourne La, Chobham, Surrey

SIMMONDS SILVER MEDAL
For the third highest place points in the open classes for single blooms at the April Daffodil Show. *12 April 1988*
Mr J. W. Blanchard
Old Rectory Garden, Shillingstone, Blandford, Dorset

For the second highest place points in the open classes for single blooms at the May Daffodil Competition. *4 May 1988*
Mr E. Jarman
Cobbles, Church Rd, Ramsden Bellhouse, Billericay, Essex

SPECIAL PRIZES
For the most meritorious dish in the single dish classes for fruit.

In the Summer Fruit and Vegetable Competition, for a dish of gooseberry 'Leveller'. *14 July 1987*
Mrs M Goodchild
Farnborough Common, Farnborough, Orpington, Kent

In the Autumn Fruit and Vegetable Show, for a dish of apple 'Jester'. *6 October 1987*
Mr G. Edwards
'Tryfan', 24 Rodney Gardens, Pinner, Middx

In the Autumn Fruit and Vegetable Show, for a dish of pear 'Conference'. *6 October 1987*
Mr W. A. Upstone
90 Biggin Hill, London SE19

In the Late Apple and Pear Competition, for a dish of apple 'Spartan'. *24 November 1987*
Mrs H. Donmjan
Denehill, Beechenlea La, Swanley Village, Kent

STEPHENSON R. CLARKE CUP
For an exhibit of four trees and/or shrubs of different genera with autumnal fruit, Class 1, shown at the Tree and Shrub Competition, 27 to 28 October 1987. *27 October 1987*
Lord Aberconway
Bodnant, Tal-y-Cafn, Colwyn Bay, Clwyd

VEITCH MEMORIAL GOLD MEDAL
Conferred on persons who have helped in the advancement and improvement of the science and practice of horticulture and for special exhibits.
Mr K. A. Beckett
Bramley Cottage, Stanhoe, King's Lynn, Norfolk

Mr V. F. Fowler
15 Kelston Rd, Bath, Avon

Mrs Paul Mellon
Oak Spring, Upperville, Virginia 22176, USA

Dr R. H. M. Robinson
Hyde Hall, Rettendon, Cheimsford, Essex

Princess Greta Sturdza
Le Vasterival, 76119 Varengeville-sur-Mer, France

Professor H. D. Tindall
8 Church Ave, Ampthill, Bedford

VICTORIA MEDAL OF HONOUR
To British horticulturists resident in the United Kingdom whom the Council consider deserving of special honour at the hands of the Society. *December 1987*
Mr W. L. Banks
13 Abercorn Place, London NW8

Mrs B. Chatto
White Barn House, Elmstead Market, Colchester, Essex

WESTONBIRT ORCHID MEDAL
For the most meritorious group of orchids staged in the Society's halls during 1987 (exhibit of March 1987). *December 1987*
McBean's Orchids Ltd
Cooksbridge, Lewes, Sussex

WIGAN CUP
For the best exhibit shown to the Society during 1987 by a local authority (carpet bedding at Chelsea). *December 1987*
Torbay Parks & Recreation Dept
Town Hall, Torquay, Devon

WILLIAMS MEMORIAL MEDAL
For a group of plants and/or cut blooms of one genus (fruit and vegetables excluded) which show excellence in cultivation, staged at one of the Society's shows during 1987. *December 1987*
Michael Jefferson-Brown Ltd
Broadgate, Weston Hills, Spalding, Lincs

WORSHIPFUL COMPANY OF FRUITERERS CERTIFICATE
For a collection of three dessert cultivars of pears at the 1987 Autumn Fruit and Vegetable Competition. *6 October 1987*
Mr C. E. England
48 Lowlands Rd, Eastcote, Pinner, Middx

For a collection of three dessert cultivars of apples at the 1987 Late Apple and Pear Competition. *24 November 1987*
Mr C. P. Hollis
180 Mawney Rd, Romford, Essex

PREVIEW
1988–1989

In the intervals between the Great Spring Shows, regular Chelsea visitors can sit back – even do a spot of gardening – confident that they will be dazzled yet again by the horticultural splendour of the next May. What to stage and how to stage it are, however, questions that 1989 exhibitors will have been asking themselves long before this publication is in the hands of readers.

Long-term planning is also needed to organize an event as complex as the Great Spring Show. As this publication goes to press arrangements for 1989 are well in hand, but final decisions have yet to be taken on details. In broad outline, the arrangements will follow those of 1988.

Seventy-six years after first being held in the grounds of the Royal Hospital, Chelsea, the Great Spring Show will still be staged on the same site. In the interests of members generally, those who attend Chelsea will have to pay for their tickets and, as part of the measures to keep numbers at acceptable levels, there will be a limit on the number of tickets each member can obtain. Once again, however, both Tuesday and Wednesday will be Private View Days. Tickets will be available in advance and it is likely that special rates will be offered to encourage attendance at off-peak hours. For those who travel long distances to Chelsea it is difficult to attend early or late in the day, but many living in or close to London can quite easily. By avoiding peak periods they will find their own visit much more enjoyable.

As details of arrangements are finalized they will be notified to members through the Society's publications and there will be public announcements well in advance of May. By telephoning 01 828 1744 you can hear a regularly updated recorded message giving information about the Society's shows.

There is no doubt that Chelsea is the major horticultural event of the year but it is part of and not a substitute for the total programme of shows organized by the Society. The Society's participation in a number of regional shows will go some way to balance a programme that in the past has favoured the south-east.

It is worth remembering that at Westminster shows anyone may stage an exhibit of plants and enter the plant competitions. For show regulations, schedules and other information about competitions write to the Secretary (Shows) at Vincent Square, enclosing a large self-addressed envelope.

CALENDAR OF SHOWS

♣ RHS shows that normally will be held in one or both of the Society's halls, which are adjacent to one another, the New Hall in Greycoat Street and the Old Hall in Vincent Square, Westminster. Shows and competitions organized by kindred societies in co-operation with the RHS are given in italics. The show at the Glasgow Garden Festival (5–7 August) will be like those at Westminster.

The shows are open on the first day from 11 am to 7 pm and on the last day from 10 am to 5 pm. The Great Autumn Show, which lasts three days, is open on the second day from 10 am to 7 pm. Entrance to all Westminster shows is free to members; non-members are charged a small fee for admission.

● Regional shows which the Society plans to visit with a mobile bookshop and a team of gardening experts from Wisley.

The dates given are correct at the time of going to press. Any changes to the programme will be published in *The Garden* (Journal of the Royal Horticultural Society) and the Society's *Newsletter*.

1988

21 & 22 June ♣
Early Summer Show
Flowering Tree and Shrub Competition
British Iris Society's Competition
British National Carnation Society's Competition
British Pelargonium & Geranium Society's Competition
Delphinium Society's Competition

4, 5, 6 & 7 July ●
Royal Show Stoneleigh

19 & 20 July ♣
Flower Show
Summer Fruit and Vegetable Competition
Hardy Flower Competition

British National Carnation Society's Competition
Delphinium Society's Competition
Lily Group's Competition

19, 20 & 21 July ●
East of England Show at Peterborough

5, 6 & 7 August
RHS Flower Show at the Glasgow Garden Festival

12 & 13 August ●
Shrewsbury Flower Show

16 & 17 August ♣
Summer Flower Show

Gladiolus Competition
Heather Competition
British Fuchsia Society's 50th Anniversary
Competition
National Begonia Society's Competition
Saintpaulia & Houseplant Society's
Competition

18, 19 & 20 August ●
Southport Flower Show

23, 24 & 25 August ●
Ayr Flower Show

31 August, 1 & 2 September ●
Bristol Flower Show

16 & 17 September ●
Harrogate Great Autumn Show

20, 21 & 22 September ♣
Great Autumn Show

11 & 12 October ♣
Flower Show
Autumn Fruit and Vegetable Competition
British National Carnation Society's
Competition
Japan Society of London's Bonsai
Competition

1 & 2 November ♣
Late Autumn Show
Tree and Shrub Competition
Exhibits of botanical paintings

29 & 30 November ♣
Flower Show
Late Apple and Pear Competition
Ornamental Plant Competition
Exhibits of botanical paintings
Orchid Society of Great Britain's
Competition

1989

31 January & 1 February ♣
Flower Show
Ornamental Plant Competition
Exhibits of botanical paintings

21 & 22 February ♣
Flower Show
Ornamental Plant Competition
Exhibits of botanical paintings
AGM at 2.30 pm on 21 February
British Iris Society's Competition

14 & 15 March ♣
Flower Show
Early Rhododendron Competition
Magnolia and Ornamental Plant
Competition
British Orchid Growers' Association Show

11 & 12 April ♣
Flower Show
Main Camellia Show
Daffodil Show
Sewell Medal Competition
Alpine Garden Society's Competition
Japan Society of London's Bonsai
Competition

3 & 4 May ♣
Flower Show
Main Rhododendron Show
Daffodil Competition
Tulip Competition
Ornamental Plant Competition
British Iris Society's Competition
Royal National Rose Society's Competition

5, 6 & 7 May ●
Spring Gardening Show at Malvern

23, 24, 25 & 26 May
CHELSEA

EXHIBITORS AT CHELSEA AND WESTMINSTER SHOWS
June 1987 to May 1988

Medals may be awarded for exhibits at all the Society's shows, each award depending on the content and standard of the exhibit.

For exhibits of flowers and ornamental plants: Gold (G), Silver-gilt Flora (SGF), Silver-gilt Banksian (SGB), Silver Flora (SF), Silver Banksian (SB) and Flora (F).

For exhibits of fruit: Gold (G), Silver-gilt Hogg (SG Hogg), Silver Hogg (S Hogg) and Hogg.

For exhibits of vegetables: Gold (G), Silver-gilt Knightian (SG Knightian), Silver Knightian (S Knightian) and Knightian.

For exhibits of special scientific or educational merit: Silver-gilt Lindley (SG Lindley) and Silver Lindley (S Lindley).

For pictures: Gold (G), Silver-gilt Grenfell (SG Gr), Silver Grenfell (S Gr) and Grenfell (Gr).

The following list indicates when exhibitors showed and the medals awarded for their exhibits. Dates for Westminster shows and Chelsea (Ch) for the period June 1987 to May 1988 were as follows:

1987

16 & 17 June
Early Summer Show
Flowering Tree and Shrub Competition

14 & 15 July
Flower Show
Summer Fruit and Vegetable Competition

11 & 12 August
Summer Flower Show
Gladiolus Competition
Heather Competition

15, 16 & 17 September
Great Autumn Show

6 & 7 October
Flower Show
Autumn Fruit and Vegetable Competition

27 & 28 October
Late Autumn Show
Tree and Shrub Competition
Exhibits of botanical paintings

24 & 25 November
Flower Show
Late Apple and Pear Competition

Ornamental Plant Competition
Exhibits of botanical paintings

1988

26 & 27 January
Flower Show
Ornamental Plant Competition
Exhibits of botanical paintings

23 & 24 February
Flower Show
Ornamental Plant Competition
Exhibits of botanical paintings
Annual General Meeting

22 & 23 March
Early Spring Show
Early Camellia Competition
Magnolia and Ornamental Plant Competition
Early Rhododendron Competition

12 & 13 April
Spring Flower Show
Daffodil Show
Main Camellia Competition
Ornamental Plant Competition
Sewell Medal Competition

4 & 5 May
Flower Show
Main Rhododendron Competition
Daffodil Competition
Tulip Competition
Ornamental Tree and Shrub Competition

24, 25, 26 & 27 May
CHELSEA

Abbey Brook Cactus Nursery
Old Hackney Lane, Matlock, Derbys ☎ 0629 55360
Cacti & succulents
1988: Ch, SGF

Mrs J. Abel-Smith
Orchard Ho, Letty Grn, Hertford SG14 2NZ
Daffodils
1988: Apr, SGF

Access Irrigation Ltd
15 Yelvertoft Road, Crick, Northants NN6 7XS
☎ 0788 822301
Garden frames & watering equipment
1988: Ch

Veronica Adams
The Mill House, Much Cowerne, Herefordshire HR7 4JJ ☎ 0432 820570
Garden design
1988: Ch

Aegon Garden Club
c/o Ennia House, High Street, Edenbridge, Kent TN8 5AB
W'box & H'basket Comp; Courtyard Garden Comp
1988: Ch, S Gr, S Gr

Agriframes Ltd
Charlwoods Road, East Grinstead, West Sussex RH19 2HG
☎ 0342 28644
Fruit cages & plant supports
1988: Ch

The Air Plant Company
55 Grove Park Rd, Chiswick, London W4 3RU
Tillandsias
1987: 27–28 Oct, SF; Nov, F

Alitex Ltd
Station Road, Alton, Hants, GU34 2PZ ☎ 0420 82860
Glasshouse attachments, cold frames & conservatory
1988: Ch

Allen Power Equipment
The Broadway, Didcot, Oxon OX11 8ES ☎ 0235 813936
Garden machinery
1988: Ch

Allibert Garden Furniture
Berry Hill Industrial Estate, Droitwich, Worcs WR9 9AB
☎ 0905 774221
Garden furniture
1988: Ch

Jacqueline Allwood
163 Charlton Church Way, London SE7 7AA
Botanical engravings in glass
1988: Jan

Allwood Bros
Mill Nursery, London Road, Hassocks, West Sussex BN6 9NB ☎ 079 18 4229
Carnations, pinks, etc
1988: Ch, SF

Alpine Garden Society
Lye End Link, St John's, Woking, Surrey
Publications & publicity
1987: 6–7 Oct; Nov; 1988: Jan; Feb; Apr; Ch

Alresford & District Hort Soc
34 Fair View, Alresford, Hants.
W'box & H'basket Comp
Ch: 1988, B Gr

Alton Garden Centre
Arterial Road, Wickford, Essex
☎ 0268 727913
Garden furniture
1988: Ch

Jacques Amand Ltd
Clamphill, Stanmore, Middx HA7 3JS ☎ 01-954 8138
Bulbous flowers
1987: June, SB; July, SB; Aug, SGF; Sept, SGB; 6 Oct, SGB; 27 Oct, SB; Nov, SB; 1988: Jan, G; Feb, SGF; Mar, SGB; Apr, SB; May, SF; Ch, G

Amateur Gardening
Kings Reach Tower, Stamford Street, London SE1 9LS
☎ 01-261 6313
Publications
1988: Ch

Amdega Ltd
Faverdale, Darlington, Co Durham DL3 0PW
☎ 0325 489209
Conservatory
1988: Ch

Anglian Windows Ltd
P O Box 65, Norwich, Norfolk, NR6 6EJ ☎ 0603-485000
Conservatory & garden room
1988: Ch

Anmore Exotics
4 The Curve, Lovedean, Portsmouth, Hants PO8 9SE ☎ 0705 596538
Tropical & sub-tropical plants
1987: Sept, SGF; Nov, SGF; 1988: Mar, G; Ch, G

Anne Countess of Rosse & The National Trust
Nymans Garden, Sussex
Conifers
1987: Nov, G

Ann's Garden
72 Heath Street, London NW3 1DE ☎ 01 794 9445
House & greenhouse plants
1987: June, SB; July, SGF; Sept, SF; Nov, SF; 1988: Jan, SF; Feb, SB

Arboricultural Association
Ampfield House, Romsey, Hants SO51 9PA
☎ 0794 68717
Woodlands of London
1988: Ch

ARC CONBLOC
Besselsleigh Road, Abingdon, Oxon OX13 6LQ
☎ 0865-730025
A courtyard garden
1988: Ch, SGF

Architectural Heritage Ltd
Taddington Manor, Taddington, Cutsdean, Cheltenham, Glos GL54 5RY
☎ 0386-73414
Antique garden statuary
1988: Ch

Ariens (UK) Ltd
Little End Road, Eaton Socon, St Neots, Cambs PE19 3JH
☎ 0480 218111
Garden machinery
1988: Ch

Army & Navy
101 Victoria Street, London, SW1 E6QX ☎ 01-834 1234
Garden equipment & furniture
1988: Ch

Cynthia Ashford
1 Lyne Road, Kidlington, Oxford OX5 1AE
☎ 08675 78850
Garden design
1988: Ch

ATCO
c/o Priory House, Friars Terrace, Stafford, ST17 4AG
☎ 0785 55146
Garden design
1988: Ch

ATCO
Suffolk Works, Stowmarket, Suffolk IP14 1EY
☎ 0449 612183
Garden machinery
1988: Ch

Auriol (Guildford) Ltd
Passfield, Liphook, Hants GU30 7RR ☎ 042 877 444
Garden sundries
1988: Ch

David Austin Roses
Bowling Green Lane, Albrighton, Wolverhampton WV7 3HB ☎ 090 722 3931
Old-fashioned roses & hardy plants
1988: Ch, G

Avon Bulbs
Upper Westwood, Bradford on Avon, Wilts BA15 2AT
☎ 022 16 3723
Bulbous plants
1987: Sept, SB; 1988: Jan, SGF; Feb, SGB; Mar, SF; Ch, G

Aylett Nurseries Ltd
North Orbital Rd, St Albans, Herts AL2 1DH
Dahlias, houseplants
1987: Sept, G; 1988: Feb, SGF

Jenny Aylott
'High Court', Dulby Hill, Doddington, Nr Sittingbourne, Kent ME9 0BY
Wild flowers
1987: June, F; July, SB; Aug, SF

Steven Bailey Ltd
Silver Street, Sway, Lymington, Hants. SO41 6TA
☎ 0590 682227
Carnations, pinks & alstroemerias
1987: 6 Oct, G; 1988: Apr, SGF; Ch, G

Valerie Baines
16 Medway Rd, Gillingham, Kent
Paintings of flowers
1987: 27 Oct, B Gr

Michael Balston
Manor Farmhouse, Patney, Devizes, Wilts SN10 3RB
☎ 038 084 533
Garden design
1988: Ch

The Bamboo Network
c/o 14 East Lane, Morton, Bourne, South Lincolnshire PE10 0NW
Courtyard Garden Comp
1988: Ch, S Gr

The B & Q Garden (Retail) Ltd
Portswood House, 1 Hampshire Corporate Park, Chandlers Ford, Eastleigh, Hants SO5 3YX
☎ 0703 256256
A Lakeside Garden
1988: Ch, G

Michael Banks Marketing Ltd
Ruxley Towers, Ruxley Ridge, Claygate, Esher, Surrey KT10 0JE ☎ 0372 67922
Ascender lift barrows
1988: Ch

Banstead Hort Soc
Greetings, 68 Shawley Way, Epsom Downs, Surrey KT18 5PG
W'box & H'basket Comp
1988: Ch, S Gr

Barbados Hort Soc Inc
Balls, Christ Church, Barbados
Plants & flowers of Barbados
1988: Ch, SGB

Constance Barnes
'Wayfarers', The Warren, E Horsley, Surrey KT24 5RH
Paintings of wild orchids
1988: Jan, B Gr

Barralets of Ealing Ltd
Pitshanger Lane, Ealing,
W5 1RH ☎ 01-997 0576
*Garden & flower-arranging
sundries, furniture &
summerhouses*
1987: June; July; Aug; Sept; 6–
7 Oct, 27–28 Oct; Nov; 1988:
Jan; Feb; Mar; Apr; May; Ch

E. P. Barrus Ltd
Launton Road, Bicester, Oxon
OX6 0UR ☎ 0869 253355
Garden machinery
1988: Ch

**Alexander Bartholomew
Conservatories Ltd**
277 Putney Bridge Road,
London SW15 2PT
☎ 01 785 7263
Conservatory
1988: Ch

**Barton on Humber &
District Flower Club**
Waysmeet, South Ferriby,
Barton on Humber, South
Humberside DN18 6HB
Floral arrangement
1988: Ch, S Gr

Felicity Baxter
50 Bratton Rd, Westbury,
Wilts BA13 3EP
Paintings of flowers from Greece
1988: Feb, SG Lindley, SG Gr

BBC in the Midlands
Pebble Mill, Birmingham,
B4 7QQ ☎ 021 4148319
*BBC Gardeners' World
exhibition*
1988: Ch

Peter Beales Roses
London Rd, Attleborough,
Norfolk NR17 1AY
☎ 0953 454707
Olf-fashioned & climbinb roses
1987: June, SGB; Sept, SF;
1988: CH, SGF

Tom Bebbington Dahlias
Lady Gate Nursery, The
Green, Diseworth, Derby,
DE7 2QN ☎ 0332 811565
Dahlias
1987: Sept, G; 1988: Ch, SF

**Beeches Road Civil Service
Hort Soc**
MAFF, Beeches Rd,
Chelmsford, Essex CM1 2RU
W'box & H'basket Comp
1988: Ch, B Gr

Tessa Begg
3 St Margaret's Crescent,
London SW15 6HL
☎ 01-788 3744
Garden design
1988: Ch

Berry & Saunders
17 Victoria Street, Burnham-
on-Sea, Somerset TA8 1AL
☎ 0278 782265
Floristry display
1988: Ch, SG Gr, Ring &
Brymer Trophy

**Berry Garden
Company Ltd**
6 Hodford Rd, London
NW11 8NP ☎ 01-209 0194
Garden design
1988: Ch

Bettina Floral Artist
Glenfern Rd,Bournemouth,
Dorset BN1 2NA
☎ 0202 290293
Floristry exhibit
1988: Ch, S Gr

**Biggleswade & District
Floral Arrangement Soc**
Russett, High Rd, Broom,
Biggleswade, Beds
Floral arrangement
1988: Ch, S Gr

**City of Birmingham Dept
of Recreation &
Community Services**
Auchinleck House, Five Ways,
Birmingham B15 1DS
☎ 021 235 2004
Foliage & flowering plants
1988: Ch, G

S. R. Blackie
Olivers Farm, Toppesfield,
Halstead, Essex CO9 4LS
☎ 0787 237602
Garden design
1988: Ch

Blackmore & Langdon Ltd
Stanton Nurseries, Pensford,
Bristol BS18 4JL
☎ 0272 332300
Begonias & delphiniums
1988: Ch, SGF

Blackwall Products Ltd
Unit 4, Riverside Ind Estate,
150 Riverway, London
SE10 0BH ☎ 01-305 1431
*Tumbler, seedhouse, planters &
wheelbarrow*
1988: Ch

Rev R. J. Blakeway-Phillips
Church Cottage, Clun, Craven
Arms, Shropshire SY7 8JW
Bulbs, cyclamen, alpines
1987: 6–7 Oct, SB; 1988: Jan,
SB; May

Blanchard Landscapes Ltd
92 Lots Rd, London
SW10 0RN ☎ 01-352 6741
Garden design
1988: Ch

Mary Bland
Augop, Evenjobb, Presteigne,
Powys, Wales ☎ 054 76 218
Second-hand books & prints
1988: Ch

Olga Blandford-Lewis
88 Friars Walk, Southgate,
London N14 5LN
Paintings of fruit & vegetables
1987: Nov, SG Gr

Walter Blom & Son Ltd
Coombelands Nurseries Ltd,
Leavesden, Watford, Herts
WD2 7BH ☎ 0923 672071
Tulips
1988: Ch, G

Blooms of Bressingham Ltd
Bressingham, Diss, Norfolk
IP22 2AB ☎ 037988-464
A Plant Lover's Garden
1988: Ch, G
*Herbaceous perennials, alpines,
shrubs & conifers*
1987: Sept, SGF; 1988: Feb,
SB; Ch, SGB

Bo-Kay
7 Bath Street, St Helier,
Jersey CI ☎ 0534 3381
Floristry exhibit
1988: Ch

**Bond Garden Care
Agencies**
202 Crofton Rd, Orpington,
Kent BR6 8JG ☎ 0689 50346
Garden sundries
1988: Ch

Bonsai Kai of London
39 West Square, London
SE11 4SP ☎ 01-735 8476
Bonsai
1987: 6–7 Oct; 1988: Apr; Ch,
SGF

Stephanie Booth
Ashley Cottage, 47 Baldwins
Hill, Loughton, Essex
IG10 1SF ☎ 01-508 3350
Garden design
1988: Ch

Bourne Garden Club
22 Ostler Drive, Bourne, Lincs
PE10 9QR
W'box & H'basket Comp
1988: Ch, S Gr

Bouts Cottage Nurseries
Bouts Lane, Inkberrow, Worcs
WR7 4HP
☎ 0386 792923
*Violas & pansies (Michaelmas
daisies)*
1987: Sept, SB; 1988: Apr, SF;
Ch, SF

Patrick Bowe
Parsley Cottage, 11 Ashfield
Avenue, Ranelagh, Dublin 6,
Eire ☎ 0001 975822
Garden design
1988: Ch

Chris Bowers & Sons
Whispering Trees Nurseries,
Wimbotsham, Norfolk
PE34 8QB ☎ 0366 388 752
*Fruit trees, flowering trees &
shrubs*

1987: June, SB; July, SF; Aug,
SF; Sept, SF; 27 Oct, SGB;
Nov, Hogg; 1988: Feb, SGB;
Mar, SB; May, SGB; Ch, SF

Rupert Bowlby
Gatton, Reigate, Surrey
RH2 0TA ☎ 073 74 2221
Bulbous plants
1987: Aug, F; Sept, SF; 6 Oct,
SB; 27 Oct, F; 1988: Feb, SF;
Mar, SB; Apr, SF; Ch, SF

Sylvia Boyd-Andrews
58E Redcliffe Gdns, London
SW10 9HD
*Paintings of plants collected in
Brit. Columbia, Yukon &
Alaska*
1987: 27 Oct, S Gr

S. & N. Brackley
117 Winslow Rd, Wingrave,
Aylesbury, Bucks HP22 4QB
☎ 0296 681384
Sweet peas
1987: 6 Oct, SGB; 1988: Ch,
SGF

Jenny Brasier
The Oaks, Merrist Wood,
Worplesdon, Guildford,
Surrey
Paintings of leaves
1988: Feb, G

Lys de Bray
Turnpike Cottage, 8 Leigh Rd,
Wimborne, Dorset BH21 1AF
Paintings of British wild flowers
1988: Feb, S Gr

**Brighton College of
Technology**
Stanmer Park Horticultural
Centre, Pelham Street,
Brighton BN1 4FA
☎ 0273 601678
Garden design
1988: Ch

**British & European
Geranium Soc**
South East Region, 85 Sparrow
Farm Rd, Ewell, Surrey
KT17 2LP ☎ 01-393 4229
Regal & zonal pelargoniums
1988: Ch, SB

**British Association of
Landscape Industries
(BALI)**
Southern Tree Surgeons Ltd,
Crawley Down, Crawley, West
Sussex RH10 4HL
☎ 0342 712215
Publicity
1988: Ch

**British Bedding Plants
Association**
160 New London Rd,
Chelmsford, Essex CM2 0AP
☎ 0245-355291
Bedding plants
1988: Ch, SGF

British Bonsai Association
Flat D, 15 St Johns Park,
Blackheath SE3 7TH
☏ 01-858 5621
Bonsai
1988: Ch, SGB

British Herb Trade Association
Sunnymead, West Pennard,
Glastonbury, Somerset
BA6 8NN ☏ 0458 33573
Herbs and their uses
1988: Ch

The British Fuchsia Society
29 Princes Crescent, Dollar,
Scotland FK14 7BW
☏ 02594 3180
Fuchsias
1987: Aug; 1988, Ch, F

British Iris Soc
c/o S. Linnegar, 6 Oban Gdns,
Woodley, Reading, Berks
RG5 3RG
Iris Competition, publicity
1987: June; Nov; 1988: Feb;
May

British National Carnation Soc
c/o Mr A. F. Robinson, 5 Chase
Court Gdns, Enfield,
Middlesex EN2 8DH
Society's competition
1987: June; July; 6–7 Oct

British Orchid Council
Church Bridge Lodge,
Batcombe, Shepton Mallet,
Somerset BA4 6EU
☏ 0749 830076
Orchids
1988: Ch, SF

The British Pelargonium & Geranium Soc
c/o 23 Beech Crescent,
Kidlington, Oxford OX5 1DW
☏ 08675 5063
Pelargoniums
1987: June; Aug, SB;
1988: Ch, F

British Teleflower Service Ltd
146 Bournemouth Road,
Chandler's Ford, Eastleigh,
Hants SO5 3ZB
☏ 0703 254123
Floral arrangements & Floral Relay Service information
1988: Ch

British Trust for Conservation Volunteers
The London Ecology Centre,
80 York Way, London N1 9AG
☏ 01-278 4293
The BTCV Recycled Garden
1988: Ch, SF

Broadleas Gardens Trust
Broadleas, Devizes, Wilts
SN10 5JQ
Bulbs
1988: Apr, SF

Broadleigh Gardens
Bishops Hull, Taunton,
Somerset TA4 1AE
☏ 0823 286231
Bulbous & foliage plants, Californian irises
1987: Sept, SGF; 1988: Feb,
SGF; Mar, SF; Ch, SGB

Bromage & Young Ltd
St Mary's Gardens,
Worplesdon, Surrey GU3 3RS
☏ 0483 232893
Bonsai
1988: Ch, SGF

Elsa Brown
17 Claremont Rd, Surbiton,
Surrey ☏ 01-399 3975
Floristry exhibit
1988: Ch

Brunel Trading
Trinity Vicarage Rd, Hinckley,
Leics LE10 0BU
☏ 0455 633414
Garden sundries
1988: Ch

Frances Buckland
21 Malvern Ct, Onslow Sq,
London SW7 3HU
Paintings of Convolvulaceae
1988: Jan, B Gr

Bulldog Tools Ltd
Clarington Forge, Wigan,
Lancs WN1 3DD
☏ 0942 44281
Garden tools
1988: Ch

Burncoose & Southdown Nurseries
Gwennap, Redruth, Cornwall
TR16 6BJ ☏ 0209 861112
Trees, shrubs & ornamental plants
1987: July, SGB; Sept, G; 6
Oct, G; 27 Oct, G; Nov, SGF;
1988: Jan, SGF; Feb, SGF;
Mar, G; Apr, SGF; Ch, G

Burnham Nurseries Ltd
Newton Abbot, Devon
TQ12 6PZ ☏ 0626 52233
Orchids
1987: June, SF; Sept, SF; Nov,
SGB; 1988: Feb. SF; Ch, SGF

Burntubes Ltd
Radway Rd, Shirley, Solihull,
West Midlands B90 4NS
☏ 021 704 2211
Garden arches & pergolas
1988: Ch

Jacquie Burrell
72 Valiant Ho, Vicarage Cres,
London SW11 3LX
Paintings of bulbous plants
1988: Jan, S Gr

Burrows' Roses
Pleasant View Nursery, Hallam
Hill, Little Ilkeston,
Derbyshire DE7 4LY
☏ 0602 320669
Roses
1987: Aug, SGF; Sept, SGB;
1988: Ch, SF

Burton McCall Ltd
Samuel Street, Leicester
LE1 1RU ☏ 0533 538781
Garden sundries
1988: CH

Busby Flower Club
5 Stewart Drive, Clarkston,
Glasgow
Floral arrangement
1988: Ch, SG Gr

Bush Hill Park Hort Soc
20 Old Park Ridings,
Winchmore Hill, London
N21 2EU
W'box & H'basket Comp
1988: Ch, SG Gr

W. H. Butler (Die Casting) Ltd
Lea Road, Dronfield,
Sheffield S18 6SB
☏ 0246 412257
Aluminium garden furniture
1988: Ch

Butterfields Nursery
Harvest Hill, Bourne End,
Bucks SL8 5JJ ☏ 06285 25455
Pleiones
1988: Mar, G; Ch, SGF

Jan Buytaert
Wolstraat 31, 2000 Antwerpen,
Belgium
Engravings of plants & flowers & drawings of landscapes
1987: 27 Oct, S Gr

Cambridge Bulbs
40 Whittlesford Rd, Newton,
Cambridge CB2 5PH
Bulbous & herbaceous plants
1988: Feb, SF; Mar, SF; Apr,
SGB; May, SB

Cambridge Flower Club
Sideways, 67 Narrow La,
Histon, Cambridge CB4 4YP
Floral arrangements
1988: Ch, SG Gr

Cambridge Glasshouse Co Ltd
Barton Road, Comberton,
Cambs CB3 7BY
☏ 0223 262395
Greenhouses
1988:Ch

I. G. Cantley
5 Breakspear Rd, Ruislip,
Middlesex HA4 7SB
☏ 0895 639507
Garden design
1988: Ch

Cants of Colchester Ltd
Nyland Rd, Colchester, Essex
CO4 5EB ☏ 0206 844008
Roses
1988: Ch, SGB

Capel Manor College of Horticulture
Bullsmoor Lane, Waltham
Cross, Herts EN7 5HR
☏ 0992 763849
Courses offered by the college
1988: Ch

Carlile's Hardy Plants
Carlile's Corner, Twyford,
Reading, Berks RG10 9PU
☏ 0734 340031
Herbaceous plants
1988, Ch, SGF

Carncairn Daffodils
Carncairn Lodge, Broughs La,
Co Antrim, N. Ireland
Daffodils
1988: Apr, G

Carnivorous Plant Society
24 Osborne Rd, Brentwood,
Essex CM15 9LE
☏ 01-929 1717
Carnivorous plants
1988: Ch, SGF

Castledyke Nurseries
Castledyke Bank, Wildmore,
New York, Lincs LN4 4XF
☏ 0526 43087
Fuchsias & regal pelargoniums
1987: July, SGF; 1988; Ch,
SGB

Richard G. H. Cawthorne
Lower Daltons Nursery,
Swanley Village, Swanley,
Kent BR8 7NU
Violas, violettas and viola species
1988: Ch, SGF

C.D.A. Ltd
Lockinge, Wantage, Oxon
OX12 8PH ☏ 0235 833314
Chemical applicators
1988: Ch

Ceka
34 Slough Rd, Datchet, Berks
SL3 9AW ☏ 0753 47790
Garden tools
1988: Ch

Chris Chadwell
c/o 158 Upper College Ride,
Camberley, Surrey
Himalayan expeditions, seed
1987: 27–28 Oct; 1988: Feb;
Apr

Myles Challis Gardens
1 Lister Rd, Leytonstone,
London E11 3DS
☏ 01-556 8962
The Vitax Golden Garden
1988: Ch, SB

**John Chambers Wild
Flower Seeds**
15 Westleigh Road, Barton
Seagrave, Kettering,
Northants NN15 5AJ
☎ 0933 681632
Wild flowers
1988: Ch
Gale's Honey Bee Garden
1988: Ch, G

Chatsworth Carpenters
Estate Office, Edensor,
Bakewell, Derbyshire
☎ 024 688 2242
Garden furniture
1988: Ch

Beth Chatto Unusual Plants
Elmstead Market, Colchester,
Essex CO7 7DB
Unusual herbaceous perennials
1987: Sept, G

The Chelsea Gardener
125 Sydney Street, London
SW1 6NR ☎ 01-352 5656
Garden furniture & ornaments
1988: Ch

**Cheam & Cuddington Hort
Soc**
24 Gomshall Rd, Sutton,
Surrey SM2 7JZ
W'box & H'basket Comp
1988: Ch, S Gr

Chempak Products
Geddings Rd, Hoddesdon,
Herts EN11 0LR
☎ 0992 441888
Fertilizers
1988: Ch

K. L. Chen
The Lodge, Kennington Pk Pl,
London SE11 4AS
Pressed-flower pictures
1987: 27–28 Oct

Chenies Landscapes Ltd
Bramble Lane, London Road
East, Amersham, Bucks
HP7 9DH ☎ 02403 28004
Garden design
1988: Ch

**China State Construction
Engineering Group**
Bai Wan Zhuang, Beijing,
China
Garden design
1988: Ch
Pen-jing
1988: Ch, SF

**City and Guilds of London
Institute**
46 Britannia Street, London
WC1X 9RG ☎ 01-278 2468
Promotion of the Institute
1988: Ch

Clear Span Ltd
Greenfield, Oldham, Lancs
OL3 7AG ☎ 04577 3244
Glasshouses
1988: Ch

Tony Clements Nurseries
Station Rd, Terrington St
Clement, Kings Lynn, Norfolk
PE34 4PL ☎ 0553 828374
*Saintpaulias & other
Gesneriaceae*
1987: June, SGB; July, SGB;
Sept, SGB; 6 Oct, SGB; 27
Oct, SGB; Nov, SGB; 1988:
Feb, SGB; Mar, SGB; Apr,
SGB; May, SGF; Ch, G

**Cochrane, Flynn-Rogers &
Williams**
13/15 Spitalfields, Dublin 8,
Eire ☎ 0001 534099
Garden design
1988: Ch

Colegrave Seeds Ltd
West Adderbury, Banbury,
Oxon OX17 3EY
☎ 0295 810632
Impatiens & pelargoniums
1988: Ch, G

Francis F. Colella
8 Woodbridge Rd, Westbury
Park, Newcastle under Lyme,
Staffs ST5 4LA
☎ 0782 661614
Garden design
1988: Ch

College of Garden Design
Administrative Office,
Hethersett, Cothelstone,
Taunton, Somerset TA4 3DP
☎ 0823 433215
Garden design
1988: Ch

**Commonwealth War
Graves Commission**
2 Marlow Rd, Maidenhead,
Berks SL6 7DX ☎ 0628 34221
Garden design
1988: Ch

Mr Ambrose Congreve
Mount Congreve, Waterford,
Eire
Magnolias
1988: Mar

Consumer Direct Ltd
Lower Street, Quainton,
Aylesbury, Bucks HP22 4BL
☎ 029 675 217
Growing frames
1988: Ch

Geoffrey K. Coombs
47 Larcombe Rd, Petersfield,
Hants GU32 3LS
☎ 0730 67417
Garden design
1988: Ch

Jill Coombs
Weald Ho, Handford Way,
Plummers Plain, Horsham, W.
Sussex RH13 6PD
Paintings of herbs
1988: Jan, G

Cooper, Pegler & Co Ltd
2 Victoria Gardens, Burgess
Hill, West Sussex RH15 9LA
☎ 04446 42526
Sprayers, pumps & accessories
1988: Ch

Corinnes Florist
3 Stoke Parade, Stoke Rd,
Gosport, Hants PO12 1QE
☎ 0705 580034
Floristry exhibit
1988: Ch

Cotswold Buildings Ltd
Standlake, Oxon OX8 7QG
☎ 086 731 711
*Conservatories, greenhouses &
garden chalets*
1988: Ch

Kathleen Cotterell Florist
8 Redcar Street, Shirley,
Southampton, Hants
SO1 5LL ☎ 0703 775210
Floristry exhibit
1988: Ch

The Country Garden
Langley House, China Lane,
Manchester M1 8LR
☎ 061 236 3764
Garden sundries
1988: Ch

**Countrylife Gallery
(Highacre Ltd)**
PO Box 12, 30 Sun Street,
Hitchin, Herts SG4 7SH
☎ 0462 33267
*Botanical watercolours & flower
paintings*
1987: 27–28 Oct; Nov; 1988:
Mar; Ch

County Forge Ltd
The Welshmill, Park Hill
Drive, Frome, Somerset
BA11 2LE ☎ 0373 72440
Wrought-iron & garden lighting
1988: ch

County Park Nursery
Essex Gdns, Hornchurch,
Essex RM11 3BU
*Alpines & shrubs, NZ &
Tasmanian plants*
1987: June, SGF; July, SGF;
Aug, SGF; Sept, SG Lindley,
SGB; 6 Oct, G; 1988: Apr,
SGF; May, SGF

Courtyard Pottery
Groundwell Farm, Cricklade
Road, Swindon, Wilts
☎ 0793 721111
*Terracotta & Terranigra Plant
Pots*
1988: Ch

**Coventry & District
Carnation, Rose &
Sweetpea Soc**
60 Winsford Ave, Allesley Pk,
Coventry CV5 9JF
W'box & H'basket Comp
1988: Ch, B Gr

Mrs Ray Cowell
Breeds Farm, 57 High St,
Wicken, Nr Ely, Cams
CB7 5XR
Paintings of British Fungi
1988: Jan, SG Gr

Cowpact Products
PO Box 595, Adstock, Bucks.
MK18 2RE ☎ 029 671 3838
Organic fertilizers, etc
1988: Ch

K. P. Coyne
32 High Rd, Essendon,
Hatfield, Herts AL9 6HW
☎ 070 72 71522
Garden design
1988: Ch

Andrew Crace Designs
Upper Bourne Lane, Much
Hadham, Herts
Gdn furniture, labels
1987: June; July; Sept; 6–7 Oct;
27–28 Oct; Nov; 1988: Jan;
Mar; Apr

Craig House Cacti
26 Marlborough Rd,
Southport, Lancs PR9 0RA
☎ 0704 33210
Cacti, euphorbias & succulents
1988: Ch, SF

Cramphorn PLC
Cuton Mill, Chelmsford, Essex
☎ 0245-466221
A Plantsman's Garden
1988: Ch, SGB

Craven's Nursery
1 Fould's Terrace, Bingley,
West Yorkshire BD16 4LZ
☎ 0274 561412
*Auriculas, primulas, dianthus &
pinks*
1988: Apr, SGF; May, SGF;
Ch, SB

Caroline L. Crawford
4373 East Links Parkway,
Littleton, Colorado 80122,
USA
*Drawings of the flora of the
Rocky Mountains & Great
Plains*
1988: Jan, S Gr

Crittal Warmlife Ltd
Crittal Road, Witham, Essex
CM8 3AW ☎ 0376 513481
*Greenhouse, conservatories &
accessories*
1988: Ch

Crowther of Syon Lodge
Bush Corner, London Road
Isleworth, Middx TW7 5BH
☏ 01-560 7978
Antique garden ornaments
1988: Ch

David Crudgington
10 King Alfred Place,
Winchester, Hants SO23 7DF
☏ 0962 60024
Garden design
1988: Ch

Fiona Bell Currie
1st Floor Flat, 9 Belmont Gro,
London SE13 5DW
Paintings of fruit & vegetables
1987: 27 Oct, B Gr

Cyclamen Society
c/o M. E. L. Jope, 130
Hermitage Woods Cres,
St Johns, Woking, Surrey
GU21 1UH
Cyclamen species
1987: Sept, SF; Nov, SGB;
1988: Feb, SB

Daily Express
121 Fleet Street, London
EC4P 4JT
☏ 01-353 8000 ex 4038
A Garden of Quality
1988: Ch, SF

Daily Mirror
Holborn Circus, London
EC1P 1DQ ☏ 01-822 3227
Your Garden for Pleasure
1988: Ch, SF

Daily Telegraph plc
Peterborough Court at South
Quay, 181 Marsh Wall,
London E14 9SR
☏ 01 866 5034
Summerhouse
1988: Ch

Patricia Dale, RMS, FSBA
Court Lodge, West Meon,
Petersfield, Hants GU32 1JG
☏ 073086 473
Botanical watercolour drawings
1988: Ch

Darlac Products
34 Slough Rd, Datchet, Berks
SL3 9AW ☏ 0753 47790
*Florida & Korso Flower
containers*
1988:Ch

Patricia Davies
23 Woodfield Rd, Rudgwick,
Nr Horsham, W. Sussex
RH12 3EP
Paintings of Leguminosae
1988: Jan, B Gr

Leonard C. Davis
Brook Ho, Lingen, Nr
Bucknell, Salop SY7 0DY
Paintings of flowers
1988: Feb, Gr

Tom Davison
24 Jessel Ho, Judd Street,
London WC1H 9NX
Paintings of plants
1987: Nov, Gr

Peggy Dawe
46 Green La, Purley, Surrey
CR2 3PJ
Paintings of clematis
1988: Feb, Gr

Deacons Florist
235 Commercial Rd,
Portsmouth, Hants PO1 4BP
☏ 0705 827270
Floristry exhibit
1988: Ch

Pauline M. Dean
'Two Trees', 27 Poltimore Rd,
Guildford, Surrey GU2 5PR
Paintings of clematis
1988: Jan, SG Gr

The Delphinium Society
'Ashton', Deanland Handley,
Salisbury SP5 5PD
☏ 0725 52586
Publicity for the Society
1987: June; July; Sept; 1988:
Mar; Ch

Denman's Florist
1 East Reach, Taunton,
Somerset
☏ 0823 331848
Floristry exhibit
1988: Ch

Judith Derby Florist
Croxton Kerrial, Grantham,
Lincs NG32 1QW
☏ 0476 870414
Floristry exhibit
1988: Ch

Dibco Trading & Eng Ltd
49 Dartford Rd, Sevenoaks,
Kent TN13 3TE
Terracotta pots, gdn ornaments
1988: Jan; Feb; Mar; Apr; May

The Diddybox
PO Box 111, Egerton, Bolton,
Lancs BL7 9RD ☏ 0204 53560
Flower arranger's sundries
1988: Ch

Diplex Ltd
PO Box 172, Watford, Herts.
WD1 1BX ☏ 0923 31784
Indicating instruments
1988: Ch

Samuel Dobie & Son Ltd
Hele Rd, Torquay, Devon
TQ2 7QW ☏ 0803 62011
Pansies
1988: Ch

B. S. Dollamoore Ltd
Castle Gresley, Burton-on-
Trent,
Staffs DE11 9HA
☏ 0283 217905
Garden frames
1988: Ch

Donnington Plants
Main Rd, Wrangle, Boston,
Lincs PE22 9AT
*Auriculas, Primula sieboldii,
Chrysanthemum frutescens*
1988: Apr, SGB; May, SGB

Julian Dowle
The Malt House, High Street,
Newent, Glos GL18 1AY
☏ 0531 820512
Garden design
1988: Ch

The Dried Flower Company
53 Chalk Farm Rd, London
NW1 8AN ☏ 01-267 0877
Dried flowers & rural items
1988: Ch

A. Du Gard Pasley
Dornden, Langton Rd,
Tunbridge Wells, Kent
TN3 0BA ☏ 0892 27836
Garden design
1988: Ch

**Dumfries & District
Flower Club**
16 Nunholm Pk, Dumfries
DG1 1JP
Floral arrangement
1988: Ch, B Gr

Daphne Eales
Nightingale Old Farm, Wood
Street Grn, Guildford, Surrey
GU3 3DU
Paintings of fruit
1987: 27 Oct, S Gr

T. J. Earles
65 William Bare Foot Drive,
Eltham, London SE9 3JD
Cacti & succulents
1988: Jan, G; Feb, SGB; Mar,
SGF; Ch, SGF

**Eastabrook Associates
(Architects) Ltd**
Enoch's Tower, Oddington
Rd, Stow on the Wold,
Cheltenham, Glos GL54 1AL
☏ 0451 30541
Garden design
1988: Ch

**East Anglian Wireworking
& Engineering Co Ltd**
Wright Rd, Ipswich, Suffolk
IP3 9RN ☏ 0473 710092
Plant supports & hort wire-work
1988: Ch

S. Easthams Ltd
Lord Square, Blackburn,
Lancs. BB1 7JA ☏ 0254 53001
Floristry exhibit
1988: Ch

**Ecology & Landscape
Design Partnership**
Ladywell House, Newtown,
Powys SY16 7JB
☏ 0686 27600
Garden design
1988: Ch

Edrom Nurseries
Coldingham, Eyemouth,
Berwickshire TD1X 5TZ
Alpines & bulbous plants
1987: Sept, G; 6–7 Oct, G;
1988: Feb, G; Mar, SGB; Apr,
SGB; May, SGF

Brigid Edwards
74 Duns Tew, Oxford
OX5 4JL
Paintings of fruit & vegetables
1987: 27 Oct, SG Gr

Efenechtyd Nurseries
Llanelidan, Ruthin, Clwyd
LL15 2LG
Streptocarpus
1987: July, SF; Aug, SGB

E. L. F. Plants
Cramden Nursery Ltd,
Harborough Rd North,
Northampton ☏ 0604 846246
*Dwarf shrubs, conifers & alpine
plants*
1987: June, SB; Sept, SB; 6
Oct, SF; 27 Oct, SGB; Nov,
SB; 1988: Feb, SB; Mar, F;
Apr, SB; May; Ch, SB

**English Country Garden
Design**
Primrose Farm, Langworthy
Lane, Holyport, Berks
SL6 2HN ☏ 0628 24173
Garden design
1988: Ch

**The English Gardening
School**
Chelsea Physic Garden, 66
Royal Hospital Rd, London
SW3 4HS ☏ 01-352 4347
Publicity & promotion
1988: Ch

Erin Marketing Ltd
33 Bancroft, Hitchin, Herts
5GS 1LA ☏ 0462 36911
Garden sundries
1988: Ch

**Europa Manor
Engineers Ltd**
Unit 2, Appletree Road Estate,
Chipping Warden, Nr
Banbury,
Oxon OX17 1LL
☏ 0295 86 588
*Aluminium greenhouses, cold
frames & accessories*
1988: Ch

Eversdens Floral Club
14 Finch's Field, Little
Eversden, Cambridge
CB3 7HG
Floral arrangement
1988: Ch, B Gr

Exmouth Garden Products
Woodville Road, Exmouth,
Devon EX8 1SE
☏ 0395 275665
Greenhouse accessories
1988: Ch

Exteriors Design Studio
The Wilderness, Wilderness
Lane, Hadlow Down, East
Sussex ☎ 082 585 552
Garden design
1988: Ch

Eynsford Gardeners' Club
Braeside, 55 Eynsford Rise,
Eynsford, Kent DA4 0HS
W'box & H'basket Comp
1988: Ch, B Gr

Fairlight Camellia Nursery
Three Oaks, Guestling, Nr
Hastings, E. Sussex
Camellias
1988: Feb, SB.; Mar, SB;
Apr, F

**Falkirk Floral
Arrangement Club**
218 Windsor Rd, Falkirk,
Stirlingshire FK1 5DR
Floral arrangement
1988: Ch, SG Gr

**Farnham Common
Nurseries**
Crown La, Farnham Royal,
Nr Slough, Bucks SL2 3SF
Shrubs, hardy perennials
1987: 27–28 Oct, SF; Nov,
SGF

**Jane Fearnley-
Whittingstall**
Merlin Haven House, Wotton
Under Edge, Glos GL12 7BA
☎ 0453 843228
Garden design
1988: Ch

Joyce Fenton
The Mill, Charlwood, Nr
Horley, Surrey RH6 0BY
Pressed-flower pictures
1987: Nov

T. D. Fenwick
Tree Tops, Penarvon Cove,
Helford, Helston, Cornwall
TR12 6JZ ☎ 032 623 214
Garden design
1988: Ch

Fibrex Nurseries Ltd
Honeybourne Rd, Pebworth,
Stratford-upon-Avon, Warks.
CV37 8XT ☎ 0789 720 788
*Hederas, ferns, pelargoniums,
gloxinias, hellebores*
1987: June, SGB; July, SF;
Aug, SB; Sept, SGB; 6 Oct,
SF; Nov, SF; 1988: Jan, SB;
Feb, F; Mar, SB; Apr, SF; Ch,
SF, SF

Annette Firth
40 Cecily Hill, Cirencester,
Glos GL7 2EF
Paintings of flowers
1988: Jan, B Gr

Fisk's Clematis Nursery
Westleton, Saxmundham,
Suffolk IP17 3AJ
☎ 072873 263
Clematis
1988: Ch, SF

Janet Flawn-Thomas
Shortbridge Mill, Piltdown, Nr
Uckfield, E. Sussex TN22 3XA
*Paintings of subtropical creepers
& climbers*
1987: Nov, Gr

Percy Flaxman
4 The Chine, London
N10 3QA ☎ 01-444 0766
Garden design
1988: Ch

Rethna Flaxman
4 The Chine, London
N10 3QA ☎ 01-444 0766
Garden design
1988: Ch

Fleurette
26a The Roundhouse, St
Thomas Street, Lymington,
Hants SO41 9ZP ☎ 0590 74828
Floristry exhibit
1988: Ch

Floral Roundabout
59 Sidbury, Worcester,
WR1 2HU ☎ 0905 24613
Floristry exhibit
1988: Ch, S Gr

Flowers & Things
1 The Green, Hersham,
Walton-on-Thames, Surrey
KT12 4JQ ☎ 0932 225260
Floristry exhibit
1988: Ch

Flowers By June
Westbourne Park Station,
Great Western Rd, London
W11 ☎ 01-229 9589
Floristry exhibit
1988: Ch

Flowers By Marcus
18 Nottingham Road, Alfreton,
Derbys DE5 7HL
☎ 0773 835878
Floristry exhibit
1988: Ch, S Gr

Flowers International
38 Eastover, Bridgewater,
Somerset
Floristry exhibit
1988: Ch, B Gr

Flower Service
The Old Rectory, Brinkworth,
Chippenham, Wilts
☎ 066 641 307
Floristry exhibit
1988: Ch

Flower Vogue
44 The Broadway, Stanmore,
Middlesex ☎ 01 954 0086
Floristry exhibit
1988: Ch, B Gr

M. A. Ford
22 Dyne Rd, London
NW6 7XE ☎ 01-624 7051
Garden design
1988: Ch

Forestry Commission
Forest Research Station, Alice
Holt Lodge, Wrecclesham,
Farnham, Surrey GU10 4LH
☎ 0420 22255
Advice on trees
1988: Ch

Fortescue Garden Trust
The Garden House, Buckland
Monachorum, Devon
☎ 0822 854769
*Hardy flowering & foliage
plants*
1988: Ch, SGF

John Mark Fothergill
c/o The Herbarium, Royal
Botanic Gardens, Kew,
Richmond, Surrey
Paintings of flower species
1987: Nov, S Gr

Rosalind Foulk
4 Moor View, Western Rd,
Ivybridge, Devon PL21 9AW
Paintings of irises
1988: Jan, G

Four Seasons
Hillhouse Farm, Cheney's
Lane, Forncett St Mary,
Norwich NR16 1JT
*Trees, shrubs & herbaceous
plants*
1987: June, SGB; July, SB;
Aug, SB; Sept, SF; 6 Oct, SB;
27 Oct, SB; 1988: Feb, SB;
Mar, F; Apr, SB; May, SGB;
Ch, SGB

**Four Seasons Garden
Equipment Ltd**
9 Dene Lane, Farnham, Surrey
GU10 3PW ☎ 0252 713462
Trailed gang mowers
1988: Ch

Foxgrove Plants
Foxgrove, Enborne, Newbury,
Berks RG14 6RE
☎ 0635 40554
*Herbaceous, alpine & rock gdn
plants*
1987: 6 Oct, SF; 1988 Feb, SF;
Mar, SB; Apr, SB; May, F;
Ch, F

Hazel Franklin Flowers
126 Burton Rd, Carlton,
Nottingham, Notts
☎ 0602 611080
Floristry exhibit
1988: Ch, B Gr

Franklin Mint Ltd
138 Bromley Rd, London
SE6 2XG ☎ 01-697 8121
Franklin Mint items
1988: Ch

Frost Conservatories
The Old Forge, Tempsford,
Sandy, Beds SG19 2AG
☎ 0767 40808
Timber conservatory
1988: Ch

Fryers Nurseries Ltd
Knutsford, Cheshire
WA16 0SX ☎ 0565 55455
Roses
1988: Ch, G

Garden Answers
EMAP, 13 Holkham Rd, Orton
Southgate, Peterborough
PE2 0UF ☎ 0733 237111
'Garden Answers' magazine
1988: Ch

**The Garden Centre
Association**
38 Carey Street, Reading,
Berks RG1 7JS ☎ 0734 393900
Planted hanging baskets
1988: Ch, SGF

**The Gardeners' Royal
Benevolent Society**
Bridge House, 139 Kingston
Rd, Leatherhead, Surrey
KT22 7NT
☎ 0372 373962
*Publicity for the work of the
Society*
1988: Ch

**Garden for the Disabled
Trust**
Dale Hill, Farm House,
Ticehurst, E. Sussex
TN5 7DQ
Publicity
1987: 27–28 Oct; 1988: Feb;
Mar

Gardening From Which?
Consumers' Association,
2 Marylebone Rd, London
NW1 4DX ☎ 01-486 5544
Publications & plant exhibits
1987: Aug; Sept; 1988: Ch
Gardening Through the Ages
1988: Ch

Garden News
EMAP, 13 Holkham Rd, Orton
Southgate, Peterborough,
PE2 0UF ☎ 0733 237111
'Garden News' Magazine
1988: Ch

Judith Garrett
Old Crown Ho, Lindsell,
Dunmow, Essex CM6 3QN
Paintings of pelargoniums
1988: Jan, B Gr

**Gateshead MBC Parks &
Recreation Department**
Prince Consort Rd, Gateshead,
Tyne & Wear
Courtyard garden
1988: Ch

Geddington Gardening Club
15 New Rd, Geddington, Nr Kettering, Northants NN14 1AT
W'box & H'basket Comp
1988: Ch, SG Gr

Geeco Div of McKechnie Consumer Products Ltd
Gore Road Industrial Estate, New Milton, Hants BH25 6SE ☏ 0425 614600
Watering, heating & propagating equipment
1988: Ch

J. Gerritsen & Son
PO Box 86, 2250 AB Voorschoten, Holland
Daffodils
1988: Apr, SGB

Glasgow Garden Festival
Princes Dock, Glasgow G51 1JA ☏ 041-429 8855
Glasgow Gdn Festival publicity
1988: May

Gloster Leisure Furniture Ltd
Universal House, Pennywell Road, Bristol BS5 0TJ
☏ 0272 540349
Teak furniture
1988: Ch

B. D. Goalby
99 Somerfield Road, Bloxwich, Walsall, West Midlands WS3 2EG ☏ 0922 401537
Primulas & auriculas
1988: Mar, SF; Apr, SGB; May, SB; Ch, SB

Goldbrook Plants
Hoxne, Eye, Suffolk
☏ 037 975 770
Hostas and other foliage & flowering plants
1987: June, G; July, G; Aug, SGF; Sept, SGB; 6 Oct, SF; Nov, SF; 1988: Jan, SB; Feb, SB; Mar, SF; Apr, SB; May, SB; Ch, G

Elizabeth Gray
Dumbles Cottage, Woodend La, Awre, Glos GI14 1EP
Paintings of rhododendrons
1987: 27 Oct, SG Gr

Green Brothers (Geebro) Ltd
South Road, Hailsham, East Sussex BN27 3DT
☏ 0323 840771
Teak furniture
1988: Ch

Gregory's Roses
The Rose Gardens, Stapleford, Nottingham NG9 7JA
☏ 0602 395454
Roses
1987: Sept, SF; 1988: Ch, SF

Julia Griffith-Jones
8 Fernlea Rd, London SW12 9RN
Paintings of flowers
1987: Nov, S Gr

Grosfillex (UK) Ltd
10 Chandos Road, London NW10 6NF ☏ 01-965 2268
Plant containers, gdn furniture
1988: Ch

S. E. Gudgeon
The Flowerpot Men, 62 Muncaster Rd, London SW11 6NU ☏ 01-350 2934
Garden design
1988: Ch

Eva Gundersen
3 Campden Grove, London W8
☏ 01-938 2581
Garden design
1988: Ch

Hadlow College of Agriculture & Horticulture
Hadlow, Tonbridge, Kent TN11 0AL ☏ 0732 850551
Composts for interior landscaping
1988: Ch

W. Halliday
RHS Garden, Wisley, Woking, Surrey GU23 6QB
Photos of Wisley Gdn
1988: Jan

Halliday Belgravia Art Florists
16 Halkin Arcade, Lowndes Street, London SW1 8JT
☏ 01-245 9619
Floristry exhibit
1988: Ch

Hallow Horticultural Society
The Heathers, Moseley Rd, Hallow, Worcester WR2 6NH
W'box & H'basket Comp
1988: Ch, B Gr

Halls Traditional Conservatories
Church Road, Paddock Wood Tonbridge, Kent TN12 6EU
☏ 089283 4444
Cederwood conservatory
1988: Ch

Harcostar Ltd
Windover Rd, Huntingdon, Cambs. PE18 7EE
☏ 0480 52323
Plant containers, watering cans etc
1988: Ch

The Hardy Plant Society
The Bell, Whitebrook, Monmouth, Gwent NP5 4TU
☏ 0600 860665
Hardy herbaceous perennials
1987: July, SB; 1988: Ch, SB

Brian Hargreaves
10 Kedleston Drive, Orpington, Kent BR5 2DR
Paintings of plants
1987: Nov, G

R. Harkness & Co Ltd
The Rose Gardens, Hitchin, Herts SG4 0JT ☏ 0462 420204
Roses
1987; Sept, SGF; 1988: Ch, G

Harrods Ltd
Knightsbridge, London SW1X 7XL ☏ 01-730 1234
Professional floristry & house plants
1988: Ch, SGF

Christine Hart-Davies
31 Shaftesbury Rd, Poole, Dorset BH15 2LT
Paintings of mosses, liverworts & lichens
1988: Jan, G

Hatchards
187 Piccadilly, London W1D 9DA ☏ 01-439 9921
Horticultural books
1988: Ch

Haws Elliott Ltd
Rawlings Rd, Smethwick, Warley, West Midlands B67 5AB ☏ 021 420 2494
Watering cans & sprayheads
1988: Ch

William Hayford
26/30 Queen Victoria Street, London EC4 ☏ 01-248 5312
Floristry exhibit
1988: Ch

Hayne-West
Unit 2, Stoneyhills Industrial Estate, Whitchurch, Ross-on-Wye, Hereford HR9 6BX
☏ 0600 890119
Cast metal signs, etc
1988, Ch

Hayters plc
Spellbrook, Bishops Stortford, Herts CM23 4BU
☏ 0279 723444
Lawnmowers
1988, Ch

Hazeldene Nursery
Dean Street, East Farleigh, Kent ME15 0PS ☏ 0622 26248
Violas & pansies
1987: June, SB; July, SB; Aug, SB; 6 Oct, SGF; 27 Oct, SGB; Nov, SB; 1988: Mar, SB; Apr, SGB; May, SGB, Ch, SGF

Richard Heanley
The Forge, St George, Woodmancote Henfield, Sussex BN5 9ST ☏ 0273 492947
Wrought ironwork & furniture
1988: Ch

The Hebe Society
7 Friars Stile Rd, Richmond, Surrey TW10 6NH
Hebes, alpine plants
1987: Sept, SG Lindley

Help The Aged
St James's Walk, London EC1R 0BE ☏ 01-253 0253
Help The Aged Garden
1988: Ch, SF

Henfield (W. Sussex) Flower Club
Claverley, Mill Drive, Henfield, W. Sussex BN5 9RY
Floral arrangements
1988: Ch, SG Gr

Henry Doubleday Research Association
National Centre for Organic Gardening, Ryton on Dunsmore, Coventry CV8 3LG ☏ 0203 303517
The benefits of mulching
1988: Ch

Heptacon Ltd
Suite 500. Chesham Ho, 150 Regent Street, London W1R 5FA
Houseplant database disc
1987: Nov

The Herb Society
77 Great Peter Street, London SW1P 2EZ ☏ 01-222 3634
Publicity
1988: Ch

Herons Bonsai Nursery
Wiremill Lane, Newchapel, Lingfield, Surrey RH7 6HJ
☏ 0343 832 657
Bonsai
1987: Aug, SF; 1988: Ch, G

Heston Floral Club
304 Lionel Rd, Brentford, Middx TW8 9QX
Floral arrangement
1988: Ch, B Gr

Hever Castle
Hever, Edenbridge, Kent TN8 7NG ☏ 0732 865224
Hydrangeas
1988: Ch, SB

Highfield Nurseries
Western Forestry Co Ltd, Whitminster, Gloucester GL2 7PL ☏ 0452-740266
1913 Garden Restored
1988: Ch, G

Helen Hiles
Pyrford Place, Pyrford, Woking, Surrey
Watercolour studies of plants
1987: Nov, S Gr

Helen Hilliard
99 Gales Drive, Three Bridges, Crawley, W. Sussex
Paintings of rhododendrons
1988: Jan, B Gr

Hillier Nurseries (Winchester) Ltd
Ampfield House, Ampfield, Romsey, Hants SO51 9PA
☎ 0794 68733
Trees, shrubs, roses & ground-cover plants
1987: Sept, SGF; 6 Oct, SGF; 27 Oct, SGF; 1988: Jan, SF; Feb, SGB; Mar, SGB; Apr, SGB; Ch, G

Hills Industries Ltd
Pontygwindy Industrial Estate, Caerphilly, Mid-Glam.
CF8 3HU ☎ 0222 883951
Garden sprayers & hose fittings
1988: Ch

Hinckley & District Flower Club
The Gables, Sharnford, Hinckley, Leicester LE10 3PE
Floral arrangement
1988: Ch, S Gr

Kathleen Hindle
Sunnyside, 48 Bull Green Rd, Longwood, Huddersfield, W. Yorks HD3 4XW
Paintings of flowers
1987: 27 Oct, S Gr

Peter Hodgkinson
110 Astbury Rd, London SE15
☎ 01-639 5485
Garden design
1988: Ch

Hoecroft Plants
3 Sheringham Rd, West Beckham, Holt, Norfolk NR25 6PQ
Variegated-leaved plants
1987: Aug, SGB; Sept, SGB; 6–7 Oct, SGB; 27–28 Oct, SF; 1988: May, SB

Holden Clough Nursery
Holden, Bolton-by-Bowland, Clitheroe, Lancs BB7 4PF
☎ 020 07 615
Dwarf shrubs, conifers, alpines & primulas
1987: June, SF; Sept, SGB; 6 Oct, SGF; 1988: Feb, SGB; Mar, SGF; Apr, SF; Ch, SF

Holly Gate Cactus Nursery
Ashington, West Sussex RH20 3BA ☎ 0903 892930
Cacti & succulents
1988: Ch, SGF

Home & Law Publishing Ltd
Greater London House, Hampstead Rd, London NW1 7QQ ☎ 01-388 3171
Horticultural magazines
1988: Ch

Home Meadows Nursery Ltd
Top Street, Martlesham, Woodbridge, Suffolk IP12 4RD ☎ 0394 32419
Hardy plants, Iceland poppies, verbascums, chrysanthemums
1987: 6 Oct, SF; 27 Oct, SGB; 1988: Ch, SF

Homes & Garden Magazine
King's Reach Tower, Stamford Street, London SE1 9LS
☎ 01-261 5678
The Urban Garden
1988: Ch, SF

Honda (UK) Ltd
Power Rd, Chiswick, London W4 5YT ☎ 01-747 1400
Garden machinery
1988: Ch

Honey Brothers Ltd
New Pond Rd, Peasmarsh, Guildford, Surrey GU3 1JR
☎ 0483 61362
Garden tools
1988: Ch

Hoopers of Chichester
14 South Street, Chichester, West Sussex PO19 1EJ
☎ 0243 786343
Floristry exhibit
1988: Ch

Mary-Jane Hopes
38 Larkhill, Wantage, Oxon OX12 8HA ☎ 02357 66793
Garden design
1988: Ch

Hopleys Plants Ltd
Much Hadham, Herts SG10 6BU ☎ 027 984 2509
Shrubs & perennial plants
1987: June, SB; Aug, SGF; Sept, SGB; 6 Oct, SB; 1988: Mar, SB; Apr, SB; Ch, SGB

Hopwood Kay Hopwood Ltd
Tufflink House, Chatburn, Clitheroe, Lancs
☎ 0200 41666
Trellis, fencing, lawn edging, etc
1988: Ch

Horley Fuchsia & Geranium Soc
66 Southlands Ave, Horley, Surrey RH6 8BX
W'box & H'basket Comp
1988: Ch, S Gr

Hortus Journal
c/o David Wheeler, The Nevadd, Rhayader, Powys LD6 5HH
Publicity
1988: Mar; May

House & Garden Magazine
Vogue House, Hanover Square, London W1
☎ 01-499 9080
The Blue & White Garden
1988: Ch, SGB

Hozelock-ASL Ltd
Haddenham, Aylesbury, Bucks HP17 8JD
☎ 0844 291881
Garden watering products
1988: Ch

V. H. Humphrey
8 Howbeck Rd, Arnold, Nottingham NG5 8AD
Irises
1988: May, F

Lucy Huntington
The Garden Forum, Riverside Place, Taunton, Somerset TA1 1JH ☎ 0823 433215
Garden design
1988: Ch

Husqvarna Forest & Garden
(Div of Hyett Adams Ltd), Oldends Lane, Stonehouse, Glos GL10 3SY
☎ 045 382 2382
Mowers, cultivators, etc
1988: Ch

Alan Hutchison Publishing Co Ltd
Studio 9, 27a Pembridge Villas, London W11 3EP
☎ 01-221 0129
Stationery & prints
1988: Ch

Brenda Hyatt Auriculas
1 Toddington Crescent, Bluebell Hill, Chatham, Kent ME5 9QT ☎ 0634 63251
Auriculas
1988: May, SGF; Ch, F

Hydon Nurseries Ltd
Clockbarn Lane, Hydon Heath, Godalming, Surrey GU8 4AZ ☎ 0486-32252
Rhododendrons, azaleas, acers, hostas and enkianthus
1988: Ch, SGF

Ichiyo School of Ikebana
c/o Cherry Trees, 4 Providence Way, Waterbeach, Cambs CB5 9QJ ☎ 0223 862470
Ikebana flower arrangements
1988: Jan, SGB; Ch, G

ICI Garden Products
Woolmead House East, Woolmead Walk, Farnham, Surrey GU9 7UB
☎ 0252 724 525
Problem weeds & an advisory bureau
1988: Ch

Iden Croft Herbs
Frittenden Rd, Staplehurst, Kent TN12 0DH
☎ 0580 891432
Aromatic plants & herbs
1987: Sept, SF; 1988: Ch

Ightham & District Hort Assoc
8 The Close, Tollgate, Borough Grn, Sevenoaks, Kent TN15 8EG
W'box & H'basket Comp
1988: Ch, S Gr

Ilford Horticultural Soc
93 Aldborough Rd, Seven Kings, Ilford, Essex IG3 8HS
W'box & H'basket Comp
1988: Ch, S Gr

Inchbald School of Design
7 Eaton Gate, London SW1
☎ 01-730 5508
Publicity
1988: Ch

W. E. Th. Ingwersen Ltd
Birch Farm Nursery, Gravetye, East Grinstead, West Sussex RH19 4LE ☎ 0342 810236
Rock garden plants & alpines
1987: June, SF; July, SB; Aug, SGB; Sept, SF; 6 Oct, SGB; 27 Oct, SF; Nov, SF; 1988: Jan, SF; Feb, SF; Mar, SGB; Apr, SGF; May, SGF; Ch, SGB

Inhome Ltd
Sharston Rd, Manchester M22 4TH ☎ 061 998 1811
Hoses, sprinklers, planters & sprayers
1988: Ch

The Institute of Groundsmanship
19–23 Church Street, The Agora, Wolverton, Milton Keynes MK12 5LG
☎ 0908 312511
A clinic on lawn care
1988: Ch

Institute of Horticultural Research
East Malling, Maidstone, Kent ME19 6BJ ☎ 0732 843833
Mushroom research
1988: Ch, S Lindley

The Institute of Horticulture
PO Box 313, 80 Vincent Square, London SW1P 2PE
☎ 01-834 4333
Courses and training for careers in horticulture
1988: Ch

Interflora (FTDA) British Unit Ltd
Interflora House, Sleaford, Lincs NG34 7TB
☎ 0509 304141
Professional floristry
1988: Ch, G

International Camellia Soc
Camellia Cottage, Pett Rd, Guestling, E. Sussex TN35 4EZ
Camellias
1988: Apr

Interpret Ltd
Interpret House, Vincent
Lane, Dorking, Surrey
RH4 3YX ☎ 0306 881033
Products for ponds & pools
1988: Ch

**London Borough of
Islington**
Parks Department, 345
Holloway Rd, Islington,
London N7 0RS
☎ 01-607 7331
Garden design
1988: Ch

R. Janssens, BVBA
Mechelse steenweg 388 2500,
Lier, Belgium
☎ 015 31 29 53
Greenhouses
1988: Ch

**Jardine Leisure
Furniture Ltd**
Rosemount Tower, Wallington
Square, Wallington, Surrey
SM6 8RR ☎ 01 669 8265
*Gdn furniture, accessories &
sundries*
1988: Ch

JAR Services
Garden Ho, Tudor Close,
Thorpe Willoughby, Selby
YO8 9NP
Garden holidays
1988: Jan; Feb

Michael Jefferson-Brown
Broadgate, Weston Hills,
Spalding, Lincs PE12 6DQ
☎ 0406 380420
Daffodils; lilies
1987: Sept, SGB; 6 Oct, SGB;
27 Oct, SGF; Nov, SGF; 1988:
Jan, SF; Feb, SGB; Mar, SGB;
Apr, SGB; Ch, SGB, SGF

Jenks & Cattell Ltd
Wednesfield, Wolverhampton
WV11 3PU ☎ 0902 731271
Garden tools
1988: Ch

States of Jersey
Dept of Agriculture, Howard
Davis Farm, Trinity,
Jersey, CI ☎ 0534 61074
Flowers & horticultural produce
1988: Ch, SGF

Eve Johnston
9 Church Walk, Wellesbourne,
Warwickshire CV35 9QT
☎ 0789 842647
Garden design
1988: Ch

C. & K. Jones
Golden Fields Nursery,
Barrow Lane, Tarvin, Chester
CH3 8JF
Roses
1987: Sept, G

Jennie Jowett
West Silchester Hall,
Silchester, Nr Reading, Berks
RG7 2LX
Paintings of irises
1988: Jan, G

Paula Joyce
63 Fairdene Rd, Coulsdon,
Surrey CR3 1RJ
Paintings of flowers & fruit
1988: Feb, SG Gr; Ch

Zowie Keating
The Studio, 19 Rosparc,
Probus, Truro, Cornwall
TR2 4TJ
Drawings of British fungi
1988: Jan, B Gr

Kelways Nurseries
Barrymore, Langport,
Somerset TA10 9SL
☎ 0458 250521
Irises; paeonies; daffodils
1988: Mar, F; Apr, SB; Ch,
SGF, G

Mrs M. Kennedy-Scott
Beacon Hill Cottages,
Thorpness, Leiston, Suffolk
IP16 4PE
Pressed-flower pictures
1987: Sept

**The Royal Borough of
Kensington & Chelsea**
Directorate of Engineering &
Works Section, 37 Pembroke
Road, London W8 6PW
☎ 01-373 6099
*Tropical & sub-tropical plants,
bedding plants*
1987: Nov, G, SB; 1988: Ch,
SGF

**Lynette Carrington
Kerslake**
35 Nightingale Drive,
Towcester, Northants
NN12 7RA
Paintings of violas
1988: Jan, S Gr

Clico Kingsbury
Dadbrook House, Cuddington,
Aylesbury, Bucks HP18 8AG
☎ 0844 290129
Garden design
1988: Ch

**Kings Park and Botanic
Garden**
West Perth, Western Australia
Conospermum – smoke bushes
1988: Ch

**Kirstenbosch Botanical
Gardens**
c/o Corinnes, 3 Stoke Parade,
Stoke Rd, Gosport, Hants
☎ 0705 580034

*Flowers & foliages of South
Africa*
1988: Ch. G
75th Anniversary of the Gardens
1988: Ch

Knap Hill Nursery Ltd
Barrs Lane, Knaphill, Woking,
Surrey GU21 2JW
☎ 04867 81212
Rhododendrons, azaleas, etc
1988: Ch, SGF

Douglas G. Knight
Wayside, 44 West Lane,
Freshfield, Formby, Lancs
L37 7BB ☎ 07048-72880
The Rock & Water Garden
1988: Ch, G

L. F. Knight Ltd
Reigate Heath, Reigate, Surrey
RH2 9RF ☎ 0737 244811
*Summerhouses, statuary &
vases*
1988: Ch

Knight Terrace Pots
West Orchard, Shaftesbury,
Dorset SP7 6LJ
☎ 0258 72685
Garden stoneware
1988: Ch

Knowle Nets
20 East Road, Bridport, Dorset
DT6 4NX ☎ 0308 24342
Fruit cages & vegetable supports
1988: Ch

Mrs Stella Lamb
c/o 22 Northcote Ave,
Berrylands, Surbiton, Surrey
KT5 9BZ
*Paintings of sarracenias &
orchids*
1987: 27 Oct, S Gr

The Landscape Institute
12 Carlton House Terrace,
London SW1Y 5AH
☎ 01-839 4044
*Careers; advice on using
consultants*
1988: Ch

Landsmans Bookshop Ltd
Buckenhill, Bromyard,
Hereford
☎ 0885 83420
Horticultural books
1988: Ch

Lanes of Teignmouth
17 Station Rd, Teignmouth,
TQ14 8PE ☎ 06267 2839
Floristry exhibit
1988: Ch

Langdon (London) Ltd
Ickford, Aylesbury, Bucks
HP18 9JJ ☎ 08447 337
Garden sundries
1988: Ch

Laurella
26 Briton Crescent,
Sanderstead, Surrey CR2 0JF
☎ 01-657 5856
Tropical plants
1988: Ch, SGF

Mark Laurence
The Studio, 37a Littlehampton
Rd, Worthing, West Sussex
BN13 1QJ ☎ 0903 692093
Garden design
1988: Ch

**The Lavers & District
Hort Soc**
1 Green Lane Cottages,
Threshers Bush, Nr Harlow,
Essex CM17 0NR
A herb garden
1988: Ch, S Gr

Lavinia Learmont
36 Lewisham Pk, London
SE13 6QZ
Paintings of Liliaceae
1988: Jan, SG Gr

A. T. Lee & Co Ltd
Regency House, 2 Bedford
Row, Worthing, West Sussex
BN11 3DR ☎ 0903 210225
Plant hangers
1988: Ch

E. B. LeGrice (Roses) Ltd
North Walsham, Norfolk
Roses
1987: Sept, SGB

Lely (UK) Ltd
Station Rd, St Neots, Cambs
PE19 1QH ☎ 0480 76971
Lawn mowers & garden tractors
1988: Ch

Arabella Lennox-Boyd
45 Moreton Terrace, London
SW1V 2NY ☎ 01 931 9995
Garden design
1988: Ch

**Lewes & District
Garden Soc**
11 Berkeley Row, Lewes,
E. Sussex BN7 1EU
W'box & H'basket Comp
1988: Ch, S Gr

Lewes Road Sawmills
Church Road, Scaynes Hill,
West Sussex RH17 7NZ
☎ 044 486 451
Garden buildings
1988: Ch

Lincluden Nursery
59 Freemantle Rd, Bagshot,
Surrey GU19 5LY
☎ 0276 74311
Dwarf & slow-growing conifers
1987: Sept, SB; 6 Oct, SB; 27
Oct, SB; 1988: Jan, SB; Feb,
SB; Apr, SF; Ch, SB

Link Stakes Ltd
Upper Boddington, Daventry,
Northants NN11 6DL
☎ 0327 60329
Link-stakes, cloches & trellis
1988: Ch

**Liphook Floral Decoration
Soc**
Timbers, 68 Kingswood Firs,
Grayshott, Hindhead, Surrey
GU26 6ER
Floral arrangement
1988: Ch, B Gr

**Michael Littlewood
Associates**
Mission House, Old Coach Rd,
Cross, Axbridge, Somerset
BS26 2EE ☎ 0934 732430
Garden design
1988: Ch

Lloyds of Kew
9 Mortlake Terrace, Kew,
Richmond, Surrey TW9 3DT
☎ 01-940 2512
Gardening & botanical books
1988: Ch

Lockside Nursery
160 Thames Rd, Crayford,
Kent DA1 4LY
*Greenhouse & conservatory
plants*
1987: July, SB; Aug, SB

C. S. Lockyer
Lansbury, 70 Henfield Rd,
Coalpit Heath, Bristol
BS17 2UZ ☎ 0454 772219
*Fuchsias, greenh'se &
conservatory plants*
1987: July, SB; Sept, SF; 1988:
May, SF; Ch, SF

**London Association for the
Blind**
14–16 Verney Rd, London
SE16 3DZ ☎ 01-732 8771
*A Garden for the Blind or
Partially Sighted*
1988: Ch, SB

London Wildlife Trust
80 York Way, London N1 9AG
Publicity
1987: July

Longmans Ltd
46 Holborn Viaduct, London
EC1 N2PB ☎ 01-583 1440
*Floral & indoor plant
arrangements*
1987: Sept, F; 1988: Ch, SB

Longstock Park Gardens
Stockbridge, Hants SO20 6EH
Moisture-loving plants
1987: June, SGF; 1988: May,
G

Suzanne Lucas
Ladymead, Mere, Warminster,
Wilts BA12 6HQ
Paintings of fungi
1988: Feb, G

McBeans Orchids Ltd
Cooksbridge, Lewes, Sussex
☎ 0273 400 228
Orchids
1988: Ch, G

Mary McMurtie
Balbithan Ho, Kintore,
Inverurie, Aberdeenshire
AB5 0UQ
Paintings of roses
1987; Nov, Gr

**Maidenhead Floral
Arrangement Soc**
Ringwood, Dunt La, Hurst,
Reading, Berks
RG10 0TA
Floral arrangement
1988: Ch, S Gr

Maidstone Hort Soc
20 Yeoman Way, Bearsted,
Maidstone, Kent ME15 8PH
W'box & H'basket Comp
1988: Ch, B Gr

**Maidstone Hort Soc Floral
Art Group**
52 Valley Drive, Loose,
Maidstone, Kent ME15 6TL
Floral arrangement
1988: Ch, B Gr

W. G. & D. M. Maishman
'Niton', Parkers Rd, Cotton,
Stowmarket, Suffolk
1P14 4QQ
Sweet peas
1987: Aug, SGF

Hester Mallin
82 Sandall House, Hewlett Rd,
London E3 5NB
☎ 01-981 2735
Garden design
1988: Ch

Mancs Bonsai Nursery
3 Meadow Close, Haughton
Grn, Denton, Manchester
M34 1QD
Bonsai
1988: May, SB

M & R Plants
73 Cecil Avenue, Hornchurch,
Essex RM11 2NA
☎ 04024 73153
*Herbaceous plants, trees &
shrubs, alpines*
1987: June, F; Sept, F; Nov,
SGF; 1988: Jan, SF; Feb, SB;
Mar, SB; Apr, SB; Ch, SF

S. E. Marshall & Co Ltd
Regal Rd, Wisbech, Cambs.
PE13 2RF ☎ 022023 2270
Vegetables
1988: Ch, S Knightian

Marshalls Mono Ltd
Southowram, Halifax, West
Yorkshire HX3 9SY
☎ 0422 57155
Paving, walling & furniture
1988: Ch

Marston & Langinger Ltd
Hall Staithe, Fakenham,
Norfolk NR21 9BW
☎ 0328 4933
Conservatory & accessories
1988: Ch

Marston Exotics
Hurst Lodge, Martock,
Somerset
☎ 0935 822352
Carnivorous plants
1988: Ch, SGF

Rosemary Mason
34 Bhylls La, Merry Hill,
Wolverhampton WV2 8DR
Paintings of poppies
1988: Feb, S Gr

Desmond Masters
32 Mount Ephraim Rd,
London SW16 1LW
Paintings of plants & flowers
1987: Nov, Gr

John Mattock Ltd
The Rose Nurseries, Nuneham
Courtenay, Oxford OX9 9PY
☎ 086 738265
Roses
1987: July, SGF; Sept, SGF;
1988: Ch, G

**Robert Mattock Container
Shrubs**
Lodge Hill, Abingdon, Oxford
OX14 2JD
Rose trees in containers
1987: Sept, SB

**Maxicrop Garden Products
Ltd**
Bridge House, 101 High Street,
Tonbridge, Kent TN9 1DR
☎ 0772 366710
*Seaweed extract & organic
compost*
1988: Ch

Meadow Herbs Ltd
Upper Clatford, Andover,
Hants SP11 7LW
☎ 0264 52998
*Pot pourri & the use of aromatic
herbs*
1988: Ch

Lindsay Megarrity
16 The Keep, London
SE3 0AF
Botanical paintings
1987: 27 Oct, G

**Merrist Wood Agricultural
College**
Worplesdon, Nr Guildford,
Surrey ☎ 0483-232424
A Secret Refuge
1988: Ch, G
Courtyard garden
1988: Ch, SG Gr
*Careers & training in
horticulture*
1988: Ch

Metpost Ltd
Mardy Rd, Cardiff CF3 8EQ
☎ 0222 777877
*Garden supports & chain link
fencing*
1988: Ch

Kenneth Midgley
Corner House, Burstall,
Ipswich IP8 3DN
☎ 047 387 337
Garden design
1988: Ch

Paul Miles
Castlemaine, Ufford Place,
Ufford, Woodbridge, Suffolk
IP13 6DR ☎ 0394 460 437
Garden design
1988: Ch

Judith Milne
20 Colemans Moor Rd,
Woodley, Reading, Berks
RG5 4DL
Paintings of flowers
1987: Nov, Gr

Mrs P. Milosevic
16 Somers Cres, London
W2 2PN
Pressed-flower collage
1987: 27–28 Oct

**Ministry of Agriculture,
Fisheries & Food**
Government Buildings,
Garrison Lane, Chessington,
Surrey KT9 2LW
☎ 01-397 9121
The Plant Health Inspectorate
1988: Ch

Minsterstone Ltd
Station Rd, Ilminster,
Somerset TA19 9AS
☎ 04605 2277
*Garden ornaments, balustrading
& paving*
1988: Ch

Lorna Minton
53 Amberley Drive, Twyford,
Reading, Berks RG10 9BX
*Paintings of wild flowers &
plants*
1988: Jan, SG Gr

John Moate
7 West End Terrace,
Winchester, Hants SO22 5EN
☎ 0962 53221
Garden design
1988: Ch

Monk Sherborne Hort Soc
Rook Hill, Monk Sherborne,
Nr Basingstoke, Hampshire
RG26 6HL
*W'box & H'basket Comp;
courtyard garden*
1988: Ch, SG Gr, SG Gr

Monks Risborough Hort Soc
Trefloyne, Westfields, Whiteleaf, Aylesbury, Bucks HP17 0LH
W'box & H'basket Comp
1988: Ch, SG Gr

Carol Moore
420 London Rd, Hilsea, Portsmouth PO2 9LB
☏ 0705 699145
Floristry exhibit
1988: Ch, SG Gr

Peter Moore
Tile Barn Nursery, Standen Street, Iden Green, Beneden, Kent TN17 4LB
Cyclamen species
1987: Sept, SGF

John Moreland
47 Wickham Rd, Brockley, London SE4 ☏ 01-691 5599
Garden design
1988: Ch

Glyn Morgan
28 Priory Rd, High Wycombe, Bucks HP13 6SL
Paintings of flowers
1988: Jan, S Gr

G. D. Mountfield Ltd
Reform Rd, Maidenhead, Berks. SL6 8DQ
☏ 0628 39161
Garden tractors, mowers, trimmers
1988: Ch

Muck & Magic Organic Supplies
c/o Derek R. Bird, 60 Wood Lane, Reading, Berks RG4 9SL
Organic garden supplies
1987: 6–7 Oct; 1988: Jan, May

Ken Muir
Honeypot Farm, Rectory Rd, Weeley Heath, Clacton-on-Sea, Essex CO16 9BJ
☏ 0255 830181
Soft fruits
1987: July, S Hogg; Aug, Hogg; Sept, Hogg; Nov, Hogg; 1988: Ch, G
Stacking pots & sundries
1988: Ch

Susan M. Muir
Penylan, Aberthin, Cowbridge, S. Glam CF7 7HB
☏ 04463 2414
Garden design
1988: Ch

The Museum of Garden History
Tradescant Trust, St Mary-at-Lambeth, Lambeth Palace Rd, London SE1 7JU
Publicity
1987: May; Aug; 1988: Mar; Apr

National Association of Flower Arrangement Societies
21 Denbigh Street, London SW1V 2HF ☏ 01-828 5145
Floral arrangements
1987: July, SGB; Sept, SGF; 1988: Feb, SF; Ch, G

National Begonia Society
c/o Mr R. G. Hopkins, 9 Dukes Ride, Silchester, Reading, Berks RG7 2PX
Society's competition
1987: Aug

National Council for the Conservation of Plants & Gardens
Cambridgeshire Group, Hardwicke House, Fen Ditton, Cambridge, Cambs CB5 8TF
☏ 01-633 6347
Herbaceous and woody plants
1987: Sept, S Lindley; 1988: Ch, SGB

National Farmers' Union/British Growers Look Ahead Ltd
Agriculture House, Knightsbridge, London SW1X 7NJ ☏ 01-235 5077
Fruit, flowers & vegetables
1988: Ch, G

National Federation of Women's Institutes
39 Eccleston Street, London SW1W 9NT ☏ 01-730 7212
A Countrywoman's Garden
1988: Ch, G; Wilkinson Sword Trophy

National Gardens Scheme Charitable Trust
57 Lower Belgrave Street, London SW1W 0LR
☏ 01-730 0359
Publicity for the Scheme
1988: Mar

National Institute of Agricultural Botany
Huntingdon Rd, Cambridge, Cambs. CB3 0LE
☏ 0223 276381
Old and new varieties of vegetables
1988: Ch

The National Trust
36 Queen Anne's Gate, London SW1H 9AS ☏ 01-222 9251
Information bureau
1988: Ch

National Trust for Scotland
Brodick Castle, Brodick, Isle of Arran KA27 8DE
Rhododendrons, etc
1987: March, SGB

The National Trust for Scotland
5 Charlotte Square, Edinburgh EH2 4DU ☏ 031 226 5922
Information bureau
1988: Ch

National Westminster Bank plc
6th Floor, Finsbury Square, 101–117 Finsbury Pavement, London EC2A 1EH
☏ 01-726 1000
Banking service
1988: Ch

Neill Tools Ltd
Handsworth Rd, Sheffield S183 9BR ☏ 0742 449911
Garden tools
1988: Ch

Netlon Ltd
Kelly Street, Blackburn, Lancs BB2 4PJ ☏ 0254 62431
Garden nets, mesh, fencing
1988: Ch

C. Newberry & Son
Bulls Green Nursery, Knebworth, Herts SG3 6SA
☏ 043 879 650
Garnette & miniature roses
1987: June, SB; Aug, SB; Sept, SB; 6 Oct, SGB; 27 Oct, SB; Nov, F 1988: Feb, SF; Mar, SF; Apr F; May; Ch, SF

Josephine Newman
Sion Cottage, Sion Rd, Twickenham, Middx TW1 3DR
Paintings of flowers
1987: Nov, S Gr

Elisabeth Norman
Elms Farm Cottage, Rempstone, Loughborough, Leics
Paintings of flowers
1987: Nov, S Gr

Norman Miniatures
3 West Dene Drive, Brighton, Sussex BN1 5HE
☏ 0273 506476
Bonsai
1987: Sept, SB; 27 Oct, SF; 1988: Ch, SF

Nortene Ltd
Linenhall House, Stanley Street, Chester CH1 2LR
☏ 0244 46193
Nets, meshes & water retention materials
1988: Ch

North Middlesex Federation Garden Club
83 Mount Drive, North Harrow, Middx HA2 7RW
W'box & H'basket Comp
1988: Ch, S Gr

Notcutts Garden Centres
Cumberland St, Woodbridge, Suffolk IP12 4AF
☏ 039 43 3344
Garden furniture
1988: Ch

Notcutts Landscape Ltd
Cumberland Street, Woodbridge, Suffolk IP12 4AF ☏ 039 43 3344
Garden design
1988: Ch

Notcutts Nurseries Ltd
Cumberland St, Woodbridge, Suffolk IP12 4AF
☏ 039 43 3344
Ornamental trees, shrubs & plants
1987: Sept, SGB; 1988, Ch, G

Ryl Nowell
c/o Exteriors, Wilderness, Wilderness Lane, Hadlow Down, East Sussex
☏ 082-585 552
A Cottage in the Country 1913
1988: Ch, SGF

Nutfield Nurseries
Crab Hill La, South Nutfield, Redhill, Surrey RH1 5PG
Cacti & succulents
1987: Sept, SGB; 27 Oct, G

Mr W. Nye
34 Lawrence Ave, Stevenage, Herts SG1 3JX
Saxifraga 'Tumbling Waters'
1987: June, SGB

Oakleigh Nurseries
Monkwood, Alresford, Hants SO24 0HB ☏ 096277 3344
Fuchsias & pelargoniums
1988: Ch, SGF

Dr Henry Oakley
London SE19
Lycastes & Angulocastes
1987: June, SF

Office National des Debouches Agricoles et Horticoles
Place de Louvain 4, Btes 6 & 7, 1000 Bruxelles, Belgium
Ornamental & house plants
1988: Ch, G

O. Ohanians
53A Mansfield Rd, London NW3
Cacti & succulents
1987: June, SF; Sept

Ohara School of Ikebana
26 West Sq, London SE11
Floral arrangements
1988: May, SGB

Oldbury Nurseries
Brissenden Green, Bethersden, Kent TN26 3BJ ☏ 023 382 416
Fuchsias
1987: Aug, SGF; 1988: Ch, G

Old Oak Florist
Wood Lane Garden Centre,
Iver, Bucks
Florist's sundries
1987: 6–7 Oct; 27–28 Oct

Orchid Society of Great Britain
c/o 120 Crofton Rd, Orpington,
Kent BR6 8HZ ☎ 0689 29777
Orchids
1987, Nov; 1988: Ch, SGF

Orchid Sundries
Rosetree Farm, 29a Nine Mile
Ride, Wokingham, Berks
RG11 4QD
☎ 0734 733883
Orchid sundries
1987: July; Aug; 6–7 Oct;
27–28 Oct; Nov; 1988: Jan;
May; Ch

Otley College of Agriculture & Horticulture
Otley, Ipswich, Suffolk
IP5 9EY ☎ 047 385 543
Publicity for courses
1988: Ch

Oxfam
58 St John's Hill, London
SW11 1VJ ☎ 01-585 0220
Oxfam's work in promoting horticulture
1988: Ch

Valerie Oxley
Brookside, Kidd La, Firebeck,
Worksop, Notts S81 8JZ
Paintings of violas
1988: Feb, S Gr

James Paine (Florists)
6/8 The Avenue, Queens Rd,
Hastings, East Sussex
☎ 0424 421823
Floristry exhibit
1988: Ch

Pamal
The Cottage, Sproxton,
Melton Mowbray, Leics
LE14 4QS ☎ 0476 860266
Garden furniture
1988: Ch

Pan Products
8/9 Faraday Rd, Bicester Road
Industrial Estate, Aylesbury,
Bucks HP19 3RY
☎ 0296 433860
Garden netting & fencing
1988: Ch

Paradise Centre
Lamarsh, Bures, Suffolk
CO8 5EX ☎ 07829 449
Plants for shady conditions, bulbous & herbaceous plants
1987: June, SF; July, SF; Aug,
SGB; Sept, SF; 6 Oct, SGB;
27 Oct, SGB; 1988: Mar, SB;
Apr, SB; May SGF; Ch, SF

Mike Park
351 Sutton Common Rd,
Sutton, Surrey SM3 9HZ
Secondhand books
1987: July; Aug; Sept; 6–7 Oct;
27–28 Oct; 1988: Jan; Feb;
Mar; Apr; May

The Pavilion
51 Brookfield, Highgate West
Hill, London N6 6AT
☎ 01-341 2067
Vases, planters, jardinieres, etc
1988: Ch

T. Pearce
241 Staines Road West,
Sunbury-on-Thames,
Middlesex TW16 7BH
☎ 0932 786958
Garden design
1988: Ch

Peper Harrow School
Godalming, Surrey GU8 6BG
Plants, produce grown at PH
1987: Nov, SGB

Pershore College/Wyevale Garden
Avonbank, Worcs WR10 3JP
☎ 0386-552443
Encompassing Britain into the 1990's
1988: Ch, SGB
Courtyard garden
1988: Ch, SG Gr

Nigel L. Philips
18a Cliffe High Street, Lewes,
East Sussex BN7 2AH
☎ 0273 474948
Garden design
1988: Ch

Phostrogen Ltd
Corwen, Clwyd LL21 0EE
☎ 0490 2662
Plant foods & insecticides
1988: Ch

Pinelog Products Ltd
Riverside Works, Bakewell,
Derbys DE4 1GJ
☎ 062 981 4481
Chalets & summerhouses
1988: Ch

Pinkneys Green Floral Club
Tudor Ho, The Causeway, off
Hibbert St, Bray on Thames,
Maidenhead, Berks
Floral arrangement
1988: Ch, S Gr

Plantpak Ltd
Mundon, Maldon, Essex
CM9 6NT ☎ 0621 740140
Garden sundries
1988: Ch

PLM Power Products
Unit 8, Birchbrook Industrial
Park, Birchbrook Lane,
Shenstone, Lichfield, Staffs
WS14 0DJ ☎ 0543 481481
Powered tools & accessories
1988: Ch

Potash Nursery
Hawkwell, Hockley, Essex
SS5 4JN ☎ 0702 202403
Fuchsias, cinerarias, cyclamen, polyanthus, etc
1987: June, SF; July SGB;
Aug, SGB; Sept, SGB; 6 Oct,
SF; 27 Oct, SB; Nov, SGB;
1988: Jan, SGB; Feb, SF; Mar;
Apr, SGB; May, SF; Ch, SGF

Helen Potter
Ivy Cottage, Grove Rd,
Wallasey, Wirral L45 3HF
Paintings of hedgerow plants
1988: Feb, Gr

Potterton & Martin/Peter Orme Landscapes
The Cottage Nursery,
Moortown Rd, Nettleton,
Lincs. LN7 6HX
☎ 0472 851792
Rock garden & alpine plants, shrubs & conifers
1987: Sept, SGF; 6 Oct, SGB;
1988: Feb, SGB; Mar, SGF;
Apr, G; Ch, G

Katherine Ann Prentice
Brookholes, Duns,
Berwickshire TD11 3RL
Paintings of rhododendrons
1988: Jan, B Gr

Primrose Hill Nurseries
Asmall Lane, Halsall,
Nr Ormskirk, West Lancs
☎ 0704-840062
A Rock and Water Garden
1988: Ch, SF

The Print Room
37 Museum Street, London
WC1A 1LP ☎ 01-430 0159
Botanical engravings & lithographs
1988: Ch

Ida Proffit
13 Allerton Drive, Liverpool
L18 6HH
Paintings of wild flowers of Spain
1988: Jan, B Gr

Pulloxhill Gardeners
23 Tyburn La, Pulloxhill,
Bedford MK45 5HG
W'box & H'basket Comp
1988: Ch, B Gr

Quality Irrigation
Interchange House, Tongham
Rd, Aldershot, Hants
GU12 4XF ☎ 0252 28017
Garden watering products
1988: Ch

Rainford Flower Club
Muncaster Ho, Cross Pit La,
Rainford, Merseyside
WA11 8AJ
Floral arrangement
1988: Ch, B Gr

Ramparts Nursery
Bakers Lane, Colchester, Essex
CO4 5BB ☎ 0206 852056
Grey foliage plants, pinks & alpines
1987: June, SGF; July, SGF;
Aug, SGB; Sept, SGF; 6 Oct,
SGB; 1988: Feb, SB; Mar, SF;
Apr, SF; May, SGB; Ch, SGB

Rapitest
London Rd, Corwen, Clwyd
LL21 0DR ☎ 0490 2804
Soil testing & plant care equipment
1988: Ch

Rathowen Daffodils
'Knowehead', Dergmoney,
Omagh, Co Tyrone, N. Ireland
Daffodils
1988: Apr, G

University of Reading
Dept of Horticulture, Earley
Gate, Reading, Berks
RG6 2AU ☎ 0734 875123
'Let Us Spray!'
1988: Ch

Rearsby Roses Ltd
Melton Rd, Rearsby, Leicester
LE7 8YP ☎ 0533 601211
Roses
1988: Ch, SF

Reeves The Florist
64 Victoria Street, Bristol
BS1 6DE ☎ 0272 214067
Floristry exhibit
1988: Ch, SG Gr, Ring & Brymer Trophy

Renaissance Bronzes Ltd
Suite 78, Kent House, 87
Regent Street, London W1
☎ 01-439 7091
Bronze statuary
1988: Ch

Renaissance Casting
19 Cranford Rd, Coventry
CV5 8JF ☎ 0203 27275
Lead statuary & ornaments
1988: Ch

G. Reuthe Ltd
Crown Point Nursery,
Sevenoaks Rd, Ightham,
Sevenoaks, Kent
TN15 0HB ☎ 0732 810694
Rhododendrons, azaleas, shrubs, trees & ground-cover plants
1988: Ch, G

The Rhododendron Group
c/o Mr John Fox, Holmwood
Ho, Glemore Rd,
Crowborough, Sussex
TN6 1TN
Rhododendron species
1988: May, SB

RHS Enterprises Ltd
RHS Garden, Wisley, Woking,
Surrey GU23 6QB
☏ 0483 224234
*Horticultural books &
stationery*
1987: June; July; Aug; Sept;
6–7 Oct; 27–28 Oct; 1988: Mar;
Apr; May; Ch

RHS Lily Group
c/o James Compton, The
Chelsea Physic Garden, Royal
Hospital Rd, London SW3
Lilies
1987: July, G

Richards & Hughes
153 Seymour Place,
London W1
☏ 01-723 5881
Floristry exhibit
1988: Ch

Alexandra Ellen Robb
3 Onslow Ave Mans, Onslow
Ave, Richmond, Surrey
Paintings of ivies
1987: Nov, Gr

Stephen Roberts Florists
Llanrhydd Mill, Ruthin,
Clwyd ☏ 082 42 5179
Floristry exhibit
1988: Ch

W. Robinson & Son Ltd
Sunny Bank, Forton, Nr
Preston, Lancs PR3 0BN
Vegetables
1987: Sept, G

Robinsons Gardens Ltd
Rushmore Hill Nurseries,
Knockholt, Sevenoaks, Kent
TN14 7NN
*Trees, shrubs, dwarf conifers,
ericas*
1987: Sept, SGB; 6–7 Oct, SF;
27–28 Oct, SF; 1988: Feb,
SGB; Mar, SF

Robinsons Hardy Plants
Greencourt Nurseries,
Crockenhill, Swanley, Kent
BR8 8HD
Alpine rock plants
1987: June, SB; July, SF; Aug,
SF; Sept, SB

**Robinsons of
Winchester Ltd**
Robinson House, Winnall
Winchester, Hants SO23 8LH
☏ 0962 61777
*Greenhouses, conservatories &
accessories*
1988: Ch

Rock UK
Penyfan Industrial Estate,
Newbridge, Gwent NP1 4AH
☏ 0495 247278
Powered equipment
1988: Ch

Peter Rogers
Northdowns, Titsey Rd,
Limpsfield, Surrey
RH8 0DF ☏ 0883 715818
Countryside Glass Garden
1988: Ch, G

Peter Rogers & Associates
Northdowns, Titsey Rd,
Limpsfield, Surrey RH8 0DF
☏ 0883 715818
Garden design
1988, Ch

Rolawn Ltd
Elvington, York YO4 5AR
☏ 0904 85 661
Lawn turf
1988: Ch

**Romilt Landscape Design &
Construction Ltd**
North Wyke Farm, Guildford
Rd, Normandy, Surrey
☏ 0483 811933
Garden design
1988: Ch

Room Outside Ltd
Goodwood Gardens,
Goodwood
Chichester, West Sussex
PO18 0QB
☏ 0243 776563
Conservatory
1988: Ch

Rosedale Engineers Ltd
9 Bridlington Rd, Hunmanby,
Filey, North Yorks YO14 0LR
☏ 0723 890 303
Solardomes
1988: Ch

Rose-Marie
73 Cecil Ave, Hornchurch,
Essex RM11 2NA
Dried-flower arrangements
1988: Apr; May

Rosemary Roses
The Nurseries, Stapleford
Lane, Toton, Beeston, Notts
NG9 5FH
☏ 0602 491100
Roses
1987: June, SGB; July, SGF;
Aug, SGB; Sept, SGB; 1988,
Ch, SGF

Roses du Temps Passé
Woodlands House, Stretton,
Stafford ST19 9LG
☏ 0785 840217
Old-fashioned roses
1987: July, SGB; Aug, SGB;
Sept, SF; 1988: Ch, SGB

Rougham Hall Nurseries
Bury St Edmunds, Suffolk
IP30 9LZ ☏ 0359 70577
*Hardy perennials, delphiniums,
Iceland poppies, myosotis*
1987: June, SB; July, SF; Aug,
SF; Sept, SGB; 6 Oct, SGB;
27 Oct, F; 1988: Jan, SGB; Feb,
SGB; Mar, SF; Apr, SB; May,
F; Ch, SGB

**Royal Botanic Gardens,
Kew, Richmond, Surrey
TW9 3AB**
Curtis's Botanical Magazine
1987: Sept

**The Royal Horticultural
Society**
Wisley, Woking, Surrey
GU23 6QB ☏ 0483 224234
*Soft fruit & apples; lesser-
grown vegetables; red
delphiniums; Advisory Bureau*
1987: July; 6–7 Oct; 1988: Ch

**Royal London Society for
the Blind**
105–109 Salusbury Rd,
London NW6 6RH
☏ 01-624 8844
Planters, trays & baskets
1988: Ch

**The Royal National Rose
Society**
Chiswell Green, St Albans,
Herts AL2 3NR
☏ 0727 50461
*Publicity & promotion for the
Society*
1988: May; Ch

The Royal Parks
The Royal Parks Division
Training Centre, Eltham
Palace Court Yard, London
SE9 5QE ☏ 01-859 4959
Woodland & herbaceous plants
1988: Ch, G

**Royal Society for Nature
Conservation**
The Green, Nettleham, Lincs
LN2 2NR ☏ 0522 752326
Display of wild flowers
1988: Ch

Charles Russell
5 Clarendon Drive, London
SW15 1AW ☏ 01-788 5571
Antiquarian prints & books
1988: Ch

**Rutland Floral
Arrangement Soc**
9 Hudson Close, Oakham,
Rutland, Leics LE15 6NA
Floral arrangement
1988: Ch, SG Gr

**Ruxley Manor Garden
Centre**
Maidstone Rd, Sidcup, Kent
DA14 5BQ ☏ 01-300 0084
Garden furniture
1988: Ch

**Saintpaulia &
Houseplant Soc**
c/o Mrs Potter, Show
Secretary, Graystone,
Brighton Rd, Godalming,
Surrey GU7 1PL
Society's competition
1987: Aug, S Lindley

**Samlesbury Bonsai
Nursery**
Potters Lane, Samlesbury,
Preston PR5 0UE
☏ 077 477 213
Bonsai
1987: 6 Oct, SGB; 1988; Ch,
SGB

Sandhurst Gardening Club
20 Brook Ave, Weybourne,
Farnham, Surrey GU9 9HB
W'box & H'basket Comp
1988: Ch, SG Gr

Sandvik Saws & Tools UK
Manor Way, Halesowen,
West Midlands B62 8QZ
☏ 021 550 4700
Garden tools
1988: Ch

**Sandwell Metropolitan
Borough Council**
Recreation & Amenities Dept,
Hales La, Smethwick, Warley,
West Midlands B67 6RS
W'Box & H'basket Comp
1988: Ch, S Gr

Scea Pepinières Jean Rey
Route de Carpentras,
84150 Jonquieres, France
Mediterranean plants
1988: Ch, SGB

Sara Anne Schofield
40 Grove Wood Hill,
Coulsdon,
Surrey CR3 2EL
Paintings of irises
1987: 27 Oct, G

Scotts of Eastbourne
5 Gildredge Rd,
Eastbourne BN21 4RB
☏ 0323 20501
Floristry exhibit
1988: Ch

**Scotts Nurseries
(Merriott) Ltd**
The Royal Nurseries,
Merriott,
Somerset TA16 5PL
*Trees, shrubs, climbers,
herbaceous perennials*
1987: July, SB; Sept, F; 27–28
Oct, SGB; 1988: Feb, SB; Mar,
SGB; Apr, SGB

Peter Seabrook
212A Baddow Rd,
Chelmsford, Essex
Chrysanthemums
1987: 27–28 Oct, SGB

Cherida Seago
Danson House,
Danson Park,
Bexley Hearth,
Kent DA6 8HL
☏ 01–304 3761
Garden design
1988: Ch

Sealand Nurseries Ltd
Sealand, Chester CH1 6BA
☏ 0244 880 501
Astilbes, paeonies & lilies; roses
1988: Ch, G, G

Serac Ltd
Nyton Rd, Aldingbourne,
Chichester, West Sussex
PO20 6TU
Greenhouses & garden rooms
1987: Aug; Nov; 1988: May; Ch

**Shades Garden Design &
Construction Ltd**
71 Frog Lane, West Overton,
Marlborough,
Wilts SN8 4ER
☏ 01–304 3761
Garden design
1988: Ch

Susan Sharkey
6 Cleveland Avenue,
Chiswick, London W4 1SN
☏ 01–995 7977
Garden design
1988: Ch

Judith Sharpe
35 Rudloe Road,
London SW12 0DR
☏ 01–673 2437
Garden design
1988: Ch

Annie Shaw
26 Park Road, East Molesley,
Surrey KT8 9LE
☏ 01–979 6612
Garden design
1988: Ch

**Heather Shaw Floral
Specialists**
98 Wide Bargate,
Boston, Lincs PE21 6SE
☏ 0205 64990
Floristry exhibit
1988: Ch

Joanna Sheen Ltd
Victoria Farm,
Stokeinteignhead, Newton
Abbot, Devon TQ12 4QN
☏ 0626 872405
Pressed-flower pictures
1988: Ch

**Sheffield Park Gardens &
The National Trust**
Nr Uckfield, Sussex
Conifers
1987: Nov, G

Ann Shelley-Lloyd
5 Hill Ct, Main Rd, Romford,
Essex RM1 3DA
Paintings of orchid species
1988: Feb, G

Sherrards
Wantage Rd, Donnington,
Newbury, Berks
Trees, shrubs, hardy plants
1987: June, SB

Silvaperl Products Ltd
PO Box 8, Harrogate,
North Yorks
Composts, hort sundries
1987: 27–28 Oct

Anthony R. Sisson
29 Northwick Ave
Kenton, Harrow,
Middlesex HA3 0AA
Sunrooms, conservatories
1987: Aug; 1988: Jan

Slough Corporation
Town Hall, Slough, SL1 3UQ
☏ 0753 875502
Herbaceous & annual plants
1988: Ch, SGB

Frederick W. Smallwood
48c Castle Hill Ave,
Folkestone,
Kent CT20 2RE
Photographs of wild flowers
1988: Feb, S Gr

Alan C. Smith
127 Leaves Green Rd
Keston, Kent BR2 6DG
*Sempervivums, jovibarbas,
dwarf conifers, alpines*
1987: June, SGB; July, SGB;
Aug, SGB; Sept, SB; 6 Oct, F;
27 Oct, SB; 1988: Mar, SF;
Apr, SB; May, SF

David Smith
3 Golden Cross Road,
Rochford, Essex SS4 3DL
☏ 0702 549161
Bonsai
1988: Ch

Marion Smith
Farm Cottage,
Puttenham, Guildford,
Surrey GU3 1AJ
☏ 0483 810352
Garden sculpture
1988: Ch

P. J. Smith
Chanctonbury Nursery,
Rectory Lane,
Ashington, West Sussex
RH20 3AS ☏ 0903 892870
Alstroemerias
1987: Aug, SGF; 1988: Ch,
SGB

**Société Nationale
d'Horticulture**
Les Amis de Fleurs de
St-Cloud, 25 rue Michel Salles,
92210 St-Cloud, France
Floral arrangement
1988: Ch, S Gr

Society of Floristry
50 Leatherhead Road,
Ashtead, Surrey KT20 2SY
☏ 0932 229730
Careers in Floristry
1988: Ch

Somerford Sheltatrees
Newleage, Great Somerford
Chippenham, Wilts SN15 5EN
☏ 0249 720442
Plant shelters & mulches
1988: Ch

**Somerset College of
Horticulture**
Cannington College,
Cannington,
Bridgwater, Somerset
☏ 0278 652226
Flowering & foliage plants
1988: Ch, SGB

South Leigh Press
The Studio, Lavender Cottage,
Chilcroft Rd, Kingsley Green,
Haslemere, Surrey GU27 3LS
☏ 0428 3459
Botanical prints
1987: Nov; 1988: Ch

**Southampton Borough
Council**
Civic Centre, Southampton,
Hants SO9 4XF
☏ 0703 832746
*Plants for woodland garden
conditions*
1988: Ch, SF

**Southern Tree
Surgeons Ltd**
Crawley Down, Crawley,
West Sussex RH10 4HL
☏ 0342 712215
Publicity & promotion
1987: Sept, 27–28 Oct; Nov;
1988: Jan; Mar; May; Ch

Southfield Nurseries
Louth Road, Holton-le-Clay,
Grimsby, South Humberside
DN36 5HL
☏ 0472 822157
Cacti & succulents
1987: Sept, SGF; 27 Oct, SGF;
1988: Apr, SGF; Ch, G

**Southport & District
Gardening Soc**
34a Park Avenue, Southport,
Lancashire PR9 9EF
Courtyard garden
1988: Ch, B Gr

Spalding Gardeners Club
Acacia, 141 Small Grove,
Weston, Spalding, Lincs
PE12 6HL
W'box & H'basket Comp
1988: Ch, B Gr

Ann Spencer
89 Park Avenue South,
London N8 8LX
☏ 01–340 8293
Garden design
1988: Ch

Sportsmark Group Ltd
Sportsmark House, Ealing
Road, Brentford, Middx
TW8 0LH ☏ 01–560 2010
Environment products
1988: Ch

Constance Spry Ltd
25 Manchester Square,
London W1M 5AP
☏ 01–486 6441
Flower arrangements
1988: Ch

**Stapeley Water Gardens
Ltd**
92 London Road, Stapeley,
Nantwich, Cheshire CW5 0EF
☏ 0270 623868
*Water lilies & aquatic plants;
fountains & aquatic accessories*
1988: Ch, G

Starborough Nursery
Starborough Road, Marsh
Green, Edenbridge,
Kent TN8 5RB
☏ 0732 865614
Ornamental trees & shrubs
1987: June, SGB; July, SF;
Aug, SF; Sept, SF; 6 Oct,
SGB; 27 Oct, SGB; Nov, SGB;
1988: Jan; Feb, SGB;
Mar, SGB; Apr, SGF; May,
SGF; Ch, SF

Margaret Stevens
1 Hen Capel, Gevlan, Nr
Bethesda, Gwynedd, Wales
Paintings of flowers
1987: 27 Oct, S Gr

**Margaret Stewart Flower
Designer**
77 Clarkston Rd, Glasgow
G44 3BQ ☏ 041 637 8466
Floristry exhibit
1988: Ch

Stone Art
Willow Thatch, Swallow
Lane, Stoke Mandeville,
Bucks HP22 5UW
☏ 029661 3281
Garden ornaments & fountains
1988: Ch

Stonehurst Orchids
Ardingley,
Sussex RH17 6TN
Orchids
1987: June, G; 1988: Jan, SGB;
Feb, SF

D. & R. Strauss
'Stonehurst', Ardingley,
Sussex
Camellias
1988: April

Susanna Stuart-Smith
7 Market St, Staplehurst,
Tonbridge, Kent
TN12 0QT
Botanical illustrations
1988: Feb, SG Gr

Stydd Nursery
Stonygate Lane, Ribchester,
Preston, Lancs PR3 3YN
☎ 025 484 797
Old-fashioned roses & perennial plants
1987: July, SF; 1988: Ch, F

Pearl Sulman
54 Kingsway, Mildenhall,
Bury St Edmunds,
Suffolk IP28 7HR
☎ 0284 712297
Dwarf pelargoniums
1987: June, SF; July, SF; 1988:
Ch, SF

**Sunbury-on-Thames
Flower Club**
258 Staines Rd East,
Sunbury-on-Thames,
Middx TW16 5AX
Floral arrangement
1988: Ch, 5 Gr

The Sunday Times
1 Pennington Street, London
E1 9XW ☎ 01-822 9797
A Swimming Pool Garden
1988: Ch, SGF

Surbiton Horticultural Soc
116 Meadow Walk, Ewell,
Epsom, Surrey KT19 0BA
W'box & H'basket Comp
1988: Ch, S Gr

Susan's Flower Shop
14 Hyde Road, Paignton,
Devon ☎ 0803 556595
Floristry exhibit
1988: Ch

Swansea City Council
Director of Development,
The Guildhall,
Swansea SA1 4PH
Flowering & foliage plants
1988: May, SB

Synchemicals Ltd
44/45 Grange Walk, London
SE1 3EN ☎ 01-232 1225
Horticultural chemicals & sundries
1988: Ch

10 Kai
92 St John's Wood Tce,
London NW8
Bonsai, bonsai sundries
1987: July; Aug; Sept; 6 Oct,
G; 27–28 Oct; Nov; 1988: Jan;
Feb; May

Diana Taylor-Lowen
Studio Flat 5, Over
Norton, Over Norton Pk,
Chipping Norton,
Oxon OX7 5PX
Paintings of rhododendrons
1987: 27 Oct, B Gr

Jessica Tcherepnine
1192 Park Ave, New York,
NY 10128, USA
Paintings of wild flowers of NY
1988: Jan, G

The Thames Polytechnic
Oakfield Lane, Dartford, Kent
☎ 0322 21328
Courses available
1988: Ch

**Thames Valley Orchid
Society**
15 Weald Rise, Tilehurst,
Reading, Berks RG3 6XB
☎ 01-560 0232
Orchids
1988: Ch, SGF

Thermoforce Ltd
Heybridge Works, Maldon,
Essex CM9 7NW
☎ 0621 58797
Greenhouse equipment
1988: Ch

Three Counties Nurseries
Marshwood, Bridport, Dorset
☎ 029 77 257
Garden pinks
1987: Aug, SGF; Sept, G; 6
Oct, SGB; 1988: Apr, SF; May
SGB; Ch, SGF

Freda Titford
9 Mark Ave, Chingford,
London E4 7NR
Paintings of fungi
1987: Nov, Gr

Philip Tivey & Sons
28 Wanlip Rd, Syston,
Leicester LE7 8PA
☎ 0533 692968
Dahlias & chrysanthemums
1987: Sept, SGF; 1988: Ch,
SGF

Thundersley GAFAG
40 Badgers Way, Thundersley,
Essex SS7 1TR
Floral arrangement
1988: Ch, B Gr

Mr & Mrs W.L. Tjaden
85 Welling Way, Welling,
Kent DA16 2RW
Cacti & succulents
1987: June, SGF; July, G; Aug,
SGB; 6 Oct, G; 27 Oct, SGF;
Nov, SGF; 1988: Jan, SGF;
Feb, SGF; Mar, SGF; Apr,
SGF

Tokonoma Bonsai Ltd
14 London Rd, Shenley,
Radlett, Herts WD7 9EN
☎ 092 76 7587
Bonsai & bonsai sundries
1988: Ch, SGB

Borough of Torbay
Parks & Recreation Dept.,
Town Hall, Torquay,
Devon TQ1 3DR
☎ 0803 296244
Carpet bedding
1988: Ch, G

James Trehane & Sons
Staplehill Rd, Hampreston,
Wimborne, Dorset BH21 7NE
Blueberries, camellias, pieris
1987: Aug, Hogg; 1988: Feb,
SGB; Mar, SGF; Apr, SGF

William Treseder Ltd
30 Cowbridge Rd East,
Canton, Cardiff, South
Glamorgan CF1 9UA
☎ 0222 382456
Floristry exhibit
1988: Ch

Julian Treyer-Evans
Magnolia House,
26 Cuckfield Rd,
Hurstpierpoint, West Sussex
☎ 0273 834833
Garden design
1988: Ch

**Hort Soc of Trinidad &
Tobago**
PO Box 252, Port-of-Spain
Trinidad, West Indies
*Flowers from Trinidad &
Tobago*
1988: Ch, G

Troon Floral Club
Oakley, 21 Bentick Drive,
Troon, Ayrshire
KA10 6HX
Floral arrangement
1988: Ch, B Gr

Marion Tumelty
37 Woodland Way,
Stevenage, Herts
SG2 8BU
*Paintings of flowers from bulbs,
corms & rhizomes*
1987: 27 Oct, SG Gr

Stuart Turner Ltd
Henley-on-Thames, Oxon
RG9 2AD ☎ 0491 572655
Pumps & accessories
1988: Ch

Twil Group Marketing Ltd
PO Box 119, Shepcote Lane,
Sheffield S9 1TY
☎ 0742 443388
Fencing, nets & meshes
1988: Ch

Two Wests & Elliott Ltd
Unit 4, Carrwood Road,
Sheepbridge Ind. Estate,
Chesterfield, Derbys S41 9RH
☎ 0246 451077
*Greenhouse equipment &
accessories*
1988: Ch

Vale Garden Houses
Melton Road, Harlaxton
Grantham, Lincs NG32 1HQ
☎ 0476 64433
Conservatory & summerhouse
1988: Ch

Van Tubergen UK Ltd
PO Box 16, Diss, Norfolk
IP22 3AA ☎ 037 988 8282
Bulbous plants
1988: Ch, G

**The Vernon Geranium
Nursery**
Cuddington Way, Cheam,
Sutton, Surrey SM2 7JB
☎ 01-393 7616
Pelargoniums
1987: June, SB; July, SF; Aug,
SB; Sept, SB; 6 Oct, F; 1988:
May, SB; Ch, SB

Vesutor Ltd
Marringdean Rd,
Billingshurst, West Sussex
RH14 9EH ☎ 040381 2420
Bromeliads
1988: Ch, SGB

The Vicarage Garden
Carrington, Urmston,
Manchester M31 4AG
☎ 061 775 2750
Herbaceous & alpine plants
1987: June, SB; Sept, SF; 1988:
Ch, F

Victa (UK) Ltd
2 Beechwood, Lime Tree Way,
Chineham Business Park,
Basingstoke, Hants RG24 0WA
☎ 0256 50301
*Mowers & turf maintenance
machinery*
1988: Ch

Victorian Lace
40 Solent Road, Havant, Hants
PO9 1JH ☎ 0705 492816
Gazebo, railings & pergola
1988: Ch

Wagtail Publications
West Cottage, Lechlade
Garden & Fuchsia Centre,
Lechlade, Glos GL7 3DP
Books
1987: Aug

Rosaleen Wain
Moorshead, Deancombe, Dean
Prior, Buckfastleigh, Devon
Paintings of clematis
1987: Nov, SG Gr

Winifred Waldron
Weather Vane, Wadenhoe,
Peterborough PE8 5SX
Paintings of Brit Wild flowers
1987: Nov, S Gr

B. Wall
4 Selbourne Close, New Haw,
Weybridge, Surrey
KT15 3RG ☎ 093 23 41390
Begonia species
1987: June, SB; July, SGB;
Aug, SF; Sept, SF; 6 Oct, SF;
27 Oct, SF; Nov, SB; 1988:
Feb, SB; Mar, F; Apr, SB;
May, F; Ch, F

Wendy F. Walsh
The Glebe Ho, Lusk, Co
Dublin, Ireland
Paintings of flowers & shrubs
1988: Feb, G

Walton Conservatories Ltd
Unit 26, Lyon Road, Hersham
Industrial Estate, Walton-on-
Thames, Surrey KT12 3PU
☎ 0932 242579
Conservatory
1988: Ch

George Ward (Moxley) Ltd
Heathfield Lane, Darlaston,
West Midlands WS10 8QZ
☎ 0902 41991
Propagators & planters
1988: Ch

Alan Watling
7 The Glade, Welshwood Pk,
Colchester, Essex CO4 3JD
Paintings of flowers
1987: 27 Oct, B Gr

Wells & Winter
Mereworth, Maidstone, Kent
ME18 5NB ☎ 0622 813627
*Herbs, variegated shrubs,
herbaceous plants*
1987: Sept, SB; 1988: Ch, B
Knightian
Gardening books & sundries
1987: June; July; Aug; Sept; 6–
7 Oct; 27–28 Oct; Nov; 1988:
Jan; Feb; Mar; Apr; May; Ch

**Welsh College of
Horticulture**
Northop, Mold, Clwyd
☎ 035 286 861
Specialised courses available
1988: Ch

West Country Plants
26 Barons Mead, Chippenham,
Wilts SN14 0LN
☎ 0249 653105
Herbaceous plants (shrubs)
1987: June, SF; July, SGB;
Aug, SB; Sept, SB; 6 Oct, SB;
27 Oct, SGB; Nov, SB; 1988:
Jan, SB; Feb, F; Apr, SB; May,
SB; Ch, SF

West Meters Ltd
Western Bank Industrial
Estate, Wigton, Cumbria
CA7 9SJ
☎ 0965 44288
*Greenhouse, garden indicators
& weatherstations*
1988: Ch

Weston Turville Hort Soc
4 Penfold, Weston Turville,
Aylesbury, Bucks HP22 5SW
W'box & H'basket Comp
1988: Ch, S Gr

Westwood Engineering Ltd
Bell Close, Newnham
Industrial Estate, Plympton,
Devon PL7 4JH
☎ 0752 346555
Tractors, mowers & accessories
1988: Ch

**Weymouth Evening Floral
Group**
19 Markham Ave, Weymouth,
Dorset DT4 0QL
Floral arrangement
1988: Ch, B Gr

Wheelbarrow Books Ltd
22 Brangwyn Ave, Brighton,
E. Sussex BN1 8XG
Antiquarian hort. books
1988: Jan

Whichford Pottery
Whichford, Shipston-on-
Stour, Warks CV36 5PG
☎ 0608 84416
Terracotta ware
1988: Ch

C. H. Whitehouse Ltd
Buckhurst Works, Frant,
Tunbridge Wells, Kent
TN3 9BN
*Cedar greenhouses, propagators,
etc*
1987: Nov; 1988: Jan

Faith & Geoff Whiten
29 Castle Row, Canterbury,
Kent CT1 2QY
*The Bradstone Anniversary
Garden*
1988: Ch, SF

Whitton Floral Club
5 Ryecroft Ave, Whitton,
Twickenham, Middx
TW2 6HH
Floral arrangement
1988: Ch, S Gr

**Metropolitan Borough of
Wigan**
Dept of Leisure, Westgate
House, Green Street, Wigan
WN3 4HJ ☎ 0942 44991
Herbaceous & annual plants
1988: Ch, SB

Wilkinson Sword Ltd
Sword House, Bridgend,
Mid Glam CF31 3YN
☎ 0656 55595
Garden sundries
1988: Ch

Robin Williams
2 Foxwood Close, Hanworth,
Middlesex TW13 7DL
☎ 01-890 3692
Garden design
1988: Ch

M. E. Wilson
28 Empson Rd, Kendal,
Cumbria LA9 5PS
*Paintings of the flora of the
French & Swiss Alps*
1988: Feb, S Gr

Isobel Wilton
Edelweiss, 93 Ipswich Street,
Stowmarket, Suffolk IP14 1BB
☎ 0449 612505
Floristry exhibit
1988: Ch

Winslow Garden Soc
23 Highfield Rd, Winslow,
Buckingham, Bucks
MK18 3DU
W'box & H'basket Comp
1988: Ch, B Gr

Ken & Barbara Winsper Ltd
72 High Street, Birmingham
B14 7JZ ☎ 021 444 2910
Floristry exhibit
1988: Ch, B Gr

Patricia Winstone
Beech Farm, Kingston,
Thornbury, Bristol BS12 1NB
Paintings of anemones
1987: 27 Oct, B Gr

Witbourne (LP) Ltd
23 Upperton Lane,
Eastbourne, East Sussex
BN21 2DB ☎ 0323 20288
Garden furniture
1988: Ch

**Wolf Tools for Garden &
Lawn Ltd**
Alton Road, Ross-on-Wye,
Hereford HR9 5NE
☎ 0432 67600
Garden tools & equipment
1988: Ch

Wood End Hort Soc
7 Russell Rd, Northolt Pk,
Middx UB5 4QR
W'box & H'basket Comp
1988: Ch, B Gr

Woodfield Bros
71 Townsend Rd, Tiddington,
Stratford-on-Avon, Warks
CV37 7DF ☎ 0789 205618
Lupins, delphiniums
1987: June, G; 1988: Ch, SGF

Woodstock Orchids
Woodstock Ho, 50 Pound Hill,
Great Brickhill, Nr Milton
Keynes, Bucks MK17 9AS
Orchids
1987: Nov, SB

**Thomas Woodward
Gardens**
Birds Cottage, Sibdon Castle,
Craven Arms, Shropshire
SY7 9AQ ☎ 058-82 6115
Garden design
1988: Ch

Jane Woollett
Spring Cottage, Loders,
Bridport, Dorset DT6 4NW
Paintings of rhododendrons
1987: 27 Oct, S Gr

H. Woolman (Dorridge) Ltd
Grange Rd, Dorridge, Solihull,
West Midlands B93 8QB
☎ 05645 6283
*Chrysanthemums & regal
pelargoniums*
1988: Ch, SF

The World of Flowers
6 Cropston Rd, Anstey,
Leicester LE7 7BJ
☎ 0533 362233
Floristry exhibit
1988: Ch, B Gr

Wendy Wright
29 Lurline Gardens, London
SW11 4DB ☎ 01-622 2088
Garden design
1988: Ch

**Writtle Agricultural
College**
Chelmsford, Essex CM1 3RR
☎ 0245 420705
*Courses and student training
offered*
1988: Ch

Wye College
Biological Sciences Division,
University of London, Wye,
Ashford, Kent TN25 5AH
☎ 0233 812 401
*Composting: the scientific
principles – the practical art*
1988: Ch, SG Lindley

Wyld Court Orchids
Hampstead Norreys,
Newbury, Berks RG16 0TN
☎ 0635 201283
Orchids
1987: 27 Oct, SF; Nov, SF;
1988: Jan, SF; Ch, SGB

John Wyndham
Westgates, Muddles Green,
Chiddingly, Lewes, East
Sussex BN8 6HW
☎ 0825 872036
Garden furniture
1988: Ch

INDEX TO PLANTS

Page numbers in italics refer to illustrations.

Acacia podalyriifolia 150
Acer palmatum 'Butterfly' 28
 platanoides 'Drummondii' 47
Adiantum venustum 116
Aesculus × *mutabilis* 'Induta' 32, *32*
Alchemilla conjuncta 34
Allium aflatunense 103
 a. 'Purple Globe' 46
 caeruleum 36, 46
 christophii 103–4, *104*
 giganteum 46, 104
 pulchellum 104
 'Purple Sensation' 36, 103
 unifolium 36, 46, 104
Alstroemeria hybrids 42
Andromeda polifolia 118
 p. 'Macrophylla' 118
Anemone nemorosa cultivars 110, *110*
 petiolulosa 110
 ranunculoides 110
 r. 'Pallida' 110
 × *seemannii* 110
apple rootstocks 62–4, *62, 63, 66–7,*
 67
Arisaema sikokiana 111
Arum creticum 110
asparagus 'Franklim' 50
asparagus pea 52
Asphodeline luteus 46, *46*
Asplenium scolopendrium cultivars 116

bamboos 28
Berberis candidula 114
 × *frikartii* 114
 verruculosa 114
Bergenia cordifolia 114
 crassifolia 114
 purpurascens cultivars 114, *115*
 × *schmidtii* 114
Betula pendula 'Golden Cloud' 24
 'Trost's Dwarf' 28
Blechnum penna-marina 116
broad bean 'The Sutton' 51

calabrese 'Romanesco' 49
Camellia 98–100
 japonica 'Miss Charleston' *149*
Cardiocrinum giganteum 104
Carex riparia 'Variegata' 36
Cassiope 'Edinburgh' 118, *118*
cauliflower 50
celtuce 54
Chamaecyparis lawsoniana cultivars
 120
 obtusa 'Nana Gracilis' 120
cherry rootstocks 66–7, *66*
Chinese artichoke 54
Chinese cabbage, flowering 54
 'Tip Top' 50
Clematis armandii 15, 120
 a. 'Apple Blossom' 120
 cirrhosa 120–1

c. var. *balearica* 121
viticella 'Purpurea Plena Elegans'
 148
Colchicum agrippinum 107
 autumnale 107
 giganteum 107
 speciosum 107
 s. album 107
 'Water Lily' 107, *107*
Convallaria majalis cultivars 45
Corydalis ochroleuca 34, 36
Cotoneaster congestus 120
 microphylla 120, *121*
 dammeri 120
Crocus banaticus 107
 goulimyi 107
 nudiflorus 107
curly endive 52
Cyclamen africanum 106
 cilicium 106
 coum 108, *108*
 cyprium 106
 graecum 106
 hederifolium 73, 106
 intaminatum 106
 libanoticum 108
 mirabile 106
 parviflorum 108
 trochoptantherum 108
Cymbidium cultivars *126*
Cynara cardunculus 45
 scolymus 45

Dactylorhiza elata 127
 foliosa 127
 maculata 126
 praetermissa 126
dandelion (as vegetable) 52, *53*
Daphne laureola 114
 odora 114
 o. 'Aureomarginata' 114
Delphinium 100–1
Dianthus Allwoodii pinks 16
 carnation 16, 41
 plumarius 16

Epipactis gigantea 126
Eucomis bicolor 106, *106*
 comosa 106
Euphorbia characias wulfenii 46, *47*

Fritillaria acmopetala 111
 alfredae ssp. *glaucoviridis* 110
 aurea 109
 caucasica 109
 hermonis ssp. *amana* 109
 imperialis 73
 liliacea 110
 meleagris 111
 pallidiflora *109*, 110
 pontica 111
 verticillata 111

Galanthus caucasicus 107
 elwesii 107
 ikariae 107
 lutescens 107
 nivalis 'Viridapicis' 107
Geranium × *cantabrigiense* 74
 cultivars 74, *74–5*
 maculatum 34, *35*
Gerbera 42
Gladiolus 'The Bride' 104

nanus cultivars 104
 primulinus 104
Gloriosa superba 42–3

Halimium lasianthum 33
Hebe albicans 119
 a. 'Prostrata' 119
 odora 119
 o. 'New Zealand Gold' 119
 rakaiensis 119, *118–9*
Hedychium aurantiacum 106
 densiflorum 'Assam Orange' 106
 gardnerianum 106
Hemerocallis dumortieri 34
herbs, decorative and useful 57–8
Hosta cultivars 24, 44, *45*, 74

Ilex crenata cultivars 114
 pernyi 114
Iris, bearded 16, *17*
 danfordiae 109
 histrioides 'Major' 109
 reticulata 'Clairette' *109*, *109*
 unguicularis lazica 92

Japanese mustard 'Mizuna' 54
Jasminum humile 'Revolutum' 32, *33*
Juniperus chinensis 'Pyramidalis' 119
 communis cultivars 119
 squamata cultivars 119

kale, flowering, 'Green Lance' 54

leek 'Winterreuzen' 49
lettuce 'Continuity' 52
 'Green Lollo' 52
 'Lobjoit's Green' 49, *50*
 'Novita' 50
 'Red Lollo' 49, 52
lilac cultivars 47
Lilium auratum 40, 104
 chalcedonicum 104
 nepalense 104
 regale 15, 104, *105*
 speciosum 104
Liquidambar styraciflua 'Worplesdon'
 148

Magnolia campbellii var. *mollicomata*
 15, 100
Masdevallia strobelii 'Muriel' 124
Miltoniopsis Hannover 'Mont Millais'
 122
miner's lettuce 52
'Mitsuba' 54
mushrooms 54

Narcissus asturiensis 108
 bulbocodium 108
 cultivars 108, *150*
 romieuxii 108
nasturtium (as vegetable) 52

Odontioda Becky Falls 'Dipper' *127*
Odontoglossum 125
onion 'Giant Fen Globe' 50
orach 52
oriental greens 54
Ornithogalum nutans 36

Paeonia officinalis 'Rubra Plena' 43,
 43
 lactiflora cultivars 44, *44*

'Phylis Moore' *146*
Pak choi 54
Papaver bracteata 'Goliath' 45
  nudicaule 45, *44–5*
  orientalis cultivars 16, 45
Paphiopedilum spp. & hybrids 125,
  127
pea 'Bikini' 50
  purple-podded 52
peach rootstocks 65–6, 67
pear rootstocks 64
Phyllodoce empetriformis 118
  × *intermedia* 118
Picea abies 'Nidiformis' 120
  omorika 'Nana' 120
Pinus mugo 72, 120
  m. cultivars 120
  sylvestris cultivars 120
Pittosporum tenuifolium 'Garnettii'
  32–3
Pleione bulbocodioides 126
  formosana cultivars 126
  forrestii 126
  Shantung 126
plum rootstocks 64–5, *65*, 67
Polemonium carneum 75
Polygonatum × *hybridum* 45
Polystichum munitum *112*, 116
  setiferum 'Acutilobum' 116
potato 'Concorde' 50
  'Dunluce' 50
Protea 42
Ptilotrichum spinosum roseum 33, *34*

Quercus robur 'Concordia' 32

raspberry 'Autumn Bliss' *148–9*
Rhamnus alaterna
  'Argenteovariegata' 33
Rhododendron calostrotum 117, *117*
  c. 'Gigha' 117
  cultivars *30*, 33, 46–7, *46*, *150*

keleticum 117
lepidostylum 117
radicans 117
williamsianum 117
Rhodohypoxis *111*
  cultivars 110
rhubarb chard 52
Ribes speciosum 33
Robinia hispida 31, *32*
Rosa 'Agnes' 34
  'Alberic Barbier' 121
  'Anne Harkness' 144
  'Ballerina' 142
  'Climbing Iceberg' 143
  'Comte de Chambord' 138, *140*
  'Cramoisi Supérieur' *142*
  × *damascena bifera* 137
  'Felicia' 139
  'Fru Dagmar Hastrup' 139, *141*
  'Général Jacqueminot' *138*
  'Geranium' *139*
  glauca 139
  'Golden Showers' *144*
  'Highdownensis' 139
  'Jacques Cartier' 138
  'Just Joey' *145*
  'La France' 138–9
  luciae 121
  macrophylla 139
  'Mme Alfred Carrière' 75, 143
  'Mme Isaac Pereire' 40–1, *41*, 138
  moyesii 142–3
  'Old Blush' 142
  'Peaudouce' *144*
  'Penelope' 139
  'Prosperity' 139
  'Roseraie de l'Hay' 139
  'Shirley Hibberd' 121
  'Stanwell Perpetual' 139, *140–1*
  sweginzowii 139
  'Trier' 142
  'Westerland' 34

wichuraiana 121
  'William and Mary' 75
  'Zéphirine Drouhin' *136–7*

Sarcococca confusa 116
  hookeriana 116
  h. vars. 116, *116*
  ruscifolia var. *chinensis* 116
Scilla peruviana 110
sea kale 52, *52*
Smilacina racemosa 34
Sorbus 'Leonard Messel' *149*
Sternbergia clusiana 107
Strelitzia reginae 40
sweet corn 'Candle' 50
sweet pea 39–40, *40*
  'Countess Spencer' 16
sweet pepper 'Clio' 50
Swiss chard 52

Tiarella wherryi 36, *37*
tomato 'Cherito' 53
  'Gardener's Delight' 49, *53*
  'Striped Cavern' 52
  'Totem' 51
Trachelospermum asiaticum 121
  jasminoides 28
Trillium erectum 110
  sessile 110, *111*
Tsuga canadensis 'Jeddeloh' 120
Tulipa *102–3*
  'Bronze Charm' 110
  linifolia 36
  sprengeri 36
turnip 'Gilfeather' 52
  'Purple Top' 50

Weigela florida 'Variegata' 46

Zantedeschia aethiopica cultivars 42,
  149

ACKNOWLEDGEMENTS

The publishers and General Editor of *The Chelsea Year*, who are indebted to many for help in the preparation of this first issue, gratefully acknowledge in particular the assistance given by the staff and officers of the Royal Horticultural Society and by exhibitors.

The publishers thank the following photographers and organizations for permission to reproduce photographs and illustrations: AFRC Institute of Horticultural Research, East Malling, 62, 63, 65, 66, 66–7; Karen Banks/British Trust for Conservation Volunteers, 22; BBC Hulton Picture Library, 12–13, 14–15, 17; Gillian Beckett, 112–13, 116, 117, 118, 118–19; Eric Young Orchid Foundation, 122; Mary Evans Picture Library, 82–3; Michael Gibson, 41, 136–7, 140, 140–1, 141, 144 top & bottom, 145; Harry Smith Collection, 8, 74–5, 96–7, 150 bottom left & bottom right; Arthur Hellyer, 133 top & bottom; Help the Aged/Robin Williams, 27; House & Garden, 29; Jenny Jowett, 92; David Joyce, 21 top & bottom, 23, 24, 28, 71; The National Trust Foundation for Art, 128–9; Notcutts Nurseries Ltd, 15; Jocelyn Nowell, 58; Photos Horticultural/Michael Warren, half-title, frontispiece, 11, 18–19, 26, 30–1, 32 top & bottom, 33, 34, 35, 37, 40, 43, 44, 44–5, 45, 46 top & bottom, 47, 48–9, 50, 51, 52, 53 top & bottom, 55, 56, 59, 60–1, 68–9, 76–7, 81, 84–5, 87, 88, 89, 91, 99, 100–1, 104, 105, 106, 107, 108, 109 top & bottom, 110, 111 top & bottom, 115, 121, 135, 142–3, 146, 148 top & bottom, 148–9, 149 top, bottom left & bottom right, 150 top; Royal Horticultural Society, 126 left & right, 127 left & right; Serac Ltd, 79; Pamela Toler/Impact, 38–9, 102–3; Paul Tucker, 25; Jane Woodward, 20.